Enhancing the Regulatory Decision-Making Approval Process for Direct Food Ingredient Technologies

Workshop Summary

Food Forum

Food and Nutrition Board

INSTITUTE OF MEDICINE

IOM

NATIONAL ACADEMY PRESS
Washington, D.C. 1999

NATIONAL ACADEMY PRESS • 2101 Constitution Avenue, N.W. • Washington, DC 20418

NOTICE: The project that is the subject of this report was approved by the Governing Board of the National Research Council, whose members are drawn from the councils of the National Academy of Sciences, the National Academy of Engineering, and the Institute of Medicine. The members of the committee responsible for the report were chosen for their special competences and with regard for appropriate balance.

The Institute of Medicine was chartered in 1970 by the National Academy of Sciences to enlist distinguished members of the appropriate professions in the examination of policy matters pertaining to the health of the public. In this, the Institute acts under the Academy's 1863 congressional charter responsibility to be an adviser to the federal government and on its own initiative in identifying issues of medical care, research, and education. Dr. Kenneth I. Shine is president of the Institute of Medicine.

This project was funded by the U.S. Department of Health and Human Services Food and Drug Administration, U.S Department of Agriculture Food Safety and Inspection Service, U.S. Department of Commerce National Marine Fisheries Service, U.S. Environmental Protection Agency, Frito-Lay, Inc.; Hershey Foods; Kellogg Company; Kraft Foods, Inc.; McDonald's Corporation, Monsanto Company; Nabisco, Inc.; Nestlé USA; Proctor & Gamble, and Ross Products. The opinions expressed herein are those of the workshop participants and do not necessarily reflect those of the funders.

International Standard Book No. 0-309-06486-4
Library of Congress Catalog Card Number 99-62305

Additional copies of *Enhancing the Regulatory Decision-Making Process for Direct Food Ingredient Technologies: Workshop Summary* are available for sale from the National Academy Press, 2101 Constitution Avenue, N.W., Box 285, Washington, DC 20055. Call (800) 624-6242 or (202) 334-3313 (in the Washington metropolitan area) or visit the NAP's on-line bookstore at **www.nap.edu**.

For more information about the Institute of Medicine, visit the IOM home page at **www2.nas.edu/iom**.

Printed in the United States of America.

The serpent has been a symbol of long life, healing, and knowledge among almost all cultures and religions since the beginning of recorded history. The image adopted as a logotype by the Institute of Medicine is based on a relief carving from ancient Greece, now held by the Staatliche Museen in Berlin.

FOOD FORUM

FERGUS M. CLYDESDALE *(Chair),* University of Massachusetts, Amherst
PERRY L. ADKISSON, Texas A&M University, College Station
DIANE FEICKERT BIRT, Iowa State University, Ames
MARSHA N. COHEN, Hastings College of the Law, University of California, San Francisco
JOHN M. CONNOR, Purdue University, West Lafayette, Indiana
MICHAEL P. DOYLE, University of Georgia, Griffin
ROBERT DROTMAN, Frito-Lay, Inc., Plano, Texas
CHARLES DUNCAN, Hershey Foods, Hershey, Pennsylvania
VICTOR FULGONI, Kellogg Company, Battle Creek, Michigan
MICHAEL J. GOLDBLATT, McDonald's Corporation, Oak Brook, Illinois
EDWARD GROTH III, Consumers Union, Yonkers, New York
RICHARD L. HALL, Consultant, Baltimore, Maryland
ARTHUR L. HECKER, Ross Products Division, Abbott Laboratories, Columbus, Ohio
JERRY HJELLE, Monsanto Company, Deerfield, Illinois
WILLIAM KELLY JONES, Nabisco Foods Group, East Hanover, New Jersey
EILEEN MADDEN, Nestlé USA, Inc., Purchase, New York
RICHARD A. MERRILL, University of Virginia School of Law, Charlottesville
SANFORD A. MILLER, Graduate School of Biomedical Sciences, University of Texas Health Science Center, San Antonio
M. JAYE NAGLE, Kraft Foods, Glenview, Illinois
MICHAEL W. PARIZA, University of Wisconsin, Madison
KEITH TRIEBWASSER, Procter & Gamble, Cincinnati, Ohio

Ex-Officio Members

E. SPENCER GARRETT, National Marine Fisheries Service, Pascagoula, Mississippi
LYNN GOLDMAN, U.S. Environmental Protection Agency, Washington, DC
DAVID A. KESSLER, Food and Drug Administration, Rockville, Maryland
DAVID R. LINEBACK, University of Idaho, Moscow
GEORGE PATERSON, Health Canada, Ottawa, Ontario
DONNA V. PORTER, Library of Congress, Washington, DC
MICHAEL TAYLOR, United States Department of Agriculture, Washington, DC

Forum Staff

SANDRA SCHLICKER, Director
KATHERINE J. GORTON, Policy Intern
GERALDINE KENNEDO, Project Assistant

FOOD AND NUTRITION BOARD

Preface

The Institute of Medicine's (IOM's) Food Forum was established in 1993 to allow science and technology leaders in the food industry, top administrators in the federal government, representatives from consumer interest groups, and academicians to discuss and debate food and food safety issues openly and in a neutral setting. The Forum provides a mechanism for these diverse groups to identify possible approaches for addressing food and food safety problems and issues surrounding the often complex interactions among industry, academia, regulatory agencies, and consumers.

On May 6-7, 1997, the Forum convened a workshop titled *Enhancing the Regulatory Decision-Making Process for Direct Food Ingredient Technologies*. Workshop speakers and participants discussed legal aspects of the direct food additive approval process, changes in science and technology, and opportunities for reform. Two background papers, which can be found in Appendix A and B, were shared with the participants prior to the workshop. The first paper provided a description and history of the legal framework of the food ingredient approval process and the second paper focused on changes in science and technology practices with emphasis placed on lessons learned from case studies. This document presents a summary of the workshop.

The workshop began with Professor Noah's overview of the Food Additives Amendment Act of 1958 and how the U.S. Food and Drug Administration (FDA), over the period of the law's existence, has interpreted and applied the law. This overview was followed by a panel of reactors who spoke about their expectations and perceptions of the congressional and administrative decisions. Members of this panel were lawyers with experience in the legal aspects of the food ingredient approval process and represented consumers, industry, and government. The afternoon session began with an overview of the changes in science and technology and related policy factors that have impacted the FDA's decision making since the passage of the Food Additives Amendment Act of 1958. Generic lessons learned from experience and case studies about direct food additives were presented. Individuals from government, industry, and consumer groups reacted to the lessons learned from the case studies. An open discussion among speakers and the audience ended the first day's program.

The second day of the workshop focused on the opportunities for reform of the current food ingredient approval system. Speakers from the FDA, industry, Congress, and consumer groups presented their views on the causes of the problems and possible remedies. Open discussion among all participants followed this panel. An agenda and list of participants can be found at the end of the workshop summary.

The purpose of a Forum at the IOM is to foster dialogue and discussion across sectors and institutions. Public forums offer a mechanism for convening individuals from a variety of government, academic, industry, and citizen groups and provide a structured opportunity for open communication among representatives of these groups. The objective, however, is to illuminate issues, not to resolve them. Unlike study committees of the IOM, Forums cannot provide advice or recommendations to any government agency or other organization. Similarly, workshop summaries or other products resulting from forum activities are not intended to reach conclusions or recommendations but, instead, are to reflect the variety of opinions expressed by the participants. The comments in this report represent the views of the workshop participants, as indicated generically in the text. The identification of a speaker as an "industry representative" or a "FDA representative" is not intended to suggest that the individual speaks for that organization or others who work there.

This report has been reviewed in draft form by individuals chosen for their diverse perspectives and technical expertise, in accordance with procedures approved by the National Research Council's Report Review Committee. The purpose of this independent review is to provide candid and critical comments that will assist the Institute of Medicine in making the published report as sound as possible and to ensure that the report meets institutional standards for objectivity, evidence, and responsiveness to the study charge. The content of the final report is the responsibility of the Institute of Medicine and the study committee and not the responsibility of the reviewers. The review comments and draft manuscript remain confidential to protect the integrity of the deliberative process. The forum wishes to thank the following individuals, who are neither officials nor employees of the Institute of Medicine, for their participation in the review of this report: Caroline Smith DeWaal, J.D., Center for Science in the Public Interest; Peter Barton Hutt, LL.M., Covington & Burling; Franklin M. Lowe, D.V.M., Ph.D., Becker College; Judith Stern, Ph.D., University of California at Davis; and Donna U. Vogt, M.A., Congressional Research Service.

While the individuals listed above have provided many constructive comments and suggestions, responsibility for the final content of this report rests solely with the authoring committee and the Institute of Medicine.

Contents

Enhancing the Regulatory Decision-Making Approval Process for Direct Food Ingredient Technologies

Workshop Summary

Opinions vary on the historical success of the U.S. Food and Drug Administration (FDA) in protecting the American public from harmful food ingredients. Industry and academic representatives credit the agency with prevention of public health emergencies associated with consumption of food substances. Consumer groups are reluctant to praise FDA, and are not convinced that the public has been adequately served by the food additive petition process. The cases of violet dye #1 and sulfites are cited as historical examples of once-approved ingredients that may have adversely affected the public's health.

In the absence of timely approval, industry is likely to rely more heavily on the statutory exception for Generally Recognized as Safe (GRAS) substances to facilitate the marketing of new ingredients. A recent FDA proposed rule (see section on "Extramural Reviews" in Appendix A), if finalized, would eliminate the FDA GRAS affirmation process and establish a FDA GRAS notification procedure in its place.

However, not all potential ingredients can detour food additive review. Reform of the formal food additive review process may significantly affect the willingness of manufacturers to invest substantial sums of money in the research and development of new technologies. Congressional intent in enacting the 1958 Food Additives Amendment to the Federal Food, Drug, and Cosmetic (FD&C) Act was to create a process that would encourage technological development, not hinder it. This statute may need updating to serve this purpose. At the same time, it must continue to protect the food supply for the consuming public.

Three major themes emerged during the workshop. First, communication is a key to enhancing the regulatory review process. Well-developed food additive petitions that include all of the necessary data can only serve to enhance scarce agency resources. However, the determination of the appropriate level of communication needs further exploration. What some may consider to be a consultative process may appear to be collaborative to others.

Second, solving complex food ingredient issues requires the involvement of many scientific disciplines that are often not available within the FDA staff. Often, outside experts residing in academia, professional scientific associations, and public interest groups may need to be involved in the evaluation process, but barriers, such as the Federal Advisory Committee Act and the confidential nature of the data submitted, limit the involvement of outside experts.

Finally, the possibility of congressional authorization of user fees to enhance FDA's diminishing resources needs further discussion. Many participants agreed with the user fee concept, but representatives of the public interest groups were opposed to the idea of manufacturers paying for FDA contractor-approved petition reviews. Manufacturers are reluctant to pay a user fee without some assurance of benefit, such as market exclusivity. Continued exploration of the fundamental public policy issues raised by user fees is critical to mutual understanding among all parties.

INTRODUCTION AND BACKGROUND

The purpose of the workshop was to allow experts in food science and policy to discuss the capacity of the current food ingredient regulatory review process to facilitate and/or impede the application of new food science and technologies into the marketplace. Prior to the workshop, Lars Noah, Assistant Professor of Law at the University of Florida, was commissioned to draft a background document, *Legal Aspects of the Food Additive Approval Process* (Appendix A). In addition, a series of case studies of the food additive review process were developed by members of the Food Forum and distributed to participants (Appendix B). This summary is based on those papers and dialogue among participants during the workshop. The views presented in this summary represent the diverse backgrounds and interests of the participants, including representatives from the FDA, academia, consumer groups, and the food industry.

Since the passage of the 1958 Food Additives Amendment to the FD&C Act of 1938, significant technological advances have tested the effectiveness of the FDA's primary tool for ensuring the safety of new food ingredients. Manufacturers of controversial new food ingredients have sought FDA approval, and the agency has experienced a rise in the number of applications seeking approval for novel food technologies, such as bioengineered foods, macronutrient substitutes, or genetically produced or modified foods or ingredients, placing additional burdens on an agency already constrained by resource limitations. As a result, the average time to approve a new direct food additive is estimated to exceed six years. Yet the formal statutory deadline for action on a food additive petition remains just 180 days (see section on "Food Additives Petitions" in Appendix A).

OVERVIEW OF THE APPROVAL PROCESS FOR FOOD USE SUBSTANCES

Food substances include food and color additives, ingredients generally recognized as safe (GRAS), new food-animal drugs, dietary supplements, and bioengineered or genetically produced or modified foods or ingredients. These substances can extend shelf life and provide taste, texture, color, and nutritional value, among other vital functions, in foods.

Food Additives

By legal definition, a food additive is "any substance the intended use of which results or may reasonably be expected to result, directly or indirectly, in its becoming a component or otherwise affecting the characteristics of any food . . . , if such substance is not generally recognized . . . to be safe under the conditions of its intended use . . . " (see the section on "Components of Food" in Appendix A). A food additive may be a direct (intentional) or an indirect (incidental) food additive. The definition specifically excludes GRAS substances, substances approved by the FDA and USDA during 1938 to 1958 (so called "prior sanctioned"), as well as color additives, pesticide chemicals, new animal drugs, and dietary supplements (see the section on "Components of Food" in Appendix A). Some substances, such as dietary supplements, were potentially eligible for food additive status, but a subsequent amendment to the FD&C Act narrowed the legal definition to exclude them.

GRAS SUBSTANCES

Substances determined to be generally recognized as safe (GRAS) are excluded from the food additive definition. GRAS status requires consensus, but not unanimity, among experts qualified by scientific training and experience. Under the FD&C Act, GRAS determination must be made "among experts qualified by scientific training and experience to evaluate its safety, as having been adequately shown through scientific procedures (or, in the case of a substance used in food prior to January 1, 1958, through either scientific procedures or experience based on common use in food) to be safe under the conditions of its intended use" (see the section on "Generally Recognized as Safe" in Appendix A). The phrase "scientific procedures" is defined under FDA regulations as data based upon "published studies which may be corroborated by unpublished studies or other data and information" (see the section on "Generally Recognized as Safe in Appendix A). Nevertheless, interpretation of the GRAS definition leaves room for judgment. The statute provides few details about the requirements of scientific substantiation, which has raised questions in GRAS determinations over the years. GRAS determinations can be made either by FDA upon petition, or by self-determination, in which case the sponsor may rely on a third party's review.

Following the enactment of the 1958 Food Additives Amendment, FDA affirmed that a number of food ingredients met the GRAS standard. After questions were raised about the safety of some GRAS ingredients, the agency initiated a review of these ingredients in 1972. The agency utilized the scientific expertise of an independent organization, the Federation of American Societies for Experimental Biology (FASEB), to assist in the evaluation, which spanned a decade. During that time, FASEB's Select Committee on GRAS Substances (SCOGS) evaluated over 450 food use ingredients, and recommended that only one percent of the ingredients on the original GRAS list be re-categorized as food additives. To date, nearly 200 substances appear on FDA's affirmed GRAS list for direct use in foods. The agency's review of the SCOGS reports has never been completed, and FDA has never intended that the GRAS lists be comprehensive.

As mentioned, a food substance does not need to be affirmed GRAS by the FDA to be eligible for GRAS status (and thus excluded from food additive requirements). An ingredient manufacturer, or a third party, may apply the scientific requirements and determine with or without notifying FDA that a substance is GRAS. In most cases, the ingredient manufacturer contracts with an independent organization to make such a determination. For example, both Proctor & Gamble and Nabisco sought FASEB review for ingredients they later marketed as GRAS. FDA has rarely challenged GRAS self-determinations, but there is some regulatory risk involved. GRAS determinations are never absolute. The agency retains the right to pursue enforcement proceedings, if it disagrees with a manufacturer's own GRAS determination.

GRAS self-determinations raise the legal question of who bears the burden of proof for a GRAS determination to be considered scientifically substantiated. There is disagreement on whether this burden lies with the agency or the ingredient manufacturer. A GRAS affirmation process whereby manufacturers submit a petition to FDA requesting the affirmation of a GRAS self-determination has been a primary mechanism for manufacturers to protect themselves from

FDA enforcement actions. A recent FDA proposed rule (see section on "Extramural Reviews" in Appendix A), if finalized, would eliminate the FDA GRAS affirmation process and establish an FDA GRAS notification procedure in its place (see the section on "Extramural Reviews" in Appendix A).

Interim Additives

Interim food additives are previously approved or long used ingredients placed in this transitional category pending further safety review. This regulatory category emerged when FDA initiated its review of food additives in 1972 after the safety of some food additives was questioned. Interim food additives may remain on the market indefinitely, pending a lack of immediate public health concern from their continued use. Interim food additives are intended either to be reconfirmed as safe or removed from the market following additional safety review. There has been significant delay, both from the agency and manufacturers, in reevaluating these substances. As a result, several food ingredients have remained in interim food additive status for many years.

LEGAL FRAMEWORK OF THE INGREDIENT APPROVAL PROCESS

Evaluation of the legal framework of the ingredient approval process demands a comprehensive understanding of the events and legal history from which current food laws emerged. Equally important are understanding the FDA's interpretation and application of the law, and recognizing that the agency is not merely an implementer of law, but an architect of the law as well, as noted by one workshop participant.

Flaws of the Current Review Process

The length of time taken by the agency to review a petition was a primary concern of workshop participants. The background paper by Lars Noah estimated that it took first-time food additive petitions more than six years, on average, from date of filing to publication of an approval order in the *Federal Register* (see section on "Track Records Compared" in Appendix A). However, it was noted that FDA is not responsible for all of the time it takes from the filing date to notification. The agency must often wait months for companies to respond to its requests for additional data. Further, decisions made at FDA must also be approved at the Office of Management and Budget (OMB) prior to public notification.

Time is only one criterion by which the regulatory process is evaluated. Although time may be over-emphasized, it is a critical issue to the food industry when awaiting approval to market a new ingredient or technology. For industry, there is a financial incentive to expedite the time taken for any new product to reach the marketplace. New food ingredients can and often do have wide appeal once available to consumers. However, one consumer representative observed that a lengthy review process concerns industry much more than it does the public. One industry spokesperson and an FDA representative also expressed the view that the quality of incoming petitions needs to be improved and that the agency and industry must work together to improve new food additive petitions.

Proposed Changes in the Approval Process

Representatives from industry, consumer groups, and FDA agreed that changes are needed to improve the regulatory review process and they suggested ways in which the system might be improved. Some changes would require statutory modifications through congressional action, while others could be initiated by FDA. The background paper by Lars Noah outlined several possible solutions (see section on "A Catalogue of Proposed Solutions" in Appendix A), and other workshop participants raised additional suggestions for change during the workshop.

Change or Enforce Deadlines for Petition Reviews

As mentioned, statutory deadlines for reviewing food additive petitions are rarely, if ever, met by the agency. FDA representatives informed workshop participants that the statutory clock is reset when the agency requests additional information for the review of a petition, but such timekeeping does not explain the gross delay in petition approval. According to the background paper by Lars Noah, some critics suggested the use of a statutory "hammer" to enforce FDA deadlines, but this suggestion has also met criticism from both within and outside the agency (see section on "Statutory Hammers" in Appendix A). Although a hammer mechanism would force the agency to make its determination within the mandated time frame, it could compromise the quality of its decisions. Most observers agree that the statutory deadlines that currently exist are too short and should be changed.

Implement User Fees

The payment of user fees was suggested by several participants as a method to supplement FDA Center for Food Science and Applied Nutrition's (CFSAN) resource base. The agency is familiar with user fees because its Center for Drug Evaluation and Review (CDER) has been collecting these fees since the passage of the Prescription Drug User Fee Act of 1992. The collection of user fees for food products would require authorization by Congress.

Grant a Period of Market Exclusivity

Congress could provide a period of market exclusivity to manufacturers of approved food additives, similar to the licensing system for new drugs. When a new drug application is approved, the manufacturer is granted an exclusive marketing period (separate from any patent protection) for a limited time.

One participant suggested that industry has not yet realized the potential benefits of user fees in expediting review times. The participant added that, if user fees were authorized, the industry should also urge Congress to provide a period of market exclusivity for approved ingredients or technologies. Without a period of market exclusivity, user fees could be problematic because food additive petitions, once approved, benefit both the petitioner and competitors. Support for willingness to pay a fee for a product's review, in addition to the financial investment already made in the development of the ingredient or technology, would be substantially reduced. Currently, patents are the only mechanism of protection extended to manufacturers of a new food additive. However, patent terms often expire by the time the agency approves a new food additive.

Re-evaluate GRAS Affirmation Process

FDA regulations have long allowed the manufacturer of a food ingredient to seek the agency's concurrence that the ingredient is GRAS. This process is similar to the process for non-exclusive over-the-counter drug monographs which has certain conditions of use written into the regulations. However, FDA recently published a proposal to change this procedure from a petition for GRAS affirmation to a notification of self-determination of GRAS status (see section on "Extramural Reviews" in Appendix A). This proposal, if finalized, would eliminate the GRAS affirmation process and replace it with a notification procedure. Public interest representatives voiced concern that the current process does not require agency notification prior to the marketing of a substance determined by a manufacturer to be GRAS. They suggested that a letter should be filed with FDA when a GRAS self-determination is made. It was noted that the notification process was designed to bring together the information needed to have a determination that is supported by the evidence. An FDA representative commented that GRAS determination is not a subjective decision by any party, but is a legal status. A substance either is or is not GRAS.

Eliminate Notice-and-Comment Procedures

Notice-and-comment procedures are not mandated by law for food additive approvals, but FDA's procedures do provide an opportunity for third party comment within 30 days after FDA publishes a final order on a petition. In addition, FDA's recent practice has been to allow, and in some cases such as the olestra petition, even solicit, external input. Consumer groups believe that this opportunity for public comment should continue to play a role in the food additive approval process, but industry representatives pointed to the delay resulting from this practice.

Abbreviate Review for Supplemental Uses

The estimated average review time to approve a supplemental use of a direct food additive is 38 months (see section on "Track Records Compared" in Appendix A). It was suggested that FDA might develop an abbreviated protocol for approving petitions for supplemental uses of previously approved food additives. In theory, it should take less time to approve supplemental uses since toxicity data and other determinants of safety have already been evaluated. However, in some cases, such as polydextrose, the agency has taken more time to approve supplemental uses than the original use (see section on "Track Records Compared" in Appendix A). The agency reports that supplemental approvals are not always simple and straightforward. FDA often must consider new exposure patterns and mediums for use because there are unique differences in how the same ingredient might be regulated and used in different types of food.

Evaluate Use of Extramural Petition Review

According to several participants, the agency needs to make greater use of scientific experts from academia or professional societies to help reach final determinations on food ingredient petitions. FDA has, in some cases, deferred completely to qualified outside review boards to conduct food ingredient reviews. As mentioned earlier, from 1972 to 1982 FDA commissioned FASEB to re-evaluate over 450 GRAS substances following concerns raised about the GRAS ingredient cyclamate. Industry associations have also set up independent review boards to evaluate ingredients. The most notable is the Flavor and Extracts Manufacturers Association (FEMA), which has evaluated over 2,000 substances.

Representatives from government, academia, and industry recognize that there can be several benefits to consultation with outside experts. Some people believe that FASEB and FEMA reviews of GRAS materials demonstrate that some topics are better handled independently. By using external resources, reviews are sometimes conducted more efficiently and economically, with little or no controversy. External bodies can operate within their own time frames, and do not have to contend with competing demands encountered within the agency. Consumer representatives, however, expressed less confidence in external reviews and raised concern that such reviews involve potential conflicts of interest. One consumer representative suggested that FDA should do all reviews internally with additional funding, either from government revenues or from small registration fees from all food manufacturing operations in the United States. However, another consumer representative commented that contracting out reviews may be an acceptable practice provided there is clearly demonstrated independence in the process.

Even though the use of outside experts could enhance the speed and breadth of expertise, workshop participants noted that they must be carefully managed by FDA. The cyclamate case study was given as an illustration that the proper use of outside experts requires their understanding of the regulatory legal framework (see case study on "Cyclamate" in Appendix B). When a panel of outside experts is convened, the agency must provide adequate guidance to those experts to ensure that the decision making criteria are clearly understood.

Prioritize Reviews

Currently FDA reviews food additive petitions in the order in which they are received. In light of the serious resource constraints on CFSAN, prioritizing reviews based on benefit could allow some petitions to move through the review process faster. This suggestion raised concerns from both representatives of consumer interest groups and the agency. Agreement on the criteria for determining which applications should get priority could become controversial. Prioritizing reviews raises the potential for petitions deemed of lesser importance by the agency to be delayed indefinitely. The background paper by Lars Noah suggested prioritizing reviews based on an initial assessment of likely public health risk and potential health benefits (see section on "Prioritizing Reviews" in Appendix A). Consideration of an ingredient's potential impact on public health is a factor used to prioritize applications in the drug review process. However, CFSAN currently does not prioritize its reviews.

Implement Safeguards to Prevent Sham Petitioning

Industry representatives raised concern about the potential for sham petitioning. Sham petitioning occurs when competitors point to what they contend is new information about a pending food additive petition in an attempt to delay or prevent approval. Virtually all aspects of a petition become available for public disclosure once it is filed with FDA. The agency has acknowledged the potential for sham petitioning. In the case of a food additive petition for the sweetener sucralose, an anonymous party, through a law firm, filed comments raising safety concerns late in the review process and submitted information to a consumer group. Imposing strict deadlines for the submission of comments used by FDA has been suggested to help combat the disruption of the review process. A consumer lawyer suggested that FDA simply refuse to accept or consider anonymous comments, unless the commenter can make a case for anonymity.

Establish a Sunset Period for Interim Additives

Establishing a moderate sunset period for current interim food additives may help eliminate food additives from this regulatory status and perhaps expedite their completion of review. Despite the intent that prompt action be taken by petitioners to provide additional substantiation for the safety of such additives, many interim food additives have remained in a semi-permanent regulatory limbo for years.

Foster Improved Communication Between Industry and FDA

Several suggestions were made for improving communications between petitioners and FDA, without compromising the maintenance of a clear administrative process and record. Both the agency and industry recognize that the current level of formality of the communication can dramatically slow the review process, as each dialogue between FDA and petitioner must be adequately recorded in writing both for historical purposes and to ensure the substantiation of the agency's position.

Improve Quality of Petitions Submitted to FDA

Representatives of FDA, consumer groups, academia, and industry all concurred that improving the quality of petitions submitted to the agency would help decrease review time. The submission of incomplete petitions or those with inadequate scientific information can substantially increase the burden on FDA and the time spent on review. Historically, the agency has worked with the industry to complete missing data, but many participants suggested that the FDA should deny review of these petitions. A suggestion was offered that the agency provide better defined data requirements or guidelines to help petitioners decide what information to submit in a petition. Due to the heterogeneity of the substances reviewed by the agency, FDA representatives commented that it would be impossible to create a single document to provide guidance for petitioners. However, it was suggested that prefiling consultations could help industry improve the quality of petitions.

SCIENTIFIC INTERPRETATION AND THE APPROVAL PROCESS

Scientific aspects of the food additive approval process were explored through discussion of generic issues and problems affecting the process as a whole. The petition process has evolved extensively since the Food Additives Amendment was enacted in 1958. Several background factors have contributed to the workload and complexity of the current food additive petition process. This discussion of the scientific and regulatory aspects of food ingredient review included key lessons learned about food safety, science and compliance infrastructure, ways in which the process has improved over recent years, and, finally, suggestions for change.

Several speakers observed that scientific advances have led to more detailed studies, more data, and increased complexity in the development of information to support food additive petitions. Several changes in technology and society identified during the discussion are found in Box 1.

BOX 1. Changes in Technology and Society Affecting Decision-Making in the Current Food Additive Petition Process

- Developments in analytical chemistry
- Developments in toxicology
- Changes in the understanding of mechanisms
- Changes in risk and safety assessment
- Changes in agriculture
- Changes in environmental concerns
- Increased consumer activity
- Changes in food marketing and consumption trends
- Increased FDA tasks with fewer resources

Criteria to Evaluate Food Additive Safety

Consensus exists that technical assessments of modern food additive petitions have become more complex. Analytical chemistry has magnified the understanding of food composition. Limits of detection and measurement have dropped from parts per million to parts per trillion. Often, questions of chemistry and biochemistry now can be raised and resolved more quickly than can questions related to toxicology. The criteria for each evaluation are unique, as are the properties and uses of each individual substance. As mentioned previously, for a food additive the statute demands neither confirmation of safety under all conditions of use, nor an absolute assurance of safety for every intended use. In the current food additive regulations, "safe" is defined as a reasonable certainty in the minds of competent scientists that the substance is not harmful under the intended conditions of use.

Evaluation of safety currently requires data and professional knowledge from many more disciplines than were required in the past. FDA representatives indicated that the agency must seek counsel from a wide range of scientific disciplines to adequately review the diverse nature of the petitions submitted. Scientists from a range of disciplines participate in the food additive review process, which often includes chemists, toxicologists, nutritionists, and microbiologists. In the case of the olestra petition, CFSAN tapped the resources of six other intra-agency centers and federal agencies, numerous outside consultants, and an FDA Food Advisory Committee special working group to assist in its review and decision making process.

FDA has attempted to specify acceptable study designs for generating the data necessary to support the approval of a food additive without imposing unduly rigid guidelines. These guidelines assist industry to assure that appropriate data are submitted to the agency. According to FDA, the agency will soon make available "Redbook II" (a revised edition of its 1982 *Toxicological Principles for the Safety Assessment of Direct Food Additives and Color Additives Used in Food,* which is referred to as the Redbook). The revised document is intended to provide updated guidance to petitioners regarding suggestions for toxicological safety data to assess direct food and color additives and GRAS ingredients. The Redbook does not mandate the submission of any specific scientific data, though in practice petitioners are reluctant to deviate far from FDA guidelines.

CURRENT EFFORTS

Workshop participants agreed that all parties with an interest in the quality of the food additive review process should work together to make sure that the process is efficient and effective. Industry and consumer interest groups can provide input into this process, but ultimately only Congress and FDA can initiate reform.

FDA representatives highlighted current efforts to improve the process within the current statutory limits. These efforts include a series of management and infrastructure initiatives designed to improve the efficiency of the approval process for direct food and color additives.

The agency has implemented several missives to help foster better lines of communication and interact with petitioners throughout the process. For example, agency representatives have expressed willingness to engage in pre-filing consultations so that petitioners have a better understanding of the types of data that are needed or that should be included in a petition submitted for review. Advance letters are a new tool of the agency to notify petitioners of a petition status, or explain why a submission may not be approved in its current form. FDA has also sponsored workshops for industry that address the food additive process and provide suggestions for petitioners.

The GRAS notification proposal is another recent initiative. It is designed to simplify the process of GRAS determination. Elimination of the lengthy GRAS affirmation procedure should help alleviate some agency resources.

FDA has organized focus teams to assist in making decisions on difficult issues that may arise during a petition review. These teams assist in moving the review process forward at times when the agency might otherwise have stalled.

Finally, FDA has entered into contractual agreements with several independent consulting organizations. One contractor assists the agency by assessing review times and analyzing the costs and resources needed to perform petition reviews most effectively. Another contractual agreement was made to assist in reducing the backlog of FDA's workload. These independent experts are assisting the agency in the scientific evaluation of more complex petitions and in the review of indirect additive petitions. Although these efforts offer initial steps in improving the food additive review process, participants recognized that long-term solutions may require statutory change.

International Efforts

While the food industry is interested in protecting the approval of new direct food additives, it is equally concerned with protecting the use of existing approvals in the global marketplace. The importance of international trade has tremendous implications for industry growth in the future. FDA may want to take a leadership role to ensure that the science-based approvals in the United States are recognized by international Codex standards. The Codex Alimentarius sets international regulatory standards useful in the case of trade disputes between countries. Currently, the Codex Commission is in the process of developing a general standard for food additives worldwide.

IMPROVING THE REGULATORY REVIEW PROCESS

Government Perspective

FDA representatives acknowledge that the current direct food additive review process has several shortcomings; the inability to process petitions within the statutory time frame is perhaps the greatest problem. Recently, the agency implemented a number of managerial and procedural changes designed to improve the system, but additional solutions are still needed. FDA seeks the suggestions of those with an interest in the process to help identify needs and propose changes.

Food additive petitions are growing more complex, and the agency cannot maintain internally the range of expertise needed for sound scientific assessments. FDA will increasingly need to call upon the expertise of outside consultants to assist in decision making. One consumer representative maintained that outside advisory committees or consultants should include consumer representatives with an understanding of the regulatory review process.

Industry Perspective

The substantial delay in the petition approval severely hinders food manufacturers from the timely introduction of new products into the marketplace. Several workshop participants suggested that the FDA needs additional resources to increase efficiency. These resources could come from congressional appropriations, petitioners, or both. Establishing a third-party review process to support FDA's activities may improve the current system. Industry and the agency could work together to determine criteria for accrediting reviewers and for the financing of these reviews. User fees for the review of direct and indirect additives may also be a viable mechanism, but would require statutory change. If user fees are imposed, a period of market exclusivity may be desirable for food ingredients that receive approval.

The quality of petitions can be improved; pre-filing consultations are useful opportunities for petitioners to better understand filing requirements. The proposed GRAS notification procedure may be useful to industry, but manufacturers who voluntarily file GRAS self-determinations are likely to seek some level of FDA recognition for these determinations. Industry will seek some incentive, such as a no objection letter, to make the filing of GRAS self-determinations worthwhile.

Industry representatives would like the Delaney clause to be replaced with a broader "reasonable certainty of no harm" standard for all additives. Finally, industry representatives emphasized the importance of protecting the integrity of the review process so that food additive approvals are upheld in the international marketplace.

Consumer Perspective

The length of the direct food additive review process is not a serious consumer concern. The imposition of user fees may also be largely inconsequential, but consumer representatives prefer user fees to an alternative that would make petitioners more directly responsible for funding the review. Consumer representatives varied in their opposition to the use of third-party reviews. Some were strictly opposed, claiming that such reviews create conflicts of interest and bias and diminish public confidence in the review process. Others were less opposed if careful guidelines are developed to ensure the independence of the process.

Consumers or their representatives would like to play an active role in providing comment to FDA on food additive petitions. The agency does provide opportunity for consumer comments in the notice-and-comment procedure and the FDA-sponsored Food Advisory Committee. Also, consumer representatives suggested that food additive approvals should never be final; rather, the agency should create a cyclical review process whereby approved ingredients are re-evaluated over time. However, if authorized, a cyclical review process would add an additional cost burden to the FDA. Most consumer representatives approve of the proposed GRAS notification procedure, but believe FDA should be notified of all GRAS self-determinations.

SUMMARY

Three major themes emerged during the workshop. First, communication is the key to enhancing the regulatory review process as better communication results in better decision making. Food additive petitions that include all of the necessary data can only serve to enhance scarce agency resources. However, what constitutes appropriate communication needs further exploration to delineate whether a consultative or collaborative process is occurring.

Second, solving complex scientific problems requires the involvement of many scientific disciplines that are often not available within the FDA staff. Accredited outside experts residing in academia, professional scientific associations, and public interest groups may need to be involved in the evaluation process, but barriers, such as the Federal Advisory Committee Act, the confidential nature of the data submitted, and concerns about potential conflict of interest, limit the involvement of outside experts. However, because the resources of FDA have remained almost level in constant dollars in recent years and the overwhelming competing pressures on the federal budget suggest that the future will be no brighter, the FDA will need to continue to rely on outside experts to resolve complex issues.

Finally, allowing user fees to enhance FDA's diminishing resources needs further discussion. Most participants agreed with the user fee concept, but public interest groups were opposed to the idea of manufacturers paying for FDA-contractor-approved petition reviews. Manufacturers are opposed to paying a user fee without a benefit such as market exclusivity. Continued discussion to further explore the public policy implications of the concept of user fees is critical to maximizing mutual understanding among all parties.

APPENDIX A

Legal Aspects of the Food Additive Approval Process

Lars Noah*

[background paper commissioned by the Institute of Medicine of the National Academy of Sciences for a Food Forum workshop entitled ENHANCING THE REGULATORY DECISION-MAKING APPROVAL PROCESS FOR DIRECT FOOD INGREDIENT TECHNOLOGIES (1997)]

---

*Associate Professor, University of Florida College of Law. I would like to thank Douglas L. Archer, Marsha N. Cohen, Catherine L. Copp, Edward Dunkelberger, Margaret Gilhooley, Richard L. Hall, Peter Barton Hutt, Richard A. Merrill, Barbara A. Noah, George M. Paterson, George H. Pauli, Donna Porter, Sidney A. Shapiro, and Keith Triebwasser for reviewing earlier drafts of the manuscript, and Lisa M.W. Hillman for her research assistance. The views expressed in this paper do not necessarily reflect the opinions of any of the reviewers or the National Academy of Sciences. For a revised and updated treatment of this subject, see Lars Noah and Richard A. Merrill, Starting from Scratch?: Reinventing the Food Additive Approval Process, 78 B.U. L. REV. 329 (1998).

Contents

What is food to one, is to others bitter poison.
—Lucretius, DE RERUM NATURA (50 B.C.)

In the past few years, novel food substances have attracted significant public attention, most notably Procter & Gamble's fat-substitute olestra and Calgene's bioengineered tomato. Some have criticized the U.S. Food and Drug Administration (FDA) for its lengthy delays in reviewing these and other substances added to food.[1] At the same time, others have argued that the agency does not adequately ensure the safety of such substances. These latest controversies pose significant and timely questions about how best to regulate substances added to food. The problems are multifaceted, and policymakers will require input from both legal and scientific perspectives to address them.

This paper focuses primarily on a description of the FDA's regulation of substances intentionally added to food as it has evolved over the last several decades, and it concludes with a discussion of several possible avenues for reform. Debates about proposals to modify existing procedures must start with a proper appreciation of the difficulties encountered in the past. Moreover, the history of the food additive approval process illuminates significant and recurring challenges faced in the design of properly functioning regulatory programs. Studies of other federal agencies have uncovered valuable lessons about effective regulation that transcend the particular program under consideration.[2]

HISTORY

The federal government first asserted authority over the quality and safety of food products early this century. In 1906, reacting to widely publicized examples of industry abuses, Congress prohibited the introduction of adulterated or misbranded food and drugs into interstate commerce.[3] The act provided that any food containing an "added poisonous or other added deleterious ingredient which may render such article injurious to health" would be deemed adulterated.[4] If they detected a safety problem, federal officials could initiate enforcement action to remove the product from the market, but the government would shoulder the burden of proving that the ingredient posed "a reasonable possibility of injury."[5] Although Congress replaced this original statute in 1938 with the federal Food, Drug, and Cosmetic (FD&C) Act,[6] the newer legislation retained the same basic system of after-the-fact policing for adulterants in food until the Food Additives Amendment of 1958[7] created a premarket review and approval system. These two enactments are discussed more fully below.

In the two decades that elapsed between the passage of the FD&C Act and the Food Additives Amendment, a number of developments rendered the original statutory design outdated. Indeed, the original legislation, based as it was on the 1906 Act, focused on the control of "adulterants" and did not fully anticipate the rapid progress in food processing technology and the growing utilization of intentional additives that would follow.[8] Technological advances spurred by World War II allowed processors to offer more nutritious, palatable, and convenient foods, and consumers increasingly demanded such improved products. Meanwhile, progress in the biomedical sciences increased the understanding of human nutritional needs as well as chronic diseases. These pressures and advances have not yet abated, and, almost four decades later, one legitimately may ask whether Congress should consider once again updating (some would say overhauling) the statutory provisions governing food additives.[9]

The Food, Drug, and Cosmetic Act of 1938

Under the original FD&C Act, the FDA enjoyed broad responsibility but fairly weak regulatory authority over substances added to food. Section 402(a) provided that a food shall be deemed to be adulterated under the following circumstances:

(1) If it bears or contains any poisonous or deleterious substance which may render it injurious to health; but in case the substance is not an added substance such food shall not be considered adulterated under this clause if the quantity of such substance in such food does not ordinarily render it injurious to health; or

(2) if it bears or contains any added poisonous or added deleterious substance which is unsafe within the meaning of section 406. . . [10]

Section 406 of the Act provided in relevant part as follows:

> Any poisonous or deleterious substance added to any food, except where such substance is required in the production thereof or cannot be avoided by good manufacturing practice[,] shall be deemed to be unsafe for purposes of the application of [the above-quoted] clause; but when such substance is so required or cannot be so avoided, the Secretary shall promulgate regulations limiting the quantity therein or thereon to such extent as he finds necessary for the protection of public health. . . [11]

The authority to promulgate food standards of identity under Section 401 provided the Agency with another, though cumbersome, regulatory mechanism for restricting the use of added substances by not authorizing their use as optional ingredients in standardized food. [12]

Under Section 402(a) of the FD&C Act, the FDA could initiate judicial proceedings to seize adulterated food or enjoin its continued marketing.[13] Unless the product exceeded one of the few tolerances established under Section 406, however, the agency would shoulder the burden of proving that the substance (1) was poisonous or deleterious and (2) may render the food injurious to health.[14] As the Supreme Court held in construing the essentially identical language in the 1906 version of the statute,[15] the government must show that the food containing a poisonous or deleterious substance creates a reasonable possibility of harm to consumers.[16] Under the 1938 Act, the FDA shouldered an even greater burden of proof in the case of non-added substances (i.e., "ordinarily render it injurious to health").[17] "Under either standard, the government must prove that the food itself probably will, or may, injure health, not merely that it contains a poisonous substance."[18] Because of the time and effort required to undertake lifetime animal feeding studies of a substance, the FDA frequently could not satisfy this burden even if it had some legitimate basis for concern about safety.[19]

On the other hand, absent a tolerance established under Section 406, any added poisonous or deleterious substance would render a food adulterated,[20] even if it was used at a level that was not "injurious" and served a useful purpose.[21] In theory, Section 402(a)(2) reduced the FDA's burden of proof in taking enforcement action against a food product by eliminating any need for it to demonstrate that an added poisonous or deleterious substance might render the food injurious to health.[22] The agency would still have to prove that an added substance was poisonous or deleterious. Once it made such a finding, however, the FDA would have difficulty authorizing the use of a safe and beneficial but technically "poisonous" substance in food.

Thus, the original statute created a safety standard for substances added to food that was both unnecessarily rigid and quite difficult for the FDA to administer. Because it shouldered the burden of proof, the agency experienced problems in regulating the introduction and marketing of foods containing potentially hazardous substances. Moreover, because the statute did not require any advance notification of the introduction of a new additive for use in food, the agency might not even learn of its use unless safety problems subsequently came to light.[23]

Although the FDA initially lacked the authority to insist on testing, chemical manufacturers and food processors nonetheless had incentives to undertake limited safety evaluations. First, companies might fear eventual enforcement sanctions under the FDA's food adulteration provisions. Second, and more importantly, companies could not risk the adverse publicity that would accompany subsequently discovered hazards in their products. Finally, though less of an issue at the time, companies might face significant tort liability if consumers suffered injuries.[24] In fact, most manufacturers did pretest new additives to some extent, but nothing prevented an unscrupulous firm from using an untested substance in food.[25]

The Food Additives Amendment of 1958

In 1950, Congress turned its attention to the growing use of chemical additives.[26] After two years of hearings on the subject,[27] a select committee of the House of Representatives chaired by James Delaney issued a report of its investigation. At the outset of its report, the committee noted the rapidly growing use of chemicals in the food supply: "There is hardly a food sold in the market place today which has not had some chemicals used on or in it at some stage in its production, processing, packaging, transportation, or storage."[28] The committee recognized the substantial value of this growing use of additives, but it also expressed concerns about the accompanying potential health hazards.[29] As noted in the report, the FDA estimated that approximately 700 chemicals were used in food at the time but that only 428 were known to be safe.[30] The committee expressed particular concern over the lack of information about the possible chronic risks of existing food-use chemicals, and it urged Congress to amend the FD&C Act so that food additives would be governed by substantially the same safety and premarket review requirements applicable to drugs at that time.[31]

In the six-year period following the investigations by the Delaney Committee, Congress considered numerous bills and held further hearings on the subject.[32] Unlike other legislative initiatives involving FDA-regulated products, which were prompted by real or perceived public health crises (most notably in the case of drugs), there was little apparent sense of urgency in crafting a proper response to the emerging concerns about new food additives. Instead, Congress acted with deliberation in designing an appropriate regulatory mechanism.[33] As an initial step, Congress amended the FD&C Act in 1954 to create a premarket approval system for pesticide residues in food, requiring the establishment of tolerances for any pesticide chemicals intended for use on a raw agricultural commodity.[34]

The food and chemical industries accepted the need for some system of premarket FDA review,[35] but initially they preferred bills demanding little more than advance notification of an intent to market a new additive rather than bills requiring the issuance of a license by the agency.[36] Administration officials objected that such an approach "would give no effect, except a delaying effect, to an adverse safety evaluation of the Secretary."[37] Such a delay would give the FDA time to institute judicial proceedings to prevent marketing, where it only would have to establish that existing studies failed to demonstrate safety (rather than the more difficult burden of proving that an added substance was poisonous or deleterious and could render a food injurious to health); however, the agency would have to prove more than a reasonable possibility of harm in the abstract, under any condition of use; it would shoulder the more difficult burden of showing inadequate pretesting related to the safety of a substance for that particular intended use.

In contrast, the Department of Health, Education, and Welfare (HEW), of which the FDA was a part, sponsored a bill that would prohibit the use of a new food additive unless and until the FDA promulgated a regulation specifically authorizing its use.[38] The agency did not conceive of this proposal as a product-specific licensing scheme authorizing a particular use by the applicant, as is the case with new drug approvals, but rather as a limitation on a proposed use uniformly applicable to all persons.[39] Under such a generic approval regime, the FDA would issue a nonexclusive public regulation authorizing the use of an additive by any person wishing to do so, subject only to any patent protection remaining for the food additive petitioner. Without any recorded discussion of the issue, Congress ultimately opted for the FDA's proposed approach.

The bills also included various deadlines for FDA review of information about a new food additive. For instance, Congressman Delaney's original bill provided that a petition would be deemed approved if the Secretary failed to act on it within 60 days of filing.[40] Under another bill, even if the Secretary concluded that an applicant had failed to demonstrate the safety of a new additive, a manufacturer or processor still could introduce the additive 30 days after notifying the agency of its intent to do so, unless the FDA first sought an injunction.[41] The agency favored a premarket approval system but protested that it would need additional time to process submissions.[42]

In 1958, Congress enacted the Food Additives Amendment to the FD&C Act.[43] By establishing a premarket review and approval system for food additives in new Section 409, Congress shifted the burden of proof on the safety issue from the FDA to the industry.[44] Food additives now could not be used unless and until the agency deemed them safe. The legislation was not, however, motivated exclusively by safety concerns. Congress sought to promote continued innovation in food technology by giving the FDA greater flexibility to authorize limited uses of substances in food even if shown in animal tests to be poisonous at higher levels.[45] The legislation also responded to proposals that had been introduced in a number of states to regulate new food additives.[46] The next three parts of this paper, focusing in turn on definitional, procedural, and substantive issues, set forth in greater detail the most important aspects of the Food Additives Amendment of 1958.

DEFINITION OF FOOD ADDITIVE

Definitional questions have assumed center stage in the application of the Food Additives Amendment over the last four decades. The statutory definition of the term "food additive" continues to pose significant interpretive difficulties. More importantly, as the food additive approval process has become increasingly cumbersome, industry has come to rely more heavily on certain exceptions enumerated in the definition. In fact, some of the recently suggested reforms focus on modifications of the existing definition in an effort to narrow the coverage of the Food Additives Amendment and, thereby, limit the scope of the FDA's premarket role.

Components of Food

The FD&C Act, as originally enacted, defined the term "food" as "articles used for food or drink . . . [and] components of any such article."[47] Putting aside the obvious tautology in the primary definition of the term, Congress clearly included "components" of food within this provision.[48] In addition, the operative provisions of the original statute—namely, the often vague prohibitions against adulteration and misbranding—refer to "substance[s]" which are added to food,[49] as well as to "ingredients" from which a food has been fabricated.[50]

Although Congress never directly modified any of these early definitions, the Food Additives Amendment effectively displaced many of the statute's broad prohibitions against adulteration insofar as they affected substances added to food.

> The term "food additive" means any substance the intended use of which results or may reasonably be expected to result, directly or indirectly, in its becoming a component or otherwise affecting the characteristics of any food . . . , if such substance is not generally recognized . . . to be safe under the conditions of its intended use. . . .[51]

By its terms, this definition does not include substances that are generally recognized as safe (GRAS), a potentially broad exception which, as discussed more fully in the next section, has become a central feature of the FDA's regulatory system. The definition enumerates a number of "indirect" additives included within its scope,[52] but, as subsequently amended, it also specifically excludes several important substances that otherwise would be covered by the broad definition, including color additives, pesticide chemicals used on raw agricultural commodities, new animal drugs, and dietary supplement ingredients.[53] Other provisions of the statute now govern each of these latter substances.[54]

At its core, the definition of "food additive" applies whenever the manufacturer or food processor actually knew or should have known that a "substance" would become a "component or otherwise affect[ ] the characteristics of any food." The FDA routinely grapples with questions about the intended use of an item in order to determine its appropriate regulatory classification as, for instance, a food, drug, medical device, or cosmetic.[55] Although Congress focused on "chemical" additives,[56] items commonly available as a food might become a food additive (e.g., tomatoes in pasta sauce) unless otherwise excluded from the definition.[57]

Indirect Additives

The definition of "food additive" clearly covers more than just intentional, functional additives; Congress expressly included substances which may indirectly become a component or otherwise affect the characteristics of food by virtue of their use in production or processing.[58] Such "indirect" or "incidental"[59] additives may, for instance, include chemical substances used in food-contact packaging which unavoidably, and often at barely detectable levels, migrate into the food.[60] Before the FDA may regulate a substance as an indirect food additive, however, it must have some evidence that the substance may reasonably be expected to migrate into food.[61] The agency then may impose conditions on the use of a substance to assure that it will not migrate into food.

In the mid-1970s, the FDA grappled with evidence suggesting that acrylonitrile, a chemical used to fabricate plastic beverage bottles and other food-contact articles, might migrate into foods and might also cause cancer.[62] After a formal hearing on the matter, the Commissioner decided that the acrylonitrile copolymer used to manufacture bottles qualified as a food additive whose safety remained unproven and, therefore, withdrew approval.[63] The manufacturers immediately and successfully challenged this decision in court.

In *Monsanto Co. v. Kennedy*,[64] the United States Court of Appeals for the District of Columbia Circuit reversed the Commissioner's decision. According to the court, the FDA had adduced no concrete evidence to support its conclusion that some residual (unpolymerized) acrylonitrile monomer would migrate from the interior surface of the plastic container into the beverage.[65] The court remanded the decision so that the Commissioner could consider migration data from recently improved detection methods and also decide, even if migration was probable at an extremely low level, whether to exercise his discretion to disregard any such migration as trivial.[66] Relying on subsequently acquired migration data, the agency again concluded that acrylonitrile qualified as a food additive, but this time it also approved the additive as safe under conditions ensuring very little risk of migration.[67]

The FDA has approved innumerable indirect food additives over the years.[68] In fact, the agency has devoted so much of its time and manpower to this task that it has, by comparison, seemingly neglected reviews of direct food additives.[69] The FDA recently established an abbreviated exemption procedure for food-contact substances where the likelihood or extent of migration is so trivial—generally less than 0.5 parts per billion (ppb)—as not to require regulation.[70] Except insofar as it affects the FDA's workload, the special questions posed by the regulation of indirect food additives are beyond the scope of this paper.

Dietary Supplements

One troubling question concerns how to differentiate between a food additive and the food itself. Before a recent amendment to the statute, this problem arose most frequently with regard to dietary supplements, but the interpretive issue is broader. Over the years, the agency has attempted to classify nutritional supplements as food additives (or drugs) so as to shift the burden of proof on questions of safety (and effectiveness) from the government to the industry. In a pair of recent cases involving black currant oil (BCO), two federal appellate courts rejected the FDA's position that BCO qualified as a food additive when sold in capsule form.[71] In both instances, the agency had seized shipments of the dietary supplement on the theory that the BCO, as a component in the dietary supplement capsules, was presumptively unsafe.[72] Notwithstanding the rule of judicial deference to reasonable agency interpretations of ambiguous language in an enabling statute,[73] neither court found the FDA's reading of the "food additive" definition persuasive.[74]

According to the courts in these cases, only those components that somehow modify a food may be regulated as food additives. In the case of the BCO capsules, the courts held that the black currant oil was the sole active ingredient and, therefore, properly regarded as the entire food rather than an additive in the food.[75] Indeed, in litigating the seizure actions, the FDA had conceded that BCO sold in bottles containing the pure liquid form would not qualify as a food additive; the courts decided that replacing the bottle with a gelatin capsule as the delivery vehicle for the BCO should not affect its regulatory status.[76] In the capsule form, two inert substances (gelatin and glycerin) encased the BCO. The dispute turned on the interpretation of the phrase "becoming a component or otherwise affecting the characteristics of any food," which the agency wished to read in the disjunctive (i.e., either becoming a component or affecting the characteristics . . .), while the processors favored an overlapping, unitary interpretation (i.e., affecting the characteristics by becoming a component or otherwise . . .).[77]

Although hardly unambiguous,[78] both courts accepted the latter construction of the statute, observing that BCO did not appear to constitute a component in the first place,[79] and explaining that BCO certainly did not affect the characteristic of the gelatin and glycerin.[80] If the FDA's interpretation were valid, then the agency could recharacterize every processed food as a food additive in order to shift the burden of proving the food's safety onto the processor, in effect reading the 1938 provisions governing food out of the statute even though Congress chose not to amend them in 1958. This judicial gloss on the definition may, however, excessively narrow the class of food additives insofar as it suggests that the "component" must meaningfully affect the characteristics of the food; it is not clear, for instance, whether the gelatin and glycerin (or an equivalent plasticizer) in the BCO capsules would fall within these courts' interpretation of the definition of the term.[81]

In earlier cases, courts have sustained efforts by the FDA to regulate similar products as food additives. Indeed, when a food contains more than one ingredient, each ingredient may be deemed a food additive, as the courts conceded in the BCO cases.[82] For example, one federal district court accepted the FDA's contention that BCO was an additive when encapsulated with fish oil, vitamins, and minerals.[83] Similarly, a federal appellate court recently decided that evening primrose oil was a food additive when encapsulated with Vitamin E.[84]

The difficult cases usually involved dietary supplements, in part because the FDA sought to find a meaningful regulatory mechanism for controlling these products. The agency also sometimes tried characterizing supplements as drugs rather than food.[85] Indeed, the references to active and inactive ingredients make little sense in the context of conventional food products. To the extent that Congress has further restricted the agency's power to control the distribution of dietary supplements, these definitional issues may become less important in the future. Nonetheless, judicial interpretations of the statutory language will continue to limit the FDA's choice of regulatory responses to concerns about more conventional foods and food components.

In 1994, Congress amended the FD&C Act to address dietary supplements,[86] and it has been suggested that food processors might utilize these special provisions to avoid the rigors of food additive review.[87] If a substance can be classified as a "dietary supplement" or as an "ingredient" in such a supplement, then it is excluded from the definition of the term "food additive."[88] Unless the substance represents a "new dietary ingredient" (because it was not marketed before October 15, 1994),[89] a manufacturer or processor would only have to file a premarket notification with the FDA 75 days prior to commercial use.[90]

The definition of the term "dietary supplement," which was added to the statute in 1994, has several elements. First, it is a product:

> intended to supplement the diet that bears or contains one or more of the following dietary ingredients: (A) a vitamin; (B) a mineral; (C) an herb or other botanical; (D) an amino acid; (E) a dietary substance for use by man to supplement the diet by increasing the total dietary intake; or (F) a concentrate, metabolite, constituent, extract, or combination of any [of these] ingredients. . . .[91]

Second, it "is intended for ingestion in tablet, capsule, powder, softgel, gelcap, or liquid form or, if not intended for ingestion in such a form, is not represented as conventional food and is not represented for use as a sole item of a meal or of the diet."[92] Third, the product must be labeled as a "dietary supplement."[93]

It is possible that the manufacturer of a conventional food (such as a candy bar) containing a new food-use substance (such as an artificial sweetener or a fat-substitute developed in the 1980s) might assert that the product (1) is intended to supplement the diet, (2) contains one or more of the enumerated dietary ingredients (even if the new food-use substance itself did not fit within any of those categories), (3) is labeled as a "dietary supplement," and (4) is not otherwise represented as a conventional food. It seems unlikely, however, that a company would take such a gamble in trying to circumvent the FDA's food additive approval requirements for new food-use substances added to conventional foods, nor is it clear that such an approach provides much of an advantage over using the existing GRAS exception.[94] Indeed, simply labeling the product as a "dietary supplement" will not by itself counteract other indicia that a product containing a new food-use substance is being represented as a conventional food, though the agency may be more hesitant to pursue enforcement efforts in such a case.

Generally Recognized as Safe

The statutory definition of "food additive" covers only a substance that "is not generally recognized . . . to be safe under the conditions of its intended use."[95] Thus, in the peculiar meaning of the term as it is used in the statute, a substance that becomes a component of a food (even as an ingredient) would not be a "food additive" if it is generally recognized as safe (GRAS). Congress further defined GRAS as requiring that a substance used in food be

> generally recognized, among experts qualified by scientific training and experience to evaluate its safety, as having been adequately shown through scientific procedures (or, in the case of a substance used in food prior to January 1, 1958, through either scientific procedures or experience based on common use in food) to be safe under the conditions of its intended use.[96]

Thus, GRAS status may exist if some level of scientific agreement about a substance's safety exists based either on appropriate testing or common use in food prior to 1958.

The GRAS exception obviously raises a number of serious interpretive difficulties. The statute provides little further elaboration about the required degree of scientific agreement, the types of scientific procedures which could provide the necessary predicate for such agreement, or, in the case of substances in widespread use before 1958, the required nature and extent of such prior use. For instance, how could a substance be GRAS without experience based on common prior use—did Congress thereby intend to give manufacturers of new food-use substances the option of submitting test results to non-FDA scientists for their evaluation and possible stamp of approval? At least one witness at the 1957 congressional hearings apparently thought so, suggesting that a company could seek the advice of private or academic consultants on the question of whether there was general recognition of safety based on existing data.[97] As discussed below, this has become a common practice.

Because the GRAS exception became a common feature of every one of the numerous bills on the subject considered by Congress,[98] the legislative history sheds some additional light on these and other questions. Although not technically a "grandfather clause" (which would permanently exempt from coverage all substances used in food prior to the enactment date),[99] the GRAS exception attempts to minimize the potentially significant and unnecessary burden that would otherwise be placed on both the industry and the FDA if the agency had to evaluate and formally approve common substances used in food.[100] In addition, for substances that were not regarded as GRAS and therefore subject to regulation as food additives, Congress initially provided a transitional period of up to 30 months for compliance with the new premarket approval requirements,[101] but it subsequently extended this phase-in period by almost five additional years.[102]

The FD&C Act included similar GRAS language in defining the term "new drug,"[103] as did the Pesticide Residues Amendment of 1954.[104] Although conceding during the congressional hearings that the language was inherently ambiguous, the agency thought that it could apply this flexible GRAS exception to food additives in a sensible manner.[105] (Interestingly, just two years after enacting the Food Additives Amendment, Congress failed to include a GRAS exception in the Color Additive Amendments.[106]) As subsequently construed by reviewing courts, the exception applicable to drugs is quite narrow,[107] in part because the statute requires that a drug be both GRAS and GRAE (generally recognized as effective). In 1973, the Supreme Court held that the exception in the definition of new drug required an "expert consensus" of both safety and effectiveness.[108]

Both the FDA and reviewing courts sometimes have struggled to make sense of the GRAS exception.[109] All agree that there must be a fairly high level of scientific agreement.[110] The

FDA's implementing regulations, finally promulgated almost two decades after passage of the Food Additives Amendment, provide as follows:

> General recognition of safety based upon scientific procedures shall require the same quantity and quality of scientific evidence as is required to obtain approval of a food additive regulation for the ingredient. General recognition of safety through scientific procedures shall ordinarily be based upon published studies which may be corroborated by unpublished studies and other data and information.[111]

Evidence of GRAS must relate to the conditions of intended use; general recognition of the safe use of a substance in a different product or at a different level would not suffice to escape the food additive definition.[112] The exception turns not on safety itself so much as on recognition of safety by scientific experts. Testimony of an absence of any evidence of a health hazard would not suffice to establish GRAS status,[113] at least not unless coupled with evidence of common prior use.[114] If GRAS status is premised on common use prior to 1958, then such use must have been fairly extensive.[115]

Originally, the FDA categorically refused to recognize use outside of the United States.[116] This policy did not, however, survive a subsequent judicial challenge.[117] The revised regulations provide that prior foreign use may support GRAS status, but only if the information about such use is readily available and corroborated.[118] In addition, GRAS status based on prior foreign use must satisfy domestic conceptions of safety.[119] If GRAS status is based on prior foreign use, the FDA urges the manufacturer to seek its concurrence.[120] Other sections of the regulations continue to define eligibility for GRAS status by reference to common use in the United States.[121]

The FDA's GRAS Lists. During the congressional hearings leading up to enactment of the Food Additives Amendment, the FDA submitted a "partial" list of what it would regard as GRAS substances including items such as butter, coffee, cream, gelatin, lard, lemon juice, margarine, molasses, mustard, olive oil, paprika, pepper, salt, sugar, vinegar, and wine.[122] During the first several years after enactment of the Food Additives Amendment, the FDA listed in its regulations hundreds of ingredients as GRAS.[123] The original GRAS lists included, for example, ascorbic acid, calcium chloride, caramel, and sodium phosphate.[124]

Because these inventories emerged without any detailed scientific assessment of the original safety data, much less of the data subsequently generated with constantly improving detection and safety assessment methods (as underscored by the discovery of evidence linking an artificial sweetener mixture containing cyclamate to cancer[125]), the FDA initiated a systematic review in 1969 in order to settle the GRAS or food additive status of a number of substances commonly added to food.[126] The agency designated several categories of food ingredients for this review: substances of natural biological origin which were widely consumed as food before 1958 but subsequently were modified in certain respects by new production processes or selective breeding; distillates, isolates, extracts, and reaction products of GRAS substances; and substances not of natural biological origin or intended for consumption for other than their nutrient properties.[127]

The National Academy of Sciences (NAS) undertook ingredient usage surveys,[128] and, in 1972, the Life Sciences Research Office (LSRO) of the Federation of American Societies for Experimental Biology (FASEB) established a Select Committee on GRAS Substances (SCOGS) to conduct reviews of the available scientific literature.[129] Over a period of 10 years, SCOGS forwarded to the FDA detailed reports on 468 food substances (of which 422 were direct ingredients).[130] The Select Committee first created an array of five standardized recommendations,[131] and it concluded that 72 percent of the food substances under review should remain GRAS and only one percent should immediately become subject to food additive requirements.[132] Although the FDA planned to review each of these reports and pursue appropriate rulemaking, it has not completed its GRAS list review 15 years after receiving the last SCOGS report.[133]

A number of substances currently appear on the GRAS affirmation list that emerged from the FDA's comprehensive review. At present, almost 200 separate ingredients are included as GRAS for direct use in food.[134] The FDA concedes, however, that its GRAS lists are not exhaustive: "Because of the large number of substances the intended use of which results or may reasonably be expected to result, directly or indirectly, in their becoming a component or otherwise affecting the characteristics of food, it is impracticable to list all such substances that are GRAS."[135] Thus, a substance "of natural biological origin that has been widely consumed for its nutrient properties in the United States prior to January 1, 1958, without known detrimental effects, which is subject only to conventional processing . . . will ordinarily be regarded as GRAS without specific inclusion" in one of the GRAS lists.[136] More specifically, "by way of illustration, the Commissioner regards such common food ingredients as salt, pepper, vinegar, baking powder, and monosodium glutamate as safe for their intended use."[137]

GRAS status does not free a substance of FDA controls. At a minimum, a GRAS substance must comply with any applicable food grade specifications appearing in the FOOD CHEMICALS CODEX,[138] and it must perform an appropriate function (and be used at a level no higher than necessary to achieve its intended purpose) in the food or food-contact article in which it is used.[139] In addition, a substance must comply with any specific usage limitations appearing in any GRAS affirmation regulation.[140] If no specific limitations apply, GRAS status is lost only if the conditions of use differ significantly from those providing the basis for eligibility.[141] Finally, "[n]ew information may at any time require reconsideration of the GRAS status of a food ingredient," and any revision of an existing GRAS regulation would be accomplished by the FDA through notice-and-comment rulemaking procedures.[142] In contrast, any revision of a food additive regulation would require more cumbersome procedures.[143]

Private GRAS Determinations. Unless the FDA previously has decided otherwise, a person may take the position that a particular food-use substance is GRAS and, therefore, exempt from food additive approval requirements.[144] In fact, there is no present requirement that the agency be advised of such private GRAS determinations. A few manufacturers have commissioned safety reviews by reputable scientific organizations, and FASEB has conducted a handful of private GRAS reviews during the last several years.[145] For example, Procter & Gamble asked the Federation to review the safety of caprenin, a reduced calorie fat-substitute; on the basis of FASEB's report, the company determined that this substance was GRAS, filed a GRAS affirmation petition with the FDA, and began selling it to food processors.[146] Similarly, Nabisco Foods sought a FASEB review of salatrim, another fat-substitute subsequently brought to market on the basis of a GRAS self-determination.[147] Some have suggested that the National Center for Food Safety and Technology, an organization recently established in the Chicago area with private and government support, might play a similar role in the future.[148]

Whether undertaken for the FDA or a private entity, FASEB's LSRO assembles an ad hoc panel of experts from several different scientific disciplines to conduct the requested reviews. These experts usually are drawn from among FASEB's more than 40,000 members, and they are hired by LSRO to serve as independent consultants.[149] The expert panels prepare study reports which are "peer-reviewed by an independent internal FASEB committee for clarity, objectivity, and scientific integrity . . . , [and] the reports of each study are published in scientific journals or are made available publicly."[150]

FASEB's review procedures depend to some extent on the terms of the particular agreement.[151] The FDA often has contracted with the LSRO to conduct safety reviews of particular substances or to formulate recommendations on broad scientific questions. These contracts may set forth precise timetables for the solicitation of public input, the scheduling of meetings, and the completion of draft and final reports. As mentioned previously, the original GRAS list review required the creation of a special standing committee (SCOGS) charged with that enormous task, and FASEB managed to review almost 500 food-use substances in just 10 years. Its more recent safety reviews of BHA and MSG, again under contract with the FDA, took more than two years to complete and cost the agency approximately $300,000 each.[152] Information about the speed and expense of FASEB's occasional private GRAS reviews is unavailable.

Similarly, a few industry associations have created their own expert panels to review the possible GRAS status of food ingredients, as the Flavor and Extract Manufacturers' Association (FEMA) has done for the last few decades.[153] FEMA's project began in 1959, initially surveying the industry about the usage of different flavoring substances. The association then established a permanent panel—composed of six to eight recognized and independent experts from various disciplines including toxicology and biochemistry—to evaluate scientific literature reviews (SLRs) assembled for its consideration and then assess the GRAS status of those flavoring substances.[154] Over the last 30 years, the expert panel's reports have been published periodically in the journal FOOD TECHNOLOGY.[155] Furthermore, the SLRs underlying the Panel's GRAS determinations were made available to the public and forwarded to the FDA.[156]

In the case of a new flavoring substance, a company seeking an opinion about the flavor's potential GRAS status must submit an application form and literature search to FEMA's staff which, after a preliminary check for completeness, forwards the request and information to the expert panel for consideration at its next regularly scheduled meeting.[157] The available literature is evaluated against FEMA's published criteria, and a GRAS designation requires a unanimous vote by the panel; otherwise, the flavoring substance will be placed in a hold category for further study or be designated as not GRAS.[158]

Since the inception of this project, FEMA has considered more than 2000 thousand flavoring substances. The expert panel's initial set of reviews identified 1,118 substances as GRAS based on prior safe use and six more as GRAS based on the available scientific information.[159] The FDA incorporated only 277 of these flavors in its own GRAS list,[160] but it also designated another 846 of these FEMA-reviewed substances as approved food additives on the strength of the existing safety data and without the need for filing separate petitions.[161] In 1985, FEMA finished a comprehensive reevaluation aimed at updating its original GRAS determinations, dropping three flavoring substances from the list.[162] In 1993, FEMA began a second reevaluation process, coupled with an effort to update and reformat all existing SLRs, which it hopes to complete in five years.[163]

The FDA has not challenged the marketing of flavors that FEMA has identified as GRAS, whether or not it has incorporated them into its own lists of GRAS substances or approved food additives.[164] In extending the date by which persons would have to comply with its bulk flavoring requirements, the agency described the FEMA list as one of the "reliable industry association GRAS lists."[165] The FDA also occasionally refers to FEMA's GRAS listing of a flavor to support a GRAS affirmation proposal.[166]

Another potentially important source of food safety expertise resides in the Joint Expert Committees on Food Additives (JECFA), first organized in 1956 by the United Nations Food and Agriculture Organization (FAO) and the World Health Organization (WHO) and now associated with these organizations' Codex Alimentarius Commission.[167] JECFA reports have influenced decisions by the FDA and other regulatory bodies, and its recommendations concerning particular additives might be relied upon by companies in making GRAS self-determinations. Under the FDA's GRAS criteria, a report by JECFA or a comparable group certainly could qualify as "general recognition" of safety, even if a substance has never before been used in food.[168]

Although nothing prevents such GRAS self-determinations, the strategy carries obvious regulatory risks. On occasion, the agency has pursued enforcement proceedings, disagreeing with a company's belated claim that a substance is GRAS.[169]

> Th[e] theoretical freedom of food processors to determine initially which ingredients require FDA licensure has little practical significance for widely used ingredients. Very few processors will purchase ingredients for which the supplier cannot provide documentation of FDA approval or acknowledgement as GRAS. Should a manufacturer independently conclude that an ingredient is GRAS it runs the risk that FDA may disagree and initiate regulatory action against its product.[170]

Some disagreement exists over who would shoulder the burden of proof on the question of GRAS status in the event that the agency challenges a company's self-determination; a few commentators have argued that the government would have to disprove that a substance is GRAS,[171] but others have suggested that the burden would rest with the manufacturer to establish general recognition of safety once questioned by the FDA.[172] (A similar question might arise when trying to determine whether a new substance falls within the scope of an existing GRAS or food additive regulation.[173]) As with the government's burden to prove adulteration under the original provisions of the FD&C Act, this is not a trivial issue.

In any case, the FDA allows any interested person to petition for an affirmation by the agency that a substance qualifies for GRAS status,[174] and the mere filing of such a petition may protect a manufacturer from enforcement action during the pendency of the agency's review.[175] Because of what some commentators have described as a complete breakdown in the food additive approval process, the GRAS exception has come to serve an essential role in the existing regulatory scheme by allowing for the use of safe food substances without necessitating agency action.[176] Whatever one thinks about the continued viability of the FDA's approval process, a matter taken up more fully later in this paper, the GRAS exception has proven to be a tremendously important feature of the current statutory design.

Prior Sanctions Exception. The statutory definition of "food additive" excludes "any substance used in accordance with a sanction or approval granted prior to the enactment of this paragraph pursuant to this Act, the Poultry Products Inspection Act . . . or the Meat Inspection Act."[177] By virtue of the date of enactment of the Food Additives Amendment, such so-called "prior sanctions" exist only if granted before September 6, 1958 (nine months later than the cut-off for prior use GRAS).[178] A prior sanction may be either formal, as when a regulation establishing a food standard of identity includes a reference to an ingredient, or informal, usually in the form of correspondence from an appropriate agency official.[179] The burden of demonstrating that a prior sanction exists rests with the person seeking to make use of this exception.

As with the exclusion for GRAS substances, a prior sanction only provides an exception for a particular food use of a substance.[180] The agency has published regulations identifying a number of prior sanctions. Apart from nitrites, which were sanctioned by the Department of Agriculture as a color fixative and preservative in cured meats,[181] the prior sanctions listed by the FDA all cover substances used in food packaging materials.[182] The agency recognizes that documentation of other sanctions may exist,[183] and it invites interested persons to request publication of any such sanction, but the FDA also warns that a prior sanction will lapse if not brought to the agency's attention once it undertakes consideration of a substance's food additive status.[184]

Unlike a GRAS determination, which the FDA always remains free to reconsider,[185] a prior sanction exception to "food additive" status technically should be irrevocable,[186] though the agency had once suggested otherwise.[187] In any case, a prior sanction would not represent a permanent safe harbor for a substance. The sanction underlying the exception may, of course, be revoked.[188] A prior sanction only provides an exception to the special statutory controls applicable to "food additives." If the FDA determines that a substance added to food "may render it injurious to health,"[189] then the agency may restrict or prohibit its further use even if prior sanctioned.[190] A prior-sanctioned substance remains a "food" subject to the FD&C Act's more general prohibitions against adulteration and misbranding.[191]

APPROVAL PROCEDURES

The definitional issues discussed above are important only because they potentially affect the regulatory status of a substance.[192] A food shall be deemed to be adulterated, thereby potentially triggering a variety of enforcement sanctions,[193] "if it is, or it bears or contains, any food additive which is unsafe within the meaning of section 409" of the FD&C Act.[194] Section 409 provides in relevant part that a food additive shall be deemed to be unsafe unless its particular use previously has been approved through the issuance of a regulation.[195] In short, if a substance qualifies as a food additive, then it may not be used unless and until the agency specifically approves the additive.

This part elaborates on the procedures involved in seeking FDA food additive approval, reserving a discussion of the applicable safety standards for the next part. Because of the procedural and substantive complexities of the food additive petition process, food processors have begun to rely more heavily on a parallel mechanism that permits them to request that the FDA affirm their own judgment that a substance is GRAS. A comparison of the two review procedures reveals that these so-called "GRAS affirmation" petitions have provided no real shortcut for securing formal FDA authorization. There is an important difference, however, because nothing prevents the use of a substance before the FDA acts on such a petition. Although some have suggested that all direct additives undergo food additive review,[196] this would surely overwhelm the agency. Others favor increased reliance on the GRAS exception to allow the FDA to allocate its resources more efficiently to review difficult food additive petitions.[197] An evaluation of these and other suggested reforms must await a fuller description of different existing procedures and, in Parts V and VI, of the agency's actual practice over the years.

Food Additive Petitions

Normally, the issuance of a regulation authorizing the use of a food additive follows from a petition filed by the manufacturer of an additive or other interested person requesting such action.[198] A food additive petition must contain information identifying the substance, its proposed use (as reflected in its labeling), all relevant data concerning its effect on food and residue detection methodologies, and full reports of safety studies.[199] In addition, upon a request, the petitioner must provide the FDA with descriptions of production methods and facilities as well as samples of the additive for testing.[200] Certain confidential information and protected trade secrets provided to the agency are exempt from public disclosure.[201]

Pursuant to its implementing regulations, which reiterate and amplify the statutory procedures for the processing of food additive petitions,[202] the agency must notify the petitioner within 15 days of receipt whether the petition is accepted for filing.[203] If a petition is not accepted for filing, the FDA will notify the petitioner in what respects the petition is incomplete.[204] Within thirty days of accepting a petition for filing, the FDA must publish a notice of filing in the *Federal Register* containing the name of the petitioner and a brief description of the proposal.[205] At any time before the agency issues an order, the petitioner may, upon its own initiative or at the FDA's suggestion, withdraw the food additive petition without prejudice to the right to refile it in the future.[206]

The statute and the FDA's regulations nowhere mention the availability of a public comment period immediately after the notice of filing and before issuance of an order.[207] Although the judicial review provisions prompted substantial debate,[208] the legislative history provides scant elaboration of the administrative procedures to be used with food additive petitions. HEW did, however, object to an industry suggestion that some sort of hearing procedure be available prior to the issuance of a final order.[209]

The agency's practice over the years confirms that no formal comment period was contemplated prior to the publication of an order.[210] Of the hundreds of notices of filing published by the FDA in the *Federal Register* since 1965, none has invited public comment. Moreover, until fairly recently, the agency's decisions on food additive petitions have never alluded to or responded to comments submitted by third parties (the boilerplate language used in these orders simply refers to "data in the petition and other relevant information"), suggesting that such comments were rarely if ever filed in response to a petition.

In practice, the FDA now allows prepublication comment. When the agency decided in 1974 that the safety data contained in food additive and other petitions should be made available to the public, prepublication comment became increasingly feasible. In fact, the hope of soliciting public comment at this early stage appears to have motivated the change in the public information regulations.[211] Although not explicitly required by the statute or the FDA's regulations governing food additive petitions, the agency now tacitly allows a post-filing opportunity for public comments on food additive petitions,[212] and it explicitly invited such comments in the case of olestra.[213]

Within 90 days of filing, the FDA must issue a regulation or deny the petition, in either case notifying the petitioner of the reasons for such action, or, if the agency needs more time to study the petition, send written notification advising the petitioner of an extension of not more than 90 additional days.[214] The agency's evaluation of a food additive petition requires input from a number of scientific and other FDA reviewers, as reflected in the accompanying diagram, and the statutory deadlines necessitate parallel rather than sequential reviews of a petition.[215] Assuming that the agency has notified the petitioner of the need for an extension, a final order must be issued within 180 days after the filing of a food additive petition. In practice, these deadlines are rarely if ever met by the FDA.[216]

The agency's implementing regulations include provisions for "tolling" the statutory clock in certain instances where the petitioner submits further information.[217] As explained by Dr. Alan Rulis, currently the Director of the Office of Premarket Approval at the FDA's Center for Food Safety and Applied Nutrition (CFSAN):

> In practice, . . . the FDA allows this clock to run only when it has in its possession adequate information to review. Should it be determined that additional information must be submitted, a letter is issued to the petitioner and the clock stops. When a substantial supplement is received by the FDA, the clock is restarted again, but it may be reset to zero. Thus, the evaluation periods for petitions may extend beyond the nominal 180 days allotted by the statute.[218]

Although some delays result from the tardy submission of supplemental information by the petitioner, the agency generally does not meet the statutory deadlines even as modified by these tolling rules. A final order granting or denying a food additive petition becomes effective immediately unless the FDA elects to stay the order pending any evidentiary hearing on objections filed after the publication of the order.[219]

The primary opportunity for external input on a food additive petition comes only after the FDA issues its final order in response to a petition. Within 30 days, "any person adversely affected by such an order may file objections thereto" and request a public hearing.[220]

> The Secretary shall, after due notice, as promptly as possible hold such public hearing for the purpose of receiving evidence relevant and material to the issues raised by such objections. As soon as practicable after completion of the hearing, the Secretary shall by order act upon such objections and make such order public. Such order shall be based upon a fair evaluation of the entire record at such hearing, and shall include a statement setting forth in detail the findings and conclusions upon which the order is based.[221]

This provision does not grant an automatic right to a hearing whenever a person files objections; within its discretion, the FDA may decide to forego a public hearing if the objections fail to raise any material issues.[222] In fact, very few orders trigger any administrative or judicial challenge; in the FDA's history, only two orders involving direct food additives have provoked successful demands for a formal hearing.[223] Apart from encouraging prompt action, the statute imposes no deadlines for responding to objections and hearing requests,[224] and the agency sometimes has been slow to make a final decision.[225]

The FDA's order in response to objections may not take effect until 90 days after publication, in part to allow any person who will be adversely affected by such an order an opportunity to seek judicial review.[226] Review is not available unless timely objections were filed to the FDA's initial order on a food additive petition.[227] On judicial review, agency findings "with respect to questions of fact shall be sustained if based upon a fair evaluation of the entire record at such [public] hearing."[228] If its order is not successfully challenged but significant new data subsequently become available, the FDA may, on its own initiative or in response to a citizen petition, issue a proposal to amend or repeal a food additive regulation.[229]

Sponsors of food additives spend approximately $20 million on average for research and development in pursuit of FDA approval.[230] Unlike a new drug application, which gives the successful applicant an exclusive private license to sell a drug product, a food additive petition results in the promulgation by the FDA of a nonexclusive public regulation authorizing the use of the additive by any person wishing to do so.[231] In this respect, food additive regulations resemble FDA monographs for over-the-counter (OTC) drug products.[232]

The food additive petitioner may benefit from any remaining patent term.[233] As delays at the agency have increased, however, this protection may dissipate soon after approval. Although limited patent term extensions may be granted by Congress, the statute does not extend to food additives the substitute market exclusivity periods now made available for approved new drugs.[234] For this reason, ingredient manufacturers may no longer choose to pursue innovations that will necessitate the filing of a food additive petition.[235]

In order to generate the safety data required for approval, researchers must have access to the substance. An unapproved food additive may be used if exempted by the agency as "intended solely for investigational use by qualified experts when . . . consistent with the public health."[236] Unlike drugs and medical devices, which routinely make use of investigational exemptions to FDA approval requirements,[237] food additives rarely are subject to an investigational use exemption.[238] Pursuant to implementing regulations, the exemption applies if an unapproved food additive is intended only for in vitro tests or investigational use in laboratory animals and is labeled as "Not for use in humans."[239] If the investigational use involves food-producing animals, more stringent restrictions apply.[240] In practice, the FDA has not objected to human studies of new food substances so long as investigators comply with the agency's informed consent and other requirements for the protection of human subjects.

GRAS Affirmation Petitions

As explained above, even if a manufacturer or processor is confident about a substance's GRAS status, there is no assurance that the FDA (or a reviewing court) will agree with such a conclusion unless it previously has been GRAS listed or affirmed. Some private GRAS determinations represent a safer bet than others—the agency routinely defers to FEMA's decisions about flavoring substances, which are unlikely to pose a serious hazard in any event because of their extremely low level of use in food. In contrast, the FDA has challenged seemingly ad hoc and poorly supported claims of GRAS status asserted by a company in response to an agency charge that a food is adulterated for containing an unapproved additive.

In lieu of gambling on a private GRAS determination, a company might seek the FDA's concurrence on a substance's purported status as exempt from food additive approval requirements. Indeed, food processors may demand such concurrence before purchasing a substance from a manufacturer. After some experience responding informally to such requests,[241] and in conjunction with its GRAS list review, the agency set forth specific procedures for seeking GRAS affirmation.[242] Unlike food additive petitions, which are governed by fairly precise statutory procedures formulated by Congress, GRAS affirmation rests wholly on procedures developed by the FDA for this purpose.[243]

A person seeking affirmation of a substance's GRAS status must file a citizen petition containing information demonstrating that the substance satisfies the agency's GRAS criteria. In particular, such a petition must include a detailed description of the substance (including names, formulae, food grade material specifications, and descriptions of its quantitative composition and the manufacturing process[244]), a history of its use (including dates of use, data on past use, foods in which it was used, levels of use, and purposes), a description of available detection methods, and information concerning its safety and functionality.[245] Unlike a food additive petition, the FDA will not recognize any claim for trade secret protection of information contained in a GRAS affirmation petition.[246] The information concerning a substance's safety and functionality may include published scientific literature (or complete bibliographic references when copies of articles are not provided) or evidence that it is identical to a GRAS counterpart of natural biological origin, and the petition must include any adverse information or consumer complaints about the substance.[247]

Within 30 days of receiving a petition, the FDA must publish in the *Federal Register* a notice of filing and allow a 60 day period for public comment.[248] After considering the petition and any comments received, the agency has two choices: if there is "convincing" evidence of GRAS status, the FDA will publish an order listing the substance in the regulations with other substances whose GRAS status it has affirmed; otherwise, it will publish a notice that the substance should be considered a food additive.[249] Neither the statute nor the FDA's regulations establish any deadline for final action on a GRAS affirmation petition,[250] and the agency has been very slow in acting on such submissions.[251] In fact, petitions affirmed during the last decade have taken more than seven years on average.[252] Thus, GRAS affirmation technically provides no shortcut over the food additive petition process,[253] though, in practice, the concept remains attractive because manufacturers can and do market substances notwithstanding FDA inaction on a GRAS affirmation petition.[254]

Interim Food Additives

In 1972, the FDA designed a special transitional category for food-use substances whose safety has been called into question.[255] The new procedural regulations emerged from the FDA's successful experience with issuing an interim order concerning brominated vegetable oil, a stabilizer in fruit-flavored beverages.[256] As it explained in the preamble to the regulation:

> The Commissioner recognizes that, with the vast increase in the quantity of scientific testing and in the sophistication of test methodology, there is virtually no[ ] natural or synthetic food substance that cannot be questioned on some technical ground. It would be impossible to require elimination from the food supply of every food substance for which such scientific questions have been or will be raised.[257]

The agency may promulgate an "interim" food additive regulation "when new information raises a substantial question about the safety or functionality of the substance but there is a reasonable certainty that the substance is not harmful and that no harm to the public health will result from the continued use of the substance for a limited period of time while the question raised is being resolved by further study."[258] In promulgating an interim regulation, the FDA must abide by the same rulemaking procedures applicable to the issuance of a final food additive order,[259] but the interim order is summarily revocable. The regulation may demand compliance "with whatever limitations the Commissioner deems to be appropriate under the circumstances."[260]

In every case, a promise by one or more sponsors to undertake additional studies represents the primary condition for continued marketing.[261] Within 60 days after the effective date of an interim food additive regulation, an interested person must certify that "adequate and appropriate" studies have been undertaken to resolve the questions raised about the substance; otherwise, an order shall be published immediately to revoke the interim food additive regulation.[262] In the preamble, the FDA emphasized that the purpose of an interim food additive regulation "is to assure that prompt action is taken to resolve the issue."[263] Progress reports are due every six months; otherwise, the same revocation sanction may apply.[264] "Promptly upon completion of the studies undertaken on the substance, the Commissioner will review all available data, will terminate the interim food additive regulation, and will either issue a food additive regulation or will require elimination of the substance from the food supply."[265]

During the past 20 or so years, the FDA has regulated the following substances as interim food additives: acrylonitrile copolymers, mannitol, brominated vegetable oil, and saccharin.[266] In each case, the regulations called for additional toxicological studies, though with different levels of specificity.[267] The original interim food additive regulation for saccharin contained a 17-month sunset provision,[268] but the FDA subsequently revised the regulation to delete any expiration date.[269]

With the exception of nitrites used in certain curing premixes,[270] no previously listed interim food additive has been made subject to permanent restrictions or an outright prohibition. The FDA recently revised the mannitol regulation to authorize an additional method of manufacture without commenting on the fact that the "interim" regulation remained in place more than two decades after promulgation.[271] Apart from saccharin, which is the subject of a continuing regulatory moratorium imposed by Congress,[272] the FDA's inaction on these interim food additives seems inexplicable.[273] Courts have invalidated a similar "holding category" designed by the agency to authorize the continued use of an OTC drug product while awaiting the results from further studies of an active ingredient.[274] Nevertheless, the FDA and the industry seem content to leave these particular additives in what has evolved into a semi-permanent regulatory limbo.

SAFETY STANDARDS

The discussion to this point has focused on definitional issues concerning which substances must undergo the food additive approval process and procedural issues about the processing of food additive and GRAS affirmation petitions. Ultimately, the FDA must evaluate such petitions in order to determine whether a substance is safe for a particular use in food. The criteria for this review raise fundamental questions of science and public policy. The definitional and procedural questions are not, however, simply a prelude for this discussion because choices about the substantive safety criteria cannot be disentangled entirely from decisions about their appropriate reach and mechanisms for their efficient application.

General Safety Standard

The FDA may not approve a food additive for a particular use unless the data presented to the agency establish that the additive is safe for that use.[275]

> In determining, for purposes of this section, whether a proposed use of a food additive is safe, the Secretary shall consider among other relevant factors—
>
> (A) the probable consumption of the additive and of any substance formed in or on food because of the use of the additive;
>
> (B) the cumulative effect of such additive in the diet of man or animals, taking into account any chemically or pharmacologically related substance or substances in such diet; and
>
> (C) safety factors which in the opinion of experts qualified by scientific training and experience to evaluate the safety of food additives are generally recognized as appropriate for the use of animal experimentation data.[276]

Unlike most drugs, food additives are likely to be consumed by all segments of the population, including children and the elderly, potentially over the full course of their lifetimes. This difference in the aggregate exposure levels, coupled with the typically less direct benefits derived from particular food substances, helps explain the FDA's generally more conservative approach to safety assessment in this area.

The intended meaning of the above-quoted safety standard was discussed in the house report accompanying the bill that would become the Food Additives Amendment of 1958:

> The concept of safety used in this legislation involves the question of whether a substance is hazardous to the health of man or animal. Safety requires proof of a *reasonable certainty that no harm will result from the proposed use* of an additive. It does not—and cannot—require proof beyond any possible doubt that no harm will result under any conceivable circumstance. This was emphasized particularly by the scientific panel which testified before the subcommittee. The scientists pointed out that it is impossible in the present state of scientific knowledge to establish with complete certainty the absolute harmlessness of any chemical substance.[277]

Thus, for food additive approvals, the statute demands neither confirmation of safety under all possible conditions of use,[278] nor an absolute assurance of safety for every intended use. In addition, pursuant to its implementing regulations, the FDA has defined GRAS to require the same quantity and quality of safety data as required for food additive approval, unless the substance was in common use prior to 1958.[279]

As explained previously, courts have interpreted the safety standard contained in the general adulteration provisions as requiring proof by the FDA of a reasonable possibility of harm to consumers in support of a seizure or injunction of a substance in use.[280] During hearings on the food additive legislation, the administration objected to the inclusion in the statute of a definition of "safe" that explicitly used a "reasonably probable" standard for deciding whether to allow for the use of a substance in food.[281] As the sponsor of the bill reiterated on the floor of the House, the legislation would not require proof of safety "beyond any possible doubt" but rather a "practical certainty" that no harm would result.[282] Although "harm" is not separately defined, Congress evidently understood the term to mean a capacity to injure or otherwise cause disease.[283] Presumably, this view would exclude undesirable side effects that posed no risk of adverse health consequences.

In its original implementing regulations, the FDA defined safe to demand "*convincing evidence* which *establishes* with reasonable certainty that no harm will result."[284] In 1971, the agency revised this definition to require proof of "no significant risk of harm,"[285] but it revised the definition again in 1976 to more closely track the legislative history quoted previously.[286] In its current food additive regulations, the FDA defines "safe" as meaning "that there is a reasonable certainty in the minds of competent scientists that the substance is not harmful under the intended conditions of use."[287] Unlike the current (though identical to the original) food additive definition, the color additive regulation demands "convincing evidence that establishes with reasonable certainty that no harm will result."[288] Although one could argue that the narrower interpretation of the statutory safety standard contained in the original implementing regulations (demanding "convincing evidence") is entitled to greater deference than the current version,[289] courts have not directly addressed the validity of the current interpretation or suggested that it imposes any particularly significant hurdle to food additive approvals.[290]

In elaborating the food additive safety standard, the FDA's regulation tracks the factors enumerated by Congress.[291] In general, the FDA has decided to follow "the principles and procedures for establishing the safety of food additives stated in current publications of the National Academy of Sciences-National Research Council."[292] For instance, unless presented with evidence justifying a different margin of safety, the agency will apply a safety factor of 100 when using data from laboratory animals; "a food additive for use by man will not be granted a tolerance that will exceed 1/100th of the maximum amount demonstrated to be without harm to experimental animals."[293] In other words, the estimated daily intake (EDI) of the additive, based on its intended use(s) and surveys of likely consumption patterns, may not exceed the allowable daily intake (ADI), which generally is set at 1/100th (as adjusted for body weight) of the no observable effect level (NOEL) derived from animal studies.[294]

Agency scientists from a number of different disciplines, including chemistry, toxicology, nutrition, and microbiology, might review a food additive petition.[295] This safety assessment task calls for the exercise of professional judgment: the "FDA's approach is better characterized as an attempt, using the best, but admittedly imperfect, tools science makes available, to manage the uncertainty inherent in food safety evaluation."[296] Agency reviewers have been criticized, however, for excessive conservatism and even paralysis in the face of such uncertainty.[297] Whether or not such criticisms are well placed, the "recursive" nature of the evaluation may consume considerable time.[298]

The FDA also has endeavored to specify acceptable study designs for generating the safety data necessary to support the approval of a food additive but without imposing unduly rigid guidelines.[299] In preparing food additive petitions, regulated firms benefit greatly from knowing in advance what types of toxicity studies the aency will deem acceptable. Although safety testing methods recommended by the NAS-NRC are presumptively acceptable, a petitioner may utilize alternative procedures if shown to be at least equally reliable.[300] In addition, upon request the agency "will advise a person who wishes to establish the safety of a food additive whether [it] believes the experiments planned will yield data adequate for an evaluation of the safety of the additive."[301]

The agency once announced plans for a "cyclic review" of all approved food additives, in effect to update its original safety decisions,[302] but it eventually discontinued work on this gargantuan task.[303] As part of the process, however, the FDA announced in 1982 the availability of its *Toxicological Principles for the Safety Assessment of Direct Food Additives and Color Additives Used in Food* (which is simply referred to as the "Redbook").[304] In recently announcing the availability of a revised draft ("Redbook II"), the agency explained that this document "is intended to provide guidance to petitioners regarding criteria used by FDA for toxicological safety assessment of direct food additives and color additives, and in the agency's evaluation of the generally recognized as safe (GRAS) status of food ingredients,"[305] arguably expanding its original scope beyond the review of food and color additive petitions.[306] The FDA continues working to finalize Redbook II.

Under its existing procedural regulations, guidelines are binding only in the limited sense that the agency must accept submissions that have been prepared in conformity with such guidelines. These regulations expressly disavow any attempt to impose binding obligations on regulated parties,[307] and the FDA has taken the position that the Redbook does not mandate the submission of particular toxicology information in food additive petitions.[308] In practice, of course, petitioners will hesitate to deviate from agency guidelines for safety testing because of a fear that the failure to adhere to those guidelines might lead to delays or even disapproval.

The FDA recently proposed revising its general administrative procedures so that agency personnel would not be bound to adhere to formally announced opinions and guidelines.[309] The utility of the new Redbook would be sharply reduced, however, if the agency ultimately makes such a revision to its generic procedural rules. It would substantially interfere with research and development efforts if sponsors could no longer conduct chronic animal studies with the assurance that these expensive and time-consuming studies would be acceptable to FDA reviewers when the studies were performed in accordance with the Redbook's guidelines.

Finally, Congress and the FDA have struggled to decide what role, if any, a consideration of benefits should play in applying the general safety standard. Earlier versions of the 1958 legislation would have premised approval on an agency finding of "functional value" in addition to safety.[310] In response to strong industry opposition,[311] the final legislation required only a consideration of functionality in the limited circumstances where considerations of safety necessitated a quantitative limitation on use and then without any judgment of social value.[312] In promulgating its revised food additive and GRAS regulations in 1976, the FDA suggested that social utility is "inevitably a factor" in the safety determination,[313] but a subsequent Commissioner expressly disavowed this statement a few years later during the course of withdrawing the new animal drug approval for DES.[314]

Carcinogenicity and the Delaney Clause

The general safety standard is modified by a proviso known as the Delaney clause which directs that "no additive shall be deemed to be safe if it is found to induce cancer when ingested by man or animal, or if it is found, after tests which are appropriate for the evaluation of the safety of food additives, to induce cancer in man or animal."[315] Professor Richard Merrill once remarked that "[t]he Delaney Clause is perhaps the most discussed, yet least used, provision of the [FD&C] Act."[316] Indeed, lay press coverage incorrectly suggested that the recently passed Food Quality Protection Act repealed the Delaney clause,[317] when Congress actually had only exempted pesticide residues remaining in processed foods and substituted a general safety standard for setting tolerances for such residues.[318] To be sure, the recent legislation reflects congressional concerns about undue rigidities in the Delaney clause, but the proviso remains fully applicable to food additives. Whatever its actual frequency of use, the Delaney clause has shaped much of the debate about the FDA's food additive approval process.

The Delaney clause appeared fairly late in the legislative process. The bill approved by the House Committee on Interstate and Foreign Commerce did not contain an anti-cancer clause, but the Committee, at Congressman Delaney's urging, added the proviso to the bill before bringing it to a vote on the House floor.[319] As explained in the subsequent report of the Senate committee considering the bill:

> We have no objections to that amendment whatsoever, but we would point out that in our opinion it is the intent and purpose of this bill, even without that amendment, to assure our people that nothing shall be added to the foods they eat which can reasonably be expected to produce any type of illness in humans or animals. We applaud Congressman Delaney for having taken this, as he has every other opportunity, to focus our attention on the cancer-producing potentialities of various substances, but we want the record to show that in our opinion the bill is aimed at preventing the addition to the food our people eat of any substances the ingestion of which reasonable people would expect to produce not just cancer but any disease or disability. In short, we believe the bill reads and means the same with or without the inclusion of the clause referred to. This is also the view of the [FDA].[320]

Although the drafters of the 1958 legislation claimed that the Delaney clause was no stricter than the general safety standard, its application has proven to be far more troublesome in practice.

The terms of the Delaney clause indicate that, if presented with data suggesting a carcinogenic effect, the FDA was to conduct a fact-based scientific inquiry. The language selected by Congress contemplated that the FDA will exercise scientific judgment in assessing the relationship between exposure to a chemical and a carcinogenic response.[321] Technically, the Delaney clause does not apply to GRAS substances (or prior sanctioned ingredients), though the FDA initially took the position that evidence of carcinogenicity would undermine GRAS status.[322]

The FDA's approach to questions concerning the putative carcinogenicity of added substances conforms with Congress' expectations that it would employ scientific judgment. Indeed, the agency has played a leading role within the federal government to ensure that the best science is brought to bear in evaluating the carcinogenicity of chemicals, such as through the Interagency Regulatory Liaison Group (IRLG) and the Interagency Staff Group on Carcinogens of the Office of Science and Technology Policy (OSTP). FDA scientists were leading participants in these efforts, and the resulting reports, one released in 1979 by IRLG[323] and the other released in 1985 by OSTP,[324] provide strong support for the role of scientific judgment in evaluating evidence relating to carcinogenicity.[325]

The FDA's own practice over the years exemplifies the central principles embodied in these reports. The agency does not accept, or act upon, the proposition that a mere temporal association between administration of a chemical to test animals and an elevation in tumor incidence justifies, much less requires, a finding that the chemical "induces cancer." Study results suggesting such an association are instead subject to critical evaluation, and any conclusion is the product of an assessment of many different scientific elements. Evidence that a test substance is associated with a statistically significant increase in tumor incidence compared with concurrent controls is a necessary, but not sufficient, basis for concluding that it "induces cancer." For example, if the increase of tumors in test animals falls within the range commonly observed in historical controls, the significance of the test results is placed in question.

The agency frequently looks beyond quantitative analysis of tumor incidence to consider, based on qualitative scientific evidence, whether the effects observed in animal studies are biologically significant: "Determination that the incidence of neoplasms increases as the result of exposure to the test compound requires a full biological, pathological, and statistical evaluation. Statistics assist in evaluating the biological conclusion, but a biological conclusion is not determined by the statistical results."[326] The OSTP guidelines make the same point: "the final judgment regarding a compound's carcinogenicity is rarely based on a single finding of statistical significance. One must be assured that the effects observed are biologically significant as well."[327] Thus, the FDA routinely considers relevant biological and biochemical data in determining whether a substance "induces cancer," including information on a variety of other biological functions such as dose response, tumor progression, and tumor latency, as well as the overall evidence from other studies.[328]

Even animal studies suggestive of significant carcinogenic activity are not relied upon by the agency without a close assessment of the overall weight of the evidence. In approving the color additive FD&C Blue No. 2, for example, the FDA stated that "the agency has consistently asserted that statistical factors must be analyzed in conjunction with biological factors in determining what, if any, conclusions can be drawn from a study."[329] The FDA relied on a similar weight-of-the-evidence analysis when it approved D&C Green No. 5, identifying the following evidence as support for its conclusion that the color additive did not induce cancer:

> (1) the fact that the incidence in the high dose group is within the normal range of background spontaneous incidence; (2) the absence of evidence of progressiveness that would be expected from a carcinogen; (3) the absence of observable non-neoplastic disease in the mouse liver; (4) the negative findings on testing D&C Green No. 5 for mutagenic activity; and (5) the atypical form of the apparent dose-response data.[330]

The agency concluded, on the basis of this weight-of-the-evidence analysis, that the color additive was noncarcinogenic and nontumorigenic, and it defended the decision a few months later when it rejected objections to the final regulation listing Green No. 5.[331]

More recently, in approving the sweetener acesulfame potassium, the FDA based its decision that this food additive is not a carcinogen on "the weight of all of the evidence; no single point provided complete proof in determining the question of carcinogenicity."[332] In denying a petition for a hearing, the FDA defended its conclusion that the incidence of mammary gland tumors in female rats was not treatment-related by pointing out that these tumors are common in old-age rats of the strain used in the bioassays, that the incidence of these tumors fell within the range for historical controls, and that there was no evidence of a dose-response relationship or evidence of progressive tumor stages.[333]

The agency also once explained that exaggerated intakes of several common products may cause tumors through a secondary mechanism, but it concluded that "these foods and drugs are not, by reason of their capacity to induce liver damage when abused by being consumed at high levels, properly classified as carcinogenic because of their potential association with a higher rate of liver cancer."[334] Over the last two decades, the FDA has continued to allow the use of a few substances that appear to cause tumors only at high-dose levels in animals, in part because it is well recognized that such substances are ubiquitous in the human diet. For instance, when the FDA approved a petition to allow selenium supplementation of livestock feed, it had to grapple with three studies that had found neoplastic lesions in the livers of rodents fed high doses of the substance. The agency ultimately concluded that there was no cancer risk to humans, discounting the observed tumors as linked to liver damage which occurred only at high doses.[335] The application of the Delaney Clause to substances suspected of causing cancer by a secondary mechanism continues to provoke controversy, and the FDA's current policy on the subject remains unclear.[336]

Finally, if the agency finds that an additive has not induced cancer, then it applies the general safety standard rather than the Delaney clause in assessing any evidence that one of the additive's constituents is a suspected carcinogen. As the FDA explained in support of its policy:

> [E]ach chemical in the complex mixture that constitutes a food additive could itself be considered to be a food additive. Each of these chemicals in some sense becomes a component of the food. . . . [T]he Delaney Clause does not apply to a carcinogenic chemical in a food additive absent a finding, after appropriate tests, that the additive as a whole induces cancer.[337]

Instead, the agency has applied the "reasonable certainty of no harm" interpretation of the general safety clause in a flexible manner that allows it to disregard truly negligible risks, and the courts have sustained the legality of the FDA's constituents policy.[338] For instance, in discussing the proper application of the Delaney clause to methylene chloride as a food additive used to decaffeinate coffee,[339] the FDA explained that it had used a one-in-one million lifetime risk of cancer standard "for determining whether the calculated upper bound risk of cancer posed by an impurity is low enough to be considered 'safe' within the meaning of the general safety clause."[340] With improvements in scientific methods for detecting substances and evaluating their potential for causing cancer, such issues will arise even more frequently in the future.[341]

Special Restrictions: Labeling

Although the Delaney clause may trigger disapproval of a carcinogenic food additive without regard to risk, the general safety standard applicable to food additives provides greater flexibility. A safety question unrelated to potential carcinogenicity would not automatically doom a food additive because the agency may be able to address such concerns by imposing restrictions on the use of the additive. The statute provides that, when the FDA issues a food additive regulation, it may prescribe the conditions for safe use:

> including, but not limited to, specifications as to the particular food or classes of food in or on which such additive may be used, the maximum quantity which may be used or permitted to remain in or on such food, the manner in which such additive may be added to or used in or on such food, and any directions or other labeling or packaging requirements for such additive deemed necessary by [the Secretary] to assure the safety of such use.[342]

In issuing food additive regulations, the agency generally has imposed only one or more of these enumerated conditions where considered necessary, though it recently has become somewhat more creative in this regard.[343] The agency may include similar limitations in GRAS affirmation regulations,[344] but it has done so only infrequently.

Labeling requirements represent one of the significant conditions that may be imposed during the food additive approval process. The FDA relies to a great extent on labeling requirements as a mechanism for regulating the numerous products subject to its jurisdiction.[345] The agency has, however, mandated relatively few warnings for food products, though it has imposed special disclosure requirements in certain cases. "The agency's primary tool for handling a situation where population subgroups may be at increased risk from a food ingredient that is safe for most people is to use [ingredient] labeling to inform those persons who need or want to avoid the ingredient."[346] Thus, food product labeling must disclose the presence of substances such as the color additive FD&C Yellow No. 5 (tartrazine)[347] and sulfiting agents used as preservatives.[348]

In addition, bulk packages of certain additives or mixtures containing these additives, such as BHA and potassium iodide, must quantify the level of the additive,[349] and curing mixes containing sodium nitrate or nitrite must include "Keep out of the reach of children" on the label.[350] Any food containing aspartame must bear a statement advising persons who suffer from phenylketonuria (a rare metabolic disorder) that the product "contains phenylalanine."[351]

Finally, the FDA sometimes mandates the disclosure of information about possible non-serious side effects.[352]

Products that may trigger allergic reactions provide one of the best justifications for choosing a labeling strategy. In the case of Yellow No. 5, the FDA found evidence of a causal link between the color additive and serious allergic-type reactions in susceptible individuals.[353] The agency rejected comments urging it to ban Yellow No. 5, explaining that it selected the label declaration because this option minimized the societal impact while providing an adequate measure of protection for those sensitive to the color.[354] In the case of sulfiting agents, the FDA did prohibit uses of these additives where labeling would be impractical (e.g., raw produce).[355] For packaged foods, however, the agency opted for a simple ingredient declaration on the label, rejecting comments urging that a "Warning" be required.[356] The FDA's recent and wide-ranging revisions of its food labeling regulations will provide even more detailed ingredient information of possible relevance for persons with allergies,[357] but the agency again rejected suggestions that explicit allergy "Warnings" appear on product labels.[358]

The FDA has taken the position that warnings on food products are appropriate only when based on sound scientific data with clear application to human health, stating that it "is unwilling to require a warning statement in the absence of clear evidence of a hazard."[359] Substances found in foods sometimes have been associated with chronic hazards, but the FDA has never suggested that every food product containing a suspected carcinogen should bear a warning statement absent evidence of a risk under actual conditions of use.

> [A] requirement for warnings on all foods that may contain an inherent carcinogenic ingredient or a carcinogenic contaminant . . . would apply to many, perhaps most foods in a supermarket. Such warnings would be so numerous they would confuse the public, would not promote informed consumer decisionmaking, and would not advance the public health.[360]

The FDA will prohibit use of the food or food additive (as it had proposed to do with saccharin[361]) if a chronic risk appears to be serious, rather than require a label warning,[362] notwithstanding objections that such a policy unduly limits consumer freedom of choice.[363]

The FDA has acknowledged the problems of information overload and dilution of warnings in a number of different contexts.[364] Even if consumers do pay attention to warnings, they may well overreact to the information, particularly when the warning statement is intended to convey a subtle message about low probability risks. Requiring warning statements about unsubstantiated or insignificant risks in the labeling of useful products can distort consumer choices. For instance, many food products contain potentially carcinogenic nitrites, but at present these preservatives provide one of the best means available for protecting against botulism.[365] In addition, the public should be more concerned with ensuring consumption of an adequate and healthy diet than with warnings about possible low-level carcinogens in food products.[366] Absent consistent and differentiated cautionary statements allowing comparisons among the risks posed by different products, narrowly focused warning requirements may distort these trade-offs. To date, the FDA has only infrequently utilized its power to condition food additive approvals on special labeling statements.

The agency's statutory authority to impose these labeling requirements is hardly clear. The FDA does enjoy broad authority to regulate the labeling of food products generally, under the statute's prohibitions against misbranding, but Section 409 does not appear to authorize the imposition of special labeling requirements for the finished food product as a condition for food additive approval.[367] Moreover, the FDA requirements for label disclosures of non-serious side effects do not represent conditions necessary to ensure safe use so much as to avoid consumer deception or product misbranding.[368] The risk of deception represents a legitimate basis for denying a food additive petition but technically not an appropriate ground under the statute for approving a petition subject to certain food labeling conditions.[369]

CASE STUDIES

Although each of the examples discussed in this part is somewhat atypical (one might even say precedent-setting), these case studies should help illustrate a variety of the challenges encountered by the FDA in applying the definitional, procedural, and substantive aspects of the Food Additives Amendment. The agency experienced special difficulties in reviewing the artificial sweetener aspartame, Calgene's bioengineered tomato, and the fatsubstitute olestra. (Several less notable but still important additives have been discussed previously where pertinent.) As scientific advances increasingly create novel food-use substances, the FDA will continue to face difficult regulatory questions.[370]

Artificial Sweeteners: Aspartame

Aspartame, a chemically bound combination of phenylalanine, aspartic acid, and methanol, is an artificial sweetener sold under the brand name NutraSweet™ and is the first sugar substitute approved in the wake of the controversies involving cyclamate and saccharin. G.D. Searle & Co. submitted a food additive petition for aspartame in 1973,[371] and, more than one year later, the FDA approved this petition, authorizing certain "dry" uses of the additive.[372] Because a rare genetic disorder prevents the metabolism of phenylalanine, which at very elevated levels poses a risk of mental retardation, the agency required that the statement "Phenylketonurics: Contains Phenylalanine" appear on the label of products containing aspartame.[373]

A few persons filed objections to the FDA's approval and requested a hearing. The agency eventually decided to stay the regulation's effective date pending a hearing on these objections because it discovered data discrepancies by a contract laboratory in the toxicological testing of other substances.[374] Four years later, the FDA convened a three-member Public Board of Inquiry to conduct the hearing.[375] The Board agreed with the FDA's initial determination that aspartame posed no risk of causing brain damage or neuroendocrine dysfunction, but it recommended against approval because of unresolved questions about brain tumors found during rodent studies of aspartame.[376] The Commissioner rejected this recommendation and finally affirmed the original food additive regulation in 1981.[377] He decided, however, to impose the following additional condition: "Searle is to monitor the actual use levels of aspartame and to provide such information on aspartame's use to the Bureau of Foods as the Bureau may deem necessary by an order, in the form of a letter, to Searle."[378] One year later, Congress extended aspartame's patent term to restore some of the time lost during the lengthy delays in securing final FDA approval.[379]

In 1982, Searle submitted a food additive petition requesting an amendment to allow the use of aspartame in carbonated beverages,[380] and the FDA approved this use the following year.[381] Several persons filed objections to the regulation, requesting an immediate stay and a public hearing, but the agency rejected the objections without conducting a hearing.[382] One consumer group brought a judicial challenge to the approval for use in carbonated beverages, but the court affirmed the FDA's decision.[383] The court held that the objections did not raise material issues concerning the wet use of aspartame and that the more general concerns about the additive's safety had been resolved during the course of the original approval for dry use.[384] In particular, the court found no material issues warranting a hearing on the objections concerning the risks of brain damage from changes in neurotransmitter production, nitrosamine formation, carcinogenicity, embryotoxicity of degradation products, increased levels of consumption, or more rapid decomposition associated with its use in carbonated beverages.[385]

The FDA subsequently amended the food additive regulation on two dozen occasions to approve additional uses of aspartame,[386] again rejecting renewed objections and denying hearing requests.[387] Although inefficient, companies apparently have found this incremental approval approach to be somewhat beneficial—the FDA may approve the initial petition for a limited use more quickly and then accord supplemental uses some presumption for approval. In 1996, the agency approved a petition requesting that aspartame be permitted for use as a general purpose sweetener, thereby consolidating the 27 narrow sweetener uses that it had approved over the last couple of decades.[388] Nonetheless, controversy about the FDA's approval of aspartame has persisted,[389] prompting the agency to continue monitoring consumer complaints.[390] Meanwhile, the attention of consumer activists has shifted to the FDA's review of newer artificial sweeteners and other direct additives.[391]

Biotechnology: Calgene's Tomato

In 1994, Calgene began marketing the FLAVR SAVR™ tomato, a tomato which can remain on the vine longer, has a longer retail shelf life, and exhibits improved viscosity when used in processed foods. Calgene created the FLAVR SAVR™ through a recombinant DNA technique, specifically by isolating the polygalacturonase gene, which is responsible for producing the enzyme that breaks down pectin in the cell walls of the tomato during the ripening process, and reintroducing the gene into the plant in the reverse or "antisense" orientation.[392] The antisense copy suppresses the production of the polygalacturonase enzyme. In this respect, Calgene's process simply rearranged the tomato's own genetic material (it was not replaced by material from a different organism), and it reduced the levels of an existing protein (it did not introduce a new chemical or increase the levels of other naturally occurring substances in the tomato).

In addition, the process required the insertion of a selectable "marker" gene, in this case the commonly used kanamycin resistance (*kan*^{r}) gene derived from certain bacteria. Marker genes help identify those plant cells which have successfully taken up the transferred gene controlling a desired trait; in this case, cells that contain the *kan*^{r} gene synthesize a protein, aminoglycoside 3'-phosphotransferase II (APH(3')II), which renders the cell resistant to the action of antibiotics.[393] By adding kanamycin or a similar antibiotic to the laboratory growth medium, a researcher can screen out the many tomato plant cells with unsuccessful gene transfers. Although the marker gene serves no useful purpose after that point, it remains part of the genetic material in every cell of the growing transgenic plant.

After the completion of field testing authorized by the USDA,[394] Calgene petitioned the FDA to issue advisory opinions on the regulatory status of both the *kan*^{r} gene[395] and the FLAVR SAVR™ tomato.[396] One year after the FDA's 1992 publication of a policy statement on foods derived from new plant varieties,[397] the company converted its initial request into a petition seeking food additive approval of the protein from the *kan*^{r} gene as a processing aid.[398]

In 1994, shortly after holding a meeting of its Food Advisory Committee, the FDA responded to Calgene's petitions. First, it "concluded that FLAVR SAVR™ tomatoes have not been significantly altered when compared to varieties of tomatoes with a history of safe use."[399] Although not stated in such terms, the FDA in effect found that this tomato was GRAS and, therefore, not a food additive when used in processed foods.[400] The agency had once before approved a GRAS affirmation petition for bioengineered versions of the milk-clotting enzyme chymosin for use in making cheese and other products, as a substitute for the animal-derived version of the enzyme which previously had been affirmed as GRAS.[401]

Second, the FDA granted Calgene's food additive petition, approving the use of APH(3')II encoded by the *kan*^{r} gene as a processing aid for developing certain new plant varieties.[402] The agency concluded that the protein produced by the *kan*^{r} gene is neither toxic nor allergenic and that estimated dietary exposure would be extremely low.[403] Although it provides antibiotic resistance and could, therefore, interfere with the therapeutic use of human antibiotics, the FDA found that the protein would be inactivated and degraded by digestion or heating.[404] Finally, the agency concluded that the proposed additive created no risk of horizontal transfer of the *kan*^{r} gene (and the spread of antibiotic resistance) into human cells lining the intestinal walls or into microorganisms found in the intestines or in the soil.[405]

Although the FLAVR SAVR™ tomato posed fairly limited complexities, the FDA and Calgene spent considerable time and effort reviewing its safety and deciding how best to regulate the product. In the future, biotechnology should become increasingly important in the development of food products, and some of the innovations will pose much more serious regulatory questions than did the Calgene tomato. In fact, DNA Plant Technology and Monsanto have developed tomatoes with even longer shelf lives by modifying the gene which controls ethylene production, and other more elaborate bioengineered food products are on the horizon.[406]

During its review of the Calgene petitions, the FDA began formulating its policies for regulating biotechnology food products. In 1992, the agency published a policy statement on foods derived from new plant varieties.[407] A rudimentary framework previously had been described in the mid-1980s,[408] but the FDA's 1992 policy statement represented the first careful elaboration of its intended regulatory approach with regard to the application of biotechnology in the development of new plant varieties for use in food products. Notwithstanding the comprehensive nature of the policy statement, the FDA continues to refine it, and subsequently published notices have requested further public comment on separate aspects of the subject, including appropriate safety testing,[409] and labeling.[410]

At the outset of the policy statement, the FDA notes that revolutionary genetic modification techniques, such as recombinant DNA and cell fusion, will lead to the development of new varieties of food plants that would not have been possible using more traditional methods of selective breeding.[411] It also recognizes that, because "these techniques are more precise, they increase the potential for safe, better-characterized, and more predictable foods."[412] In discussing genetic modification techniques to achieve desirable traits, the agency distinguished between agronomic characteristics of the plant (e.g., yield and resistance to pests or disease) and quality characteristics of the food (e.g., preservation, nutrition, and flavor).[413]

The policy statement canvasses a variety of potential safety issues posed by genetic modification—some shared with traditional selective breeding and some unique to the new methods—including unexpected chromosomal effects, changes in the levels of naturally occurring toxins in plants, reductions in nutrient bioavailability, production of new substances, introduction of allergens, and increased antibiotic resistance from marker genes.[414] The FDA decided, however, that it need not adopt any special regulatory approach for foods derived from genetically modified plants, preferring instead to "utiliz[e] an approach identical in principle to that applied to foods developed by traditional plant breeding."[415] The policy statement embraces a functional rather than literal approach to the food additive issue: the agency will "require food additive petitions in cases where safety questions exist sufficient to warrant formal premarket review by FDA to ensure public health protection."[416] The FDA did not, however, explain how it would become aware of bioengineered foods for which it might require the submission of food additive petitions.

In short, according to the policy statement, the agency plans to rely on its enforcement authority under the general adulteration provisions to ensure the safety of whole foods derived from genetically modified plants, though it pointed out that the transferred genetic material and the intended expression products could be subject to regulation as food additives if not GRAS.[417] Because nucleic acids appear in the genetic material of all foods and have posed no safety problems in the past, the "FDA does not expect that there will be any serious question about the GRAS status of transferred genetic material."[418]

The intended expression product also generally will not alter the GRAS status of any food derived from the new plant variety, unless it is "a protein, carbohydrate, fat or oil, or other substance that differs significantly in structure, function, or composition from substances currently found in food."[419] Thus, if transferred genetic material introduces an unusual protein and/or alters a metabolic pathway to produce a new carbohydrate or other substance, then the FDA may call for the submission of a food additive petition. Furthermore, apart from the possibility that a new component in a whole food might be regulated as a food additive, the whole food itself could be regulated as a food additive when used as a component of a processed food. The agency notes, however, that it rarely has passed on the presumptive GRAS status of a whole food when used as a component in a processed food because most food plants "have been widely recognized and accepted as safe."[420]

The policy statement provides detailed guidance for industry in conducting safety evaluations of new plant varieties and in determining the need for a food additive petition.[421] The "FDA believes that a scientific basis should exist to establish that new plant varieties do not exhibit unacceptable effects with respect to toxicants, nutritional value or allergens."[422] It also invites companies unsure about a new product's regulatory status to consult with the FDA on an informal basis rather than having to submit a petition requesting an advisory opinion.[423] In materials distributed at a 1994 Food Advisory Committee meeting, the agency announced its intention to propose a regulation which would require formal premarket notification for all bioengineered foods, including the submission of safety and nutritional information to the FDA.[424] Although the agency has not yet published such a proposal, a number of companies have consulted with the FDA to discuss the status of bioengineered food products under development.[425]

Finally, the FDA rejected suggestions that all bioengineered foods disclose their origin in labeling, but it would require disclosure if a risk of allergenicity has been introduced by the insertion of genetic material from another source.[426] The labeling question proved quite contentious in the wake of the agency's approval of the new animal drug recombinant bovine somatotropin (rBST).[427] Because it found no difference between milk from cows administered rBST and other milk, the FDA did not require any special disclosure statement in labeling, but it also declined to prohibit truthful and nonmisleading claims that a dairy product was derived from cows that had not received rBST.[428] In hopes of avoiding similar controversy over the FLAVR SAVR™ tomato, Calgene plans to provide point-of-sale information for consumers.[429]

Comments from consumer and environmental groups criticized the regulatory framework described in the 1992 policy statement, arguing that the FDA instead should use its food additive authority to require premarket notification, premarket safety testing, and labeling disclosures for all bioengineered foods.[430] In a recent report, the GAO elaborated on the premarket notification suggestion as follows:

> In principle, such a system would bridge the gap between the absence of a requirement for premarket approval of whole foods and of substances that manufacturers and others have determined are GRAS and the requirement for extensive premarket review of new food additives. Several premarket notification systems have been proposed that range in formality and complexity from relatively simple letters from food companies to notify FDA about the introduction of a new product to mandatory FDA premarket reviews of data submitted by manufacturers to support the safety and/or GRAS status of their food product.[431]

For the moment, the agency continues to rely on a flexible approach to determine in each case whether to impose any special requirements.

Although flexibility has obvious advantages in dealing with an emerging technology, some observers have called for a clearer regulatory response to bioengineered food products. The FDA's 1992 policy statement represents a first step in that direction, notwithstanding its emphasis on informal, ad hoc review. Reliance on the food additive approval process would not, however, provide the added certainty about the safety criteria needed to address the special questions posed by bioengineered substances. As the GAO concluded, "controversies over FDA's policy on biotechnology are reviving old questions about the adequacy of the existing regulatory framework for food and food ingredients."[432] In the future, as food biotechnology becomes more sophisticated, the agency's policies will continue to evolve.

Novel Macroingredients: Olestra

On January 30, 1996, the FDA approved Procter & Gamble's food additive petition for the noncaloric fat substitute olestra for use in certain snack foods.[433] Olestra's history is remarkable in a number of respects. Nearly 25 years elapsed between the company's initial contacts with FDA officials and final approval, though there was no food additive petition pending during most of that interval, and Procter & Gamble spent more than $200 million in the process.[434] Olestra represents one of the first macroingredients approved as a food additive,[435] and the final regulation conditions its use on special labeling, vitamin fortification, and the submission of postmarketing surveillance reports to allow for further agency review.[436] No doubt the company will seek approval of supplemental petitions for additional uses in the future.

In 1991, anticipating that the FDA would not complete its regulatory review before the expiration of the 17-year term on the various patents covering olestra, Procter & Gamble petitioned Congress for special legislation to extend several of its patents well beyond 1994.[437] The resulting hearings provided a detailed history of the company's R&D efforts.[438]

In 1969, company scientists synthesized olestra, a molecule with a sucrose core surrounded by six, seven, or eight medium- or long-chain fatty acids (classified as a sucrose polyester).[439] Triglycerides, by contrast, have a glycerol core surrounded by three fatty acids. Olestra tastes, smells, and cooks like ordinary fats, and it can absorb fat-soluble substances. The human GI tract cannot, however, absorb olestra because it lacks enzymes capable of breaking it down. Because it passes through the intestines undigested, olestra provides no calories, but it also may interfere with the absorption of substances such as fat-soluble vitamins or certain lipophilic drugs,[440] and it may cause unpleasant gastrointestinal side effects in some individuals.[441]

After initially pursuing approval of the substance as a human drug,[442] the company filed its food additive petition in 1987.[443] The precise explanation for the tardy decision to seek food additive approval remains unclear,[444] but Procter & Gamble did encounter some delays while the FDA worked with it to define appropriate testing protocols for a substance intended for use at a fairly high level in the diet.[445] In 1990, the FDA convinced Procter & Gamble to amend the petition to request approval of only a limited use in snack foods and also asked the company to undertake another long-term animal study.[446]

In reviewing the olestra petition, the FDA drew upon special expertise from other centers and federal agencies as well as external scientific consultants, and it assembled a six-member Regulatory Decision Team of senior agency managers to resolve issues that arose during the petition review process.[447] In November 1995, after the agency convened a meeting of a special working group of the Food Advisory Committee to discuss olestra's safety,[448] a majority of the full Food Advisory Committee concluded that there was a reasonable certainty that no harm would result from the use of olestra in snack foods but also recommended the imposition of certain conditions on any approval.[449] The FDA announced a final deadline for the submission of public comments in response to the food additive petition,[450] which it then approved less than two months after the close of the comment period.[451] The Center for Science in the Public Interest (CSPI) filed objections to the decision and requested a hearing but not a stay of the approval.[452] In the meantime, test marketing has begun in several cities.[453]

Shortly after finally approving olestra, the agency invited comments on the safety assessment of novel macroingredients,[454] and scientists in and out of the FDA have begun to consider the subject more closely.[455] Because olestra is virtually not absorbed, traditional toxicology studies were less important than efforts to assess various digestive effects in humans.[456] In addition, because of the relatively high consumption levels of macroingredients, it is extremely difficult to conduct animal studies at the exaggerated intake levels necessary in chronic feeding tests,[457] leading some scientists to recommend greater reliance on postmarketing evaluations of such additives.[458]

In approving olestra, the FDA evaluated a wealth of scientific data.[459] In doing so, it emphasized the irrelevance in its safety determination of either concerns about unpleasant (but not otherwise harmful) side effects or the social benefits of reducing levels of dietary fat.[460] According to the GAO's chief investigator on olestra, the "FDA feels that they really learned a lot by going through this process."[461] Ultimately, the FDA concluded that the use of olestra in certain snack foods was safe, but it imposed several unusual conditions. First, to compensate for the projected interference with the absorption of certain fat-soluble micronutrients, foods containing olestra must be fortified with precise quantities of vitamins A, D, E, and K.[462]

Second, the labels of snack foods containing olestra must bear the following boxed disclosure statement:

> **This Product Contains Olestra**. Olestra may cause abdominal cramping and loose stools. Olestra inhibits the absorption of some vitamins and other nutrients. Vitamins A, D, E, and K have been added.[463]

Unlike most of the other labeling requirements appearing in food additive regulations, which call for warnings or ingredient disclosures to alert consumers who may be allergic to the substance, the FDA concedes that this statement does not represent a condition necessary to ensure the safe use of olestra.[464] Instead, it argues that the statute's general misbranding prohibitions,[465] as cross-referenced in Section 409 as a ground for denying a food additive petition,[466] authorize the imposition of such a condition in this case.[467] The agency did, however, invite further comments on whether it should revise what it characterized as only an "interim" labeling requirement.[468] Procter & Gamble filed comments urging a less explicit labeling requirement, while at the same time CSPI sought a more conspicuous warning.[469]

The requirement for postmarketing surveillance represents one of the most interesting features of the approval. The regulation itself does not mandate further testing by the petitioner; it only provides that the FDA "will review and evaluate all data and information bearing on the safety of olestra received by the agency."[470] In the preamble, however, the agency explains that "as a condition of approval, Procter and Gamble is to conduct the studies that it has identified in its letter to FDA [dated January 24, 1996], consistent with the timetables identified in that letter,"[471] and it warned that, "if Procter and Gamble does not conduct the identified studies and does not conduct them according to the articulated timetable, FDA will consider the approval . . . to be void *ab initio* and will institute appropriate proceedings."[472]

This threat is remarkable insofar as it treats the food additive approval as a private license rather than a public regulation available, subject only to patent limitations, to any firm wishing to manufacture and sell the additive.[473] The FDA did not purport to approve olestra as an interim food additive. The agency added that such a condition "is not without precedent," citing the more limited data collection requirement imposed on the manufacturer of aspartame,[474] and it also emphasized that the imposition of this condition "is not, and should not be interpreted as, an indication that FDA has somehow not determined that there is a reasonable certainty that no harm will result from the use of olestra in savory snacks."[475] Six months after approval, Procter & Gamble reported fewer consumer complaints than expected.[476] In the meantime, the FDA must review and eventually respond to CSPI's objections and hearing request.

THE COMPOSITE PICTURE

Aggregate data provide a different and equally valuable perspective on the FDA's experience with the food additive approval process. Lengthy reviews of petitions for novel macroingredients may be unavoidable, but quantitative measures suggest habitual administrative delays for both simple and complex submissions. During the last decade, direct food additive petitions (original and supplemental) and GRAS affirmation petitions have languished at the agency for an average of more than five years. As more fully explained below, a number of factors may account for these delays, especially growing resource constraints faced by the FDA,[477] and an associated variety of reforms have been proposed.

Track Records Compared

As explained previously, the FD&C Act establishes a maximum 180-day review clock for food additive petitions, but, pursuant to FDA regulations, this clock runs only intermittently after filing—the agency stops the clock while awaiting additional information from the petitioner and resets it at zero whenever substantial new information arrives.[478] No deadlines exist for action on GRAS affirmation petitions, and the FDA has been even slower in reviewing these submissions.[479]

In fact, the FDA has approved very few direct food additives during the last quarter of a century. In addition to aspartame and olestra, these include the antioxidant TBHQ,[480] the multipurpose additive polydextrose,[481] the sweetener acesulfame potassium,[482] and the stabilizer and thickener gellan gum.[483] The bulk of the agency's food additive review caseload has involved petitions for indirect food additives.[484] In addition, as happened most notably in the case of aspartame, the FDA has processed a number of supplemental petitions requesting amendments to authorize additional uses of previously approved additives.[485] Ironically, the agency occasionally takes more time to approve these supplemental petitions than the original. For instance, the original petition for polydextrose took two years to approve, but supplemental petitions for expanded uses required up to six years.[486]

In the early 1990s, the FDA's Center for Food Safety and Applied Nutrition (CFSAN) undertook a series of internal management studies, including an evaluation of the food additive review process using data from 1979 through 1992.[487] In the case of direct food additive petitions (both original and supplemental) approved during this period, the agency found a bimodal distribution, with review times ranging from one to three years and three to six years.[488] Only three of the ninety petitions approved during this period required less than six months to review and six of the petitions required more than six years.[489] Of the 42 substances affirmed as GRAS between 1979 and 1992, none took less than one year to review and 26 took more than four years.[490]

In 1995, Congress for the first time held oversight hearings concerning the FDA's food additive approval process.[491] As summarized in the committee report issued several months after the completion of these hearings:

> FDA has a backlog of 295 food additive petitions under review, some of which have been pending since the 1970s. Approximately 100 new food and color additive petitions are submitted to the FDA each year. . . . Direct additives comprise approximately 17% of pending petitions and may be under review for up to 10 years . . . . Seventy-five GRAS affirmation petitions are currently pending at FDA, the oldest of which was filed on August 31, 1972.[492]

Several witnesses provided graphical representations of the flow of the food additive approvals and GRAS affirmation petitions, and some of the more relevant graphs have been reproduced in the accompanying pages. For instance, over the course of a decade, review times for both food additive and GRAS affirmation petitions had doubled.[493] FDA officials conceded that significant delays existed and announced various initiatives to speed reviews,[494] but they also testified that the statute's 180-day deadline was totally unrealistic.[495] Certain members of the subcommittee expressed dismay with the agency's position, recognizing that the deadline may be too short but disagreeing that the FDA could, therefore, simply choose to ignore it.[496]

In addition, agency officials explained that companies bore some of the blame for the delays in the process because of inadequacies in their submissions.[497] Although it could reject such petitions without prejudice to a resubmission in the future, the FDA generally has worked to help petitioners correct any deficiencies in a pending petition.[498] Companies apparently have tolerated lengthy delays as preferable to the stigma associated with an FDA rejection of a food additive petition.[499] Apart from the unfavorable (and somewhat misleading) impact of this policy on average review times, one witness objected to what he regarded as the FDA's goal of eventually approving all additives unless patently unsafe.[500] CFSAN officials subsequently advised industry that they plan to start rejecting incomplete petitions.[501]

Some of the subcommittee members commented on the unwillingness of officials from individual companies to testify,[502] and one witness suggested that their reluctance might reflect fear of retaliation for criticizing the FDA.[503] Even so, representatives from several trade associations appeared at the hearings. They and others commented on what they perceived to be the FDA's significant risk aversion, complaining that reviewers evidently preferred to ask additional questions rather than exercise well-informed scientific judgment and recommend closure on a petition.[504] Whatever the precise explanation, however, no one seriously disputes the fact that reviews of new food additives have become extremely slow.

Because so few petitions are approved in any single year,[505] aggregate measures for the last decade are more valuable than year-to-year comparisons, especially reflecting the average review times for (1) first approvals of direct food additives, (2) approvals of supplemental petitions for additional uses of a direct additive (sometimes referred to as follow-on petitions), and (3) affirmations of GRAS petitions for direct ingredients.

Substances Added Directly to Foods:

Average Review Times for Approvals

(Jan. 1, 1987–Dec. 31, 1996)

Food Additive Petitions = 73.5 months (n = 10).[506]

Supplemental Use Petitions = 38.0 months (n = 33).[507]

GRAS Affirmation Petitions = 87.2 months (n = 22).[508]

Thus, for direct food additives approved during the last decade, an average of more than six years elapsed between filing and first approval. Not surprisingly, the FDA approved follow-on uses for previously approved additives more quickly (in just over three years), though still long past the three- and six-month deadlines imposed by the statute. Finally, GRAS affirmation petitions approved during the last decade required more than seven years on average, by far the slowest review process for substances added directly to food products.

It is difficult, of course, to measure these review periods with any real precision. For example, some significant but unreported portions of time are consumed while the FDA awaits submission of additional information by the petitioner.[509] On the other hand, because of substantial delays in publishing notices of filing after the receipt of a petition, average review times may be understated if calculated from the notice of filing.[510] Although FDA officials have pointed to trend data as evidence of recent improvements,[511] the numbers for any particular year are too limited to justify such a conclusion and, as the backlogs of long-pending petitions are cleared, the average review times initially should worsen rather than improve.

After Congress subjected drugs to rigorous premarket FDA review for safety and effectiveness, some critics argued that the resulting delays in approval kept valuable therapeutic agents out of the hands of needy patients.[512] More than 30y years later, complaints about a "drug lag" continue.[513] Although similar delays in approvals of direct food additives may seem less consequential,[514] access to innovations in food technology does have some public health dimensions.[515] Wholly apart from delays in reviewing particular applications, the inevitability of substantial delays and confusion about applicable regulatory controls may inhibit research and development efforts.[516] The lengthy delays in FDA reviews of GRAS affirmation petitions pose fewer such concerns because, for the most part, petitioners proceed to market once the agency initially accepts their submissions and seem to care little about how much time may elapse before formal affirmation.

A Catalogue of Proposed Solutions

A number of factors may account for the delays observed in the agency's review of food additives, and a corresponding range of reforms has been suggested. Some of the solutions would require fairly modest revisions in the FDA's internal procedures, but other proposals call for radical overhauls of the current system. This section summarizes the most salient flaws in the system and suggested reforms.

Internal Management Initiatives

The FDA recently reorganized CFSAN, in part as an attempt to streamline its food additive review activities,[517] and it announced renewed efforts at publishing guidelines and tracking work flow among reviewers.[518] To be sure, the lack of coordination and frequent turnover among reviewers has created significant inefficiencies in the past.[519] Moreover, clearer guidelines and other outreach efforts such as pre-filing meetings with petitioners may help minimize reported problems with the submission of incomplete food additive petitions.

Such initiatives promise only modest improvements in efficiency,[520] however, and there are no guarantees that the FDA will make good on its assurances of streamlining the process.[521] Although they would represent dramatic improvements over the existing time frames, none of the announced performance goals—to be phased in gradually only after the agency begins reducing the current backlog—would meet the statutory deadlines.[522] One recent bill would have codified performance goals for the FDA,[523] but Congress failed to enact the proposed reforms. In any event, the agency will be free to ignore such goals unless some action-forcing mechanism accompanies any new deadlines.

Statutory Hammers

Some critics have suggested the establishment of a statutory "hammer" to force the FDA to act by a specified deadline.[524] A type of hammer appeared in some of the early food additive bills,[525] and this mechanism is currently in vogue to prompt the timely promulgation of broad regulations.[526] But such a tool seems ill-suited to the task of forcing expeditious action on food additive petitions.

Instead of tolling and ignoring the statutory clock as it does now, the FDA could circumvent a statutory hammer simply by issuing repeated denials of a petition until it was satisfied about the safety of a food additive.[527] Such a response might be desirable insofar as it encourages greater initial care in compiling petitions. The sole benefit for industry would be a much earlier opportunity to seek judicial review, but this opportunity would provide only an illusory advantage over the present system—the petitioner still would shoulder the burden of proof, and courts accord significant deference to the FDA's scientific judgments.[528]

If it could not circumvent a hammer, the agency would in theory be forced to approve food additives about which it may harbor some lingering safety concerns. The FDA might then routinely insist on the submission of postmarketing reports in such instances, as a backstop against a rushed approval decision. Even if no serious problems materialize, future backlogs may develop as FDA scientists have to spend their time reviewing these periodic reports. Statutory hammers might have some place in a revised food additive approval procedure, but, as a freestanding mechanism for reform, they suffer from significant shortcomings.

Prioritizing Reviews

Resource constraints provide one obvious explanation for the delays in FDA reviews of food additive and GRAS affirmation petitions. CFSAN staffing levels have remained constant even while food additive petitions have become more complicated and its other regulatory responsibilities have burgeoned.[529] The agency could improve utilization of these resources by better prioritizing its review activities. For instance, reducing the intensity of reviews for substances likely to pose little or no public health risk, such as indirect food additives or additional uses of direct additives, would allow reviewers to focus on the more significant petitions involving novel ingredients.

The FDA recently exempted some indirect food additives from full review if estimated human exposure falls below a "threshold of regulation,"[530] thereby allowing CFSAN to allocate more of its resources to direct additives.[531] Pursuant to this new regulation, the FDA may issue a letter exempting a food-contact substance from food additive petition requirements if a request for an exemption demonstrates, through migration data and any existing toxicological studies, that the likelihood or extent of migration to food is so trivial as not to require further regulation.[532] Although it recognized the need for timely reviews of exemption requests, the FDA declined to impose any deadlines on itself.[533] The resulting potential for internal delays may limit the policy's value as a mechanism for redirecting agency resources to nontrivial additives.[534]

By requiring FDA action on exemption requests,[535] the threshold of regulation policy is more like an abbreviated premarket review procedure than a premarket notification system. Congress recently enacted a simplified premarket notification procedure for "new dietary ingredients,"[536] though as part of an effort to deregulate the dietary supplement industry rather than to free up resources for the FDA's direct food additive reviews. Over the last 20 years, the premarket notification system for medical devices—designed by Congress as a temporary procedure for exempting "substantially equivalent" devices from full premarket approval requirements—has evolved to become the FDA's primary review mechanism and, as a result, also more cumbersome than the simple notification procedure originally envisioned by Congress.[537] Unless reoriented, a similar fate may befall the new threshold of regulation policy or similar premarket notification reforms.

In addition to exempting inconsequential food-contact substances, the agency might use an abbreviated review process for supplemental petitions seeking approval for additional uses of a previously approved additive.[538] The FDA also might assign higher priority to the review of novel food additives which promise important public health benefits. At present, the agency reviews submissions in the order that they are received, and existing backlogs may mean that scientific reviews of a newly filed petition do not even begin for a lengthy period of time.[539] Although the statute apparently prohibits any consideration of benefits in making safety determinations,[540] the FDA could prioritize its reviews on the basis of such criteria.[541] Similar prioritization systems exist for new drug reviews, though the statute expressly authorizes the consideration of benefits in the drug approval process.[542] Instead, however, the FDA's announced performance goals—varying for three tiers of petitions based on their length, complexity, or novelty of the issues—promise relatively faster reviews of petitions for the least complex and novel additives.[543]

Imposing User Fees

Some have recommended legislative authorization of user fees to address the resource problem,[544] as Congress recently did in the prescription drug area.[545] Indeed, the FDA specifically requested user fees during congressional hearings which eventually led to the enactment of the Food Additives Amendment.[546] Such a provision had been included in the Pesticide Residues Amendment of 1954,[547] and it also appeared in Congressman Delaney's food additive bills.[548] The 1958 legislation did not, however, provide the FDA with the authority to impose such fees.

By definition, user fees are intended to reimburse agencies for the particular benefits they provide to regulated entities. More than two decades ago, the Supreme Court held that the imposition of user fees on regulated companies for the benefit of the general public is nothing more than another tax on industry.[549] As explained previously, a food additive petition directly benefits competitors as well as the petitioner. Unlike a new drug application, which gives the successful applicant an exclusive private license to sell a drug product, a food additive petition results in the publication by the FDA of a regulation authorizing use of the additive by any person wishing to do so, subject only to any remaining patent term.[550]

If only the petitioner were required to pay for an FDA service that inures to the benefit of the entire food industry, developers of innovative additives would be unfairly penalized.[551] Congress could avoid this concern by converting food additive approvals into more of a private licensing system like that used for new drugs. In fact, in addition to attacking the causes of existing delays (whether by imposing user fees or otherwise), some have emphasized the need to soften the negative competitive effects of such delays by ensuring a period of market exclusivity to the petitioner in the event that patents are unavailable or about to expire.[552] Even then, however, the level of user fees would have to be far lower than currently charged for new drugs in recognition of the generally smaller R&D investment and limited commercial potentional of most new food additives. Otherwise, the imposition of user fees would further discourage companies from pursuing FDA approval.

Extramural Reviews

Frustration with delays in the FDA's drug approval process has triggered calls for extramural reviews by scientific organizations.[553] A similar approach has been suggested as a way of expediting food additive reviews. The FDA frequently involves scientific organizations in an advisory capacity, for instance, when it sought NAS and FASEB input during the GRAS list review,[554] and, in 1995, the agency announced plans to contract out reviews of routine toxicity studies in currently pending food additive petitions.[555]

Many academic scientists and industry representatives favor greater reliance on such outside organizations.[556] Under one suggested model, a petitioner willing to pay for it could ask the FDA to contract out the review of its safety data, and both the FDA and the third-party organization would have a limited opportunity to request that the petitioner first collect additional information. A number of issues would have to be resolved, including how to comply with or modify the Federal Advisory Committee Act (FACA),[557] whether fees should be channeled through the agency,[558] and what force to give the third party's recommendation. Some have suggested that the recommendations of an outside organization should be deemed adopted by the FDA unless it could demonstrate (within a limited period of time after the issuance of a report) that the petitioner had failed to establish the safety of a substance.[559]

In a related vein, some have suggested that the agency place greater reliance on the GRAS exception, though not necessarily through the formalized GRAS affirmation process that exists at present.[560] Perhaps this could be accomplished by contracting out the review of GRAS petitions, much as the FDA did in the 1970s when it contracted out data reviews for substances appearing on the initial GRAS lists,[561] or by giving presumptive weight to the conclusions of certain organizations when commissioned by the petitioner to review the GRAS status of a food substance.[562] The agency recently proposed a simplified GRAS notification procedure to replace the affirmation petition procedure in hopes of redirecting its resources to higher priorities.[563]

* * *

Efforts at constructive revisions of the statute and regulations should continue, utilizing one or more of the reforms discussed above. In the meantime, because of the breadth of the GRAS exception, industry already has the unusual opportunity to reform the food additive approval process by itself and substantially reduce existing delays. After all, GRAS is a definitional *exception* (or exclusion) rather than an *exemption* procedure, and self-determinations premised on published extramural reviews by reputable scientific organizations could almost totally supplant the industry's existing dependence on the FDA. For instance, companies can and have commissioned extramural reviews by FASEB and then submitted a GRAS affirmation petition primarily to advise the FDA of their self-determination.[564] This approach could become routine, requiring not a change in the law but in the industry's attitude.

Although food processors traditionally have insisted on some sort of FDA seal of approval, chemical manufacturers need to better explain to their customers that such approvals are neither necessary, rapidly acquired, nor terribly meaningful in some cases.[565] Why should processors feel more comfortable using an interim food additive such as mannitol (which theoretically could be withdrawn by the FDA with little or no advance warning[566]) than a substance that FASEB or FEMA found to be safe under the agency's GRAS criteria? No doubt the food processors fear the possibility of a seizure or injunction by the FDA and a resulting loss of public confidence. But the agency's past actions against unapproved food-use substances all have involved in-house and poorly documented GRAS self-determinations rather than those based on published extramural reviews.

In the highly unlikely event that the FDA initiated enforcement proceedings or sent a warning letter to a food processor, the additive's manufacturer could respond and perhaps even file a declaratory judgment action in federal court to settle the GRAS question. The FDA also could take a less adversarial approach and initiate—perhaps at the behest of a public interest organization—a rulemaking proceeding that might eventually require a food additive petition for the substance, but the agency also might do that with a substance previously affirmed as GRAS. If an additive manufacturer has assembled good safety data and chooses to present these data to a qualified and independent panel of experts (or regulatory authorities in another country), the GRAS exception currently allows the manufacturer to do so instead of filing a food additive petition with the FDA. If food processors would come to understand the limited practical value of an FDA affirmation or approval, a market for private certifications could emerge without any changes to the FD&C Act or the agency's regulations.[567]

Unless the agency chooses to obstruct such a change because it fears a loss of power or control, it also could reap substantial benefits from the development.[568] In fact, the FDA could facilitate this process by issuing guidelines for ensuring the independence of third-party organizations.[569] Of course, if FASEB or another organization concludes that a substance is not GRAS for a particular use on the basis of the evidence presented, then a company could attempt to "appeal" this conclusion by filing a food additive petition with the FDA, perhaps after first undertaking additional studies. Moreover, Congress could decide to encourage manufacturers of innovative but unpatentable substances to seek food additive approval by providing them with some form of market exclusivity.

Public interest groups surely will object to any loss of FDA control over the food additive approval process.[570] In some respects, privatization would bring us full circle, back to the time when food companies assured themselves of the safety of any substance used in food, and the FDA shouldered the burden of proving otherwise.[571] But now another expert body would review and publish the industry's judgments, applying more uniform and stringent safety assessment criteria than had existed prior to 1958.[572]

The industry frequently calls for the repeal of the Delaney clause. Even if otherwise sensible, such a reform probably would have little impact on the pace of reviews—petitioners would still have to conduct chronic toxicity studies in appropriate cases, and the FDA would apply the general safety standard conservatively even without the added strictures of the Delaney clause. Although some critics have complained of excessive risk aversion by the agency, no one seriously suggests that Congress should water down the general safety standard. Reforms in the food additive approval process will come from changes in definitions and procedures (and attitudes), not from modifications in the substantive approval criteria.

Combatting Sham Petitioning

Competitive manipulation of the FDA's procedures provides another possible explanation for delays, at least in a few cases, and deserves separate consideration. The food additive approval procedures may be vulnerable to "sham" petitioning, defined as the improper use of administrative procedures by firms seeking to delay or prevent entry into the market by a would-be competitor.[573] As I recently have concluded elsewhere, "real opportunities exist for sham petitioning in administrative proceedings, especially when market entry requires some sort of agency licensing as in the pharmaceutical, transportation, communications, and energy industries."[574] The same may be said of the food additive industry.

Upon the acceptance or refusal of a food additive petition for filing, virtually the entire petition becomes available for public disclosure.[575] The petition thus becomes an easy target for comments from interested persons, both from well-intentioned scientists and public interest groups and from competitors motivated chiefly by a desire to delay approval of the petitioner's product. In recent cases, taking advantage of the FDA's de facto comment period,[576] parties have made anonymous submissions late in the agency's internal review process apparently to create unwarranted delays in the issuance of food additive regulations.

For example, the FDA published a notice of filing for the sucralose petition almost 10 years ago.[577] Three years later, it sent the company a draft of the *Federal Register* order approving the petition, but, later that same year, a law firm submitted comments on behalf of an unnamed client raising concerns about the safety of sucralose. After a lengthy interruption in the FDA's internal processing of the final regulation, a revised draft of the final regulation reached the Office of General Counsel for approval, but the same law firm submitted a letter to the agency reiterating its original concerns, and thereafter it again wrote to the FDA purporting to raise new questions about sucralose. More than a year later, CSPI sent the FDA unsolicited information it had received from an anonymous source concerning an early draft of one of the company's studies.[578] Each of these submissions apparently interrupted the approval process. In the meantime, regulatory authorities in Canada and Australia have approved sucralose.[579]

The bizarre chronology of events surrounding the sucralose petition may reflect bad faith intervention by third parties, possibly for purposes of retaining a competitive advantage in the artificial sweeteners market. Extremely tardy comments were submitted with exquisite timing, apparently calculated to yield the greatest disruption of the FDA's internal processing of the food additive regulation and to delay eventual approval.[580] Even if this interpretation of events is unwarranted,[581] the experience with sucralose suggests that the food additive petition process may be susceptible to such abuse, and FDA officials have conceded that this may represent a problem.[582] Comments submitted several years after a notice of filing is published, and just as the agency appears ready to approve a food additive petition, can only serve to needlessly delay approval of important and legitimate new products.

Unfettered opportunities for prepublication comment may cause excessive delays which are contrary to the purpose of the act.[583] Courts will order agency action when delays become unreasonable.[584] Congress imposed a strict deadline for agency action in response to food additive petitions, and FDA delays in responding to food additive petitions have been subject to judicial scrutiny in at least two instances. In a challenge to the FDA's failure to act promptly on a food additive petition for cyclamate, the court allowed discovery to proceed because it found sufficient merit in "Plaintiff's claim that its petition is being studied into oblivion."[585] In another case, involving the additive gentian violet used in premixed medicated feed for livestock, a court found that the FDA's "failure and refusal to act upon the [food additive] petition . . . constitute[d] a clear denial of the rights of Plaintiffs [which] effectively takes their property without due process."[586]

The FDA's practice of accepting and responding to comments whenever submitted before publication of a food additive order contravenes an explicit statutory deadline requiring that the agency issue a final order within 90 days of filing, up to a maximum of 180 days if necessary to fully study and investigate the petition.[587] In practice, this deadline may be impossible for the agency to comply with, particularly when submissions include large amounts of scientific data. At a minimum, however, the deadline prescribed by Congress requires that the agency not entertain or respond to comments received after the statutory 90-day deadline has passed.[588] The FDA itself has recognized the importance of placing some strict limits on the time for filing comments and other responses. For example, in setting an explicit comment deadline with respect to olestra, the agency explained that, "[a]bsent such boundaries, it will be difficult for FDA to reach a decision because the underlying data set could be shifting continuously."[589] In addition, the FDA's revised procedural regulations for the review of OTC drug products provide strict time limits for comments submitted in response to a proposed monograph.[590]

If the FDA plans to accept and respond to comments before publication, it should place a strict limit on the time for filing comments. Otherwise it could never comply with the 90-(or 180-)day deadline contained in the statute; if the FDA were to adopt a regulation allowing a comment period on food additive petitions exceeding 180 days, the agency's action would be patently unlawful.[591] A 60-day prepublication comment period for food additive petitions would provide a reasonable time frame. For instance, the FDA's Center for Veterinary Medicine, acting pursuant to identical statutory and regulatory authority, often includes an explicit 60-day comment period in the notice of filing.[592]

Late filed comments addressing a food additive petition would not be ignored by the agency. In the unlikely event that tardy comments happen to suggest innovative interpretations of existing safety data that escaped the FDA's attention prior to approval, these issues can be raised in objections to the final regulation.[593] This is the procedure used by the agency in its OTC Drug Review. Any comments received after the 90-day comment period following publication of a proposed monograph are deferred by the agency until after a tentative final monograph (TFM) is published and interested persons are given an opportunity to file objections and request a public hearing.[594] New data and information submitted after this period but before the final monograph is published would be treated as a petition to amend the monograph.[595] New information discovered after a food additive regulation becomes final is handled in essentially this fashion.[596]

The proposed 60-day comment period would not prevent the FDA from considering important new safety data submitted any time prior to the publication of the food additive order. The agency could create conditions for the prepublication consideration of such late-filed information to ensure against submissions that contain no new safety data but are interposed for the purpose of delay. Certification requirements could ensure that the food additive petition process is not subject to abuse and unreasonable delay while at the same time retaining sufficient flexibility to take legitimate new information into account no matter when it is submitted.[597] The FDA already employs certification requirements in connection with other submissions such as citizen petitions.[598]

CONCLUSION

Almost four decades after the enactment of the Food Additives Amendment and 20 years after the political controversy over saccharin, public attention again has turned to the regulation of food additives in the United States. Food additive petitioners have become frustrated with lengthy delays in the review process, while other interested parties engage in obstructionist tactics and then vocally criticize approved additives as unsafe. The FDA is caught between these competing factions, struggling to do more with fewer resources. Out of necessity, the agency has been forced to improvise, sometimes ignoring its unrealistic statutory directives.

The GRAS exception has functioned tolerably well and created an important route to market, and the food industry could make even broader use of this definitional exclusion. For its part, the FDA could facilitate GRAS self-determinations, continue efforts at streamlining the review process, exempt certain types of substances altogether to allow a reallocation of its scarce resources, and revise its procedures to minimize the risk of sham petitioning. Finally, Congress might require the agency to implement one or more of these steps, authorize the imposition of user fees in exchange for some period of market exclusivity, and codify procedures for the extramural reviews of GRAS affirmation and food additive petitions.

Although controversy inevitably will surround the choice among these and other reforms, the FDA cannot simply continue "muddling along" in its current fashion. Unless someone fixes the food additive approval process, existing regulatory hurdles will inhibit future scientific advances in food technology. Generally, the standards for safety assessments should remain in place, but the time may have come for an overhaul of the mechanisms used to ensure the safety of substances added to food.

APPENDIX: INTERNATIONAL COMPARISONS

Different countries' approaches to food additive regulation often are characterized as either "positive" or "negative" listing systems. In a positive list system, only those additives identified as permissible by the designated regulatory authority may be used in food. In a negative list system, any additive may be used so long as it is not specifically restricted by the designated regulatory authority, which normally shoulders the burden to prove that a substance is unsafe. The Food Additives Amendment represented a shift in the United States from a negative to a positive list system. Actually, however, because of its special definition of the term food additive, the 1958 amendment established a "mixed" system, imposing a positive listing requirement for food additives while subjecting GRAS food substances to something that resembles a negative listing approach.[599] Many other nations also have hybrid systems, though their particular mixes differ depending in part on how the term food additive is defined.[600]

The following sections briefly sketch out the regulation of food additives in several industrialized countries, identifying relevant differences in approach. Although the FDA participates in international harmonization efforts, notably with regard to acceptable designs for the testing of pharmaceuticals,[601] reciprocal recognition of foreign approvals remains unlikely. Some argue that the United States encounters the difficult regulatory problems before other countries do.[602] Others have suggested that excessive FDA delays drive companies to seek initial regulatory approvals in foreign countries.[603] Unfortunately, comparative data on review times are not readily available,[604] though anecdotal evidence discussed herein suggests that food-use substances often enter foreign markets more rapidly.

Canada

Under the Canadian Food and Drugs Act,[605] the Health Protection Branch (HPB) of the department of Health controls the safety of food products sold in the country.[606] The statute prohibits the sale of food that "has in or on it any poisonous or harmful substance," and it delegates broad authority to the Department to issue regulations governing "the use of any substance as an ingredient in any food."[607]

Pursuant to the HPB's implementing regulations, originally promulgated in 1964, the term "food additive" means "any substance the use of which results, or may reasonably be expected to result, in it or its by-products becoming a part of or affecting the characteristics of a food."[608] Like the Food Additives Amendment of 1958, the definition excludes agricultural chemicals (such as pesticides) and animal drugs, but it also excludes the following: various flavors; vitamins, mineral nutrients, and amino acids; and food packaging materials.[609] Most of the substances excluded from the definition are governed by separate sections of the regulations. Although indirect additives in food packaging are not subject to a premarket review requirement in Canada, an informal (and expeditious) system has developed to respond to industry requests for letters of opinion.[610]

Although the HPB regulations do not include a GRAS or prior sanction exception in the definition of food additive, they do exclude "any nutritive material that is used, recognized or commonly sold as an article or ingredient of food."[611] The department recently proposed regulations to require that a company file a premarket notification along with safety data 90 days before introducing for sale a "novel" food or a food produced through a novel process, with novelty defined as a lack of significant previous use in Canada.[612]

Food products sold in Canada may contain only those food additives appearing on a list of approved substances.[613] In order to add a substance to the list, a company would have to submit an application to the Department of Health which includes, inter alia, "data establishing that the food additive will have the intended physical or other technical effect," and "detailed reports of tests made to establish the safety of the food additive under the conditions of use recommended."[614] Within 90 days after the filing of such a submission, the department shall advise the applicant whether, and under what terms, it intends to recommend listing.[615] The HPB approves an additive if it is safe, does not lead to deception, and offers some benefit to consumers.[616]

The United Kingdom

In the past, some have criticized the regulation of food additives in the United Kingdom as weak.[617] The relevant statute prohibits adding "any article or substance to the food, [or] using any article or substance as an ingredient in the preparation of the food," so as to render the food "injurious to health," and it authorizes the issuance of regulations governing the use of substances in food.[618] Two agencies, the Ministry of Agriculture, Fisheries and Food (MAFF) and the Department of Health and Social Security (DHSS), share responsibility for implementation of the act.

The MAFF has issued lists of permitted additives, subdivided into roughly two dozen functional categories, but certain other categories (including flavorings, starches, and enzymes) currently are not subject to positive lists.[619] The MAFF recently modified its food additive lists—for instance, by authorizing the use of cyclamate—as required under the latest directives issued by the Council of the European Union (EU) and its predecessor, the European Economic Community (EEC).[620]

In order to use an additive falling within a regulated category but not appearing on an existing list, a firm would have to seek permission by submitting safety and utility information to the MAFF. Evidence of utility must be provided because, "no matter how safe an additive might be, it is policy to prohibit compounds unless they are, in some sense, needed."[621] The ministry refers any request and accompanying information to its Food Advisory Committee and the DHSS's Committee on Toxicity, and both committees report back a recommendation to the

MAFF, which, after inviting public comment on the reports, may then publish a draft regulation for further comment and eventual finalization.[622]

The European Union

EU policy on foodstuffs directly affects domestic food additive regulation in the United Kingdom and much of the rest of Europe.[623] The free movement of goods among member states is promoted both through the principle of "mutual recognition" and efforts at the "approximation" (harmonization) of national laws. Because of difficulties and delays in harmonizing product standards, the EEC's largely self-executing mutual recognition principles initially provided an important mechanism for increased trade.[624] As explicated by the European Court of Justice in a series of cases involving food products, a member state may not prohibit the sale of food containing an unapproved additive which is authorized in another state unless: (1) an importer is given an opportunity to seek approval of the additive through an authorization procedure that will be completed in a reasonable time and subject to judicial review, and (2) the failure to approve the additive is justified on public health grounds or lack of utility.[625]

The harmonization of food additive regulations in the EU recently has accelerated, making the need for mutual recognition among inconsistent domestic regulations less relevant. A framework directive adopted in 1989 defines the term "food additive" as follows:

> [A]ny substance not normally consumed as a food in itself and not normally used as a characteristic ingredient of food whether or not it has nutritive value, the intentional addition of which to food for a technological purpose in the manufacture, processing, preparation, treatment, packaging, transport or storage of such food results, or may be reasonably expected to result, in it or its by-products becoming directly or indirectly a component of such foods.[626]

The definition specifically excludes processing aids, agricultural chemicals, flavoring substances (which are the subject of a separate framework directive), and added nutrients such as vitamins and minerals.[627] The definition lacks a GRAS exception, though it does exclude "characteristic ingredient[s]" of food and, as in Canada, the recently proposed regulations on novel food and food ingredients incorporate such a concept.[628]

The 1989 framework directive sets forth general criteria for the use of food additives. The commission will approve a food additive only under the following circumstances:

> [T]here can be demonstrated a reasonable technological need and the purpose cannot be achieved by other means which are economically and technologically practicable; they present no hazard to the health of the consumer at the level of use proposed, so far as can be judged by the scientific evidence available; [and] they do not mislead the consumer.[629]

Unlike the limitations on the FDA's ability to consider utility, the EU demands evidence that "the proposed use of the additive would have demonstrable advantages of benefit to the consumer."[630] Only then will questions of safety be considered, for which an additive "must be subjected to appropriate toxicological testing and evaluation."[631]

After the establishment of a list for a particular category of food additives, only those substances included on the list may be used in food.[632] In 1962, the EEC issued its first positive list to regulate additives throughout the European Community, reducing the number of color additives for use in food previously permitted by member states.[633] Over the course of the next decade, the EEC issued similar directives applicable to such ingredients as preservatives, antioxidants, and emulsifiers.[634] These lists subsequently were amended on several occasions, most recently in 1994 through the issuance of comprehensive new lists covering colors and sweeteners,[635] and a 1995 consolidated list of miscellaneous other additives (including over 250 individual substances for preservative and numerous other uses) which are not otherwise the subject of a final or pending list.[636] In order to become operative, these positive lists must be transposed into the national laws of each member state, as accomplished in the United Kingdom through the MAFF's regulatory amendments late in 1995.[637]

The EU continues to work on directives for the regulation of food packaging[638] and flavoring substances.[639] In addition, it appears ready to issue regulations requiring premarket approval of "novel" foods and ingredients, defined as substances (other than additives subject to other council directives) not previously consumed to a significant degree in the EU which contain or are derived from genetically modified organisms (GMOs) or are otherwise the result of significant new processing methods.[640] The proposed regulations call for the submission of a technical dossier to demonstrate the safety of novel foods for review by national authorities and, in certain cases, the EU's Standing Committee on Foodstuffs.[641] Labeling disclosures would be mandatory in most cases.[642]

Japan

The regulation of food additives in Japan is somewhat difficult to discern from the available literature. Indeed, lack of information about or transparency in the standard-setting process has complicated market penetration by foreign firms in the past.[643] The United States has included food additives as one of the many sectors over which it continues to have trade disputes with Japan.[644]

Like most other countries, Japan utilizes a positive or mixed list system. The Ministry of Health and Welfare, with input from the Subcommittee on Food Additives and Toxicology of the Ministry's Food Sanitation Investigation Council, regulates substances used in food.[645] The ministry has approved ("designated") approximately 350 substances as food additives,[646] and it will now begin regulating "natural" food additives.[647] Moreover, the ministry recently proposed revisions to streamline its food additive approval procedures—in addition to more clearly specifying the array of safety studies required in an application, the revision calls for a standard period of one year for processing a food additive application.[648]

Japanese officials have been active in developing appropriate regulatory strategies for applications of biotechnology in the food and other industries.[649] Guidelines issued by the Ministry of Health and Welfare call for manufacturers to file applications comparing their bioengineered substances to existing additives.[650] For instance, after spending six months reviewing applications for recombinant chymosin preparations, the ministry affirmed that the substance satisfied its biotechnology guidelines.[651] By comparison, the FDA took two years longer to affirm the GRAS status of this substance.[652]

References

1. *See, e.g.*, *Delays in the FDA's Food Additive Petition Process and GRAS Affirmation Process: Hearings Before the Subcomm. on Human Resources and Intergovernmental Relations of the House Comm. on Government Reform and Oversight*, 104th Cong., 1st Sess. (1995) [hereinafter *1995 Hearings*]; Peter Barton Hutt, *Approval of Food Additives in the United States: A Bankrupt System*, FOOD TECH., Mar. 1996, at 118.

2. *See, e.g.*, THOMAS O. MCGARITY & SIDNEY A. SHAPIRO, WORKERS AT RISK: THE FAILED PROMISE OF THE OCCUPATIONAL SAFETY AND HEALTH ADMINISTRATION (1993); JERRY L. MASHAW & DAVID L. HARFST, THE STRUGGLE FOR AUTO SAFETY (1990); GLEN O. ROBINSON, THE FOREST SERVICE: A STUDY IN PUBLIC LAND MANAGEMENT (1975); JAMES Q. WILSON ed., THE POLITICS OF REGULATION (1980).

3. Pure Food and Drugs Act, Pub. L. No. 59-384, ch. 3915, § 2, 34 Stat. 768 (1906) (superseded by the FD&C Act in 1938).

4. *Id.* § 7.

5. United States v. Lexington Mill & Elev. Co., 232 U.S. 399, 411 (1914); *see also* United States v. Coca Cola Co., 241 U.S. 265, 279-85 (1916) (holding that caffeine added to syrup used for making beverages was an "added" ingredient and that the government's evidence that caffeine was poisonous or deleterious should have been submitted to the jury).

6. Pub. L. No. 75-717, ch. 675, 52 Stat. 1040 (1938) (codified as amended at 21 U.S.C. §§ 321-393 (1994)). The statute refers throughout to the Secretary of Health and Human Services (previously the Secretary of Health, Education and Welfare (HEW) and before that the Secretary of Agriculture (USDA)), *id.* § 321(d), but the Secretary has delegated most powers under the FD&C Act to the Commissioner of Food and Drugs. *See id.* § 393(b); 21 C.F.R. §§ 5.10(a)(1), 5.11(a) (1996).

7. Pub. L. No. 85-929, 72 Stat. 1784 (1958) (codified as amended in scattered sections of title 21 U.S.C.).

8. *See* 104 CONG. REC. 17,417 (1958) (statement of Hon. John B. Williams) ("The 1938 law gave no recognition to substances deliberately added to food for beneficial purposes, such as retarding natural spoilage or keeping food moist or tasty. There is a gap in our pure food law as a result of advancing technology.").

9. *See, e.g.*, GENERAL ACCOUNTING OFFICE, FOOD SAFETY AND QUALITY: INNOVATIVE STRATEGIES MAY BE NEEDED TO REGULATE NEW FOOD TECHNOLOGIES, No. RCED-93-142 (1993), at 1-2, 5 [hereinafter GAO, NEW FOOD TECHNOLOGIES].

10. FD&C Act § 402(a) (codified as amended at 21 U.S.C. § 342(a) (1994)). *See generally* Richard A. Merrill, *Regulating Carcinogens in Food: A Legislator's Guide to the Food Safety Provisions of the Federal Food, Drug, and Cosmetic Act*, 77 MICH. L. REV. 171 (1978); James D. Poliquin, Comment, *The Incremental Development of an Extra-Statutory System of Regulation: A Critique of Food and Drug Administration Regulation of Added Poisonous and Deleterious Substances*, 33 ME. L. REV. 103 (1981).

11. FD&C Act § 406(a) (codified as amended at 21 U.S.C. § 346 (1994)) ("In determining the quantity of such added substance to be tolerated in or on different articles of food the Secretary shall take into account the extent to which the use of such substance is required or cannot be avoided in the production of each such article, and the other ways in which the consumer may be affected by the same or other poisonous or deleterious substances."); *see also* H.R. REP. NO. 2139, 75th Cong., 3d Sess. 6 (1938) (explaining that the tolerance setting provision would provide greater flexibility in dealing with pesticide residues); Merrill, *supra* note 10, at 175 ("In substance, Congress authorized the FDA to license the use of some potentially toxic substances in food, apparently in recognition of their utility or of the importance of foods from which they cannot practicably be eliminated.").

12. FD&C Act § 401 (codified as amended at 21 U.S.C. § 341 (1994)); *see also* Federal Security Admin. v. Quaker Oats Co., 318 U.S. 218, 227-31 (1943); Atlas Powder Co. v. Ewing, 201 F.2d 347, 350-55 (3d Cir. 1952) (upholding FDA decision, after almost one decade of hearings, not to permit the use of certain emulsifiers in bread because of unresolved safety concerns and the risk of consumer deception), *cert. denied*, 345 U.S. 923 (1953); Richard A. Merrill & Earl M. Collier, *"Like Mother Used to Make": An Analysis of FDA Food Standards of Identity*, 74 COLUM. L. REV. 561, 600 (1974). The FDA did have limited premarket approval powers under the 1938 Act through the listing and batch certification provisions applicable to coal-tar colors used in food. *See* FD&C Act § 406(b), 52 Stat. 1049 (1938), repealed and replaced by the Color Additive Amendments of 1960, Pub. L. No. 86-618, tit. I, 74 Stat. 397 (codified as amended at 21 U.S.C. § 379e (1994)).

13. *See* 21 U.S.C. §§ 331(a)-(c) (1994) (designating the adulteration of food, or its delivery or receipt, in interstate commerce as a prohibited act), 332(a) (authorizing injunctions to restrain violations of the Act), 334(a) (authorizing seizure of products in violation of the Act); *see also id.* § 333(a) (authorizing the imposition of criminal penalties for violations of the Act).

14. *See, e.g.*, United States v. 29 Cartons ... An Article of Food, 987 F.2d 33, 35 (1st Cir. 1993) ("[T]he FDA can prevent sale of bottled BCO or any other 'food' only if it proves by a preponderance of the evidence that the food is 'injurious to health.'"); United States v. Boston Farm Center, Inc., 590 F.2d 149, 153 (5th Cir. 1979) ("[I]n this case the expert evidence is uncontradicted that 20 ppb of aflatoxin may render corn harmful."); United States v. 2,116 Boxes of Boned Beef . . . , 516 F. Supp. 321, 328-30 (D. Kan. 1981) (holding that, under the identically-phrased adulteration provision in the Federal Meat Inspection Act, the government must prove a reasonable possibility of harmfulness), *aff'd*, 726 F.2d 1481 (10th Cir.), *cert. denied*, 469 U.S. 825 (1984); United States v. Anderson Seafoods, Inc., 447 F. Supp. 1151, 1155-56 (N.D. Fla. 1978) (holding that the injuriousness requirement does not mean harmfulness under any conceivable conditions of use), *aff'd*, 622 F.2d 157, 159 (5th Cir. 1980) ("The 'may render' standard has been interpreted to mean that there is a reasonable possibility of injury to the consumer."); *see also* United States v. Coca Cola Co., 241 U.S. 265, 284-85 (1916) (construing similar language in predecessor statute).

15. Pure Food and Drugs Act, Pub. L. No. 59-384, ch. 3915, § 7, 34 Stat. 768 (1906) (superseded by the FD&C Act).

16. *See* United States v. Lexington Mill & Elevator Co., 232 U.S. 399, 411 (1914) ("If it cannot by any possibility, when the facts are reasonably considered, injure the health of any consumer, such [bleached] flour, though having a small addition of poisonous or deleterious ingredients, may not be condemned under the [1906] act."); *see also* Flemming v. Florida Citrus Exchange, 358 U.S. 153, 161 (1958) (applying the holding of *Lexington Mill* to the adulteration provisions of the FD&C Act).

17. *See* Merrill, *supra* note 10, at 189 ("The sparse case law suggests that the agency would have to demonstrate a probability of harm to some significant number of consumers"). Thus, the FDA often has stretched the concept of "added" so that it could act against harmful substances even though they were not intentionally added to food. *See, e.g.*, Continental Seafoods, Inc. v. Schweiker, 674 F.2d 38, 42-43 (D.C. Cir. 1982) (salmonella in shrimp); United States v. Anderson Seafoods, Inc., 622 F.2d 157, 160-61 (5th Cir. 1980) (mercury contamination in fish); Richard A. Merrill & Michael Schewel, *FDA Regulation of Environmental Contaminants of Food*, 66 VA. L. REV. 1357 (1980); *cf.* United States v. Ewig Bros. Co., 502 F.2d 715, 722-24 (7th Cir. 1974) (upholding "food additive" designation for DDT residues in fish), *cert. denied*, 420 U.S. 945 (1975).

18. Merrill, *supra* note 10, at 193 ("The two adulteration standards in section 402(a)(1) appear to be distinguished chiefly by the greater probability of harm the government must show to restrict a natural constituent and by its ability, under the 'may render' standard, to take account of specially vulnerable segments of the population."). As another commentator explained, "[o]ften this allocation of the burden of proof determines substantive outcomes." Peter Huber, *The Old-New Division in Risk Regulation*, 69 VA. L. REV. 1025, 1034 (1983) ("Even when the substantive standard for acceptability is the same in the two systems, some sources of hazard will be excluded under the screening system, but tolerated under the standard-setting one because degrees of hazard can never be evaluated with absolute precision."). In

addition, the cost of acquiring necessary information and the risks associated with delay are shouldered by the regulated entity rather than the agency under a screening system. *See id.* at 1034-36.

19. *See* H.R. REP. NO. 2284, 85th Cong., 2d Sess. 1 (1958) ("[T]o prove an untested substance poisonous or deleterious may require approximately 2 years or more of laboratory experiments with small animals and during this period the Government cannot prevent the use of such a substance in food."); *Federal Food, Drug, and Cosmetic Act (Chemical Additives in Food): Hearings Before a Subcomm. of the House Comm. on Interstate and Foreign Commerce*, 84th Cong., 2d Sess. 71 (1956) [hereinafter *1956 Hearings*] (statement of Glenn G. Paxton, appearing as counsel for various food industry associations) ("Today FDA must do its own testing and experimentation on an additive—admittedly a difficult task—and must sustain the burden of proof that it is poisonous or deleterious—admittedly a difficult burden—before it can obtain a court order to restrain its use."); Merrill, *supra* note 10, at 194 ("To enforce section 402(a)(1), the FDA ordinarily must locate contaminated food, conduct chemical analyses, find witnesses prepared to testify that the amount of the contaminant is potentially harmful to some portion of consumers, and prove these facts in court.").

20. *See* 21 U.S.C. §§ 342(a)(2), 346 (1994); Young v. Community Nutrition Inst., 476 U.S. 974, 977, 981-84 (1986) (noting that any added poisonous or deleterious substance for which no tolerance existed would be unsafe, but holding that the statute did not compel the Agency to regard such a substance as adulterated); *Ewig Bros.*, 502 F.2d at 720 (describing the "per se" adulteration approach established by Section 406 for any poisonous or deleterious substance for which no tolerance had been promulgated). The phrase "poisonous or deleterious" is not separately defined in the statute, and the FDA has declined to include a definition in its implementing regulations. *See* 42 Fed. Reg. 52,814, 52,816 (1977).

21. *See* H.R. REP. NO. 2284, 85th Cong., 2d Sess. 1-2 (1958) ("[P]resent law entirely prohibits the use of these additives even if their use at safe levels would advance our food technology and increase and improve our food supplies."); *1956 Hearings*, *supra* note 19, at 194 (statement of George P. Larrick, Commissioner of Food and Drugs) ("Once it was shown that the proposed additive was a poison, it was excluded unless it was necessary in production or unavoidable in good manufacturing practice. Over the years, only the pesticide chemicals have met this test of necessity.").

22. *See* Merrill, *supra* note 10, at 195-98 & nn.89 & 92; Poliquin, *supra* note 10, at 111-15.

23. *See 1956 Hearings*, *supra* note 19, at 112 (statement of James M. Gillet, Manufacturing Chemists' Association) ("Under the present law there is no requirement that the [FDA] be advised in advance of the use of any new chemical, and it has been up to them to find out that such chemical is being used," though most manufacturers voluntarily provide notification.).

24. *See, e.g.*, R.D. Hursh, Annotation, *Liability of Manufacturer or Seller for Injury Caused by Food or Food Product Sold*, 77 A.L.R.2d 7 (1961); Robert C. Brown, *The Liability of Retail Dealers for Defective Food Products*, 23 MINN. L. REV. 585, 596-610 (1939) (discussing the potential tort liability of producers). For a more recent survey of decisions in this area, see Jane M. Draper, Annotation, *Liability for Injury or Death Allegedly Caused by Spoilage, Contamination, or Other Deleterious Condition of Food or Food Product*, 2 A.L.R.5th 1, 41-82 (1992).

25. *See Food Additives: Hearings Before a Subcomm. of the House Comm. on Interstate and Foreign Commerce*, 85th Cong., 1st Sess. 421-22 (1957) [hereinafter *1957 Hearings* (even though the final session of the hearings took place in 1958)] (statement of Elliot L. Richardson, Assistant Secretary of Health, Education, and Welfare (HEW)) ("The commendable actions of the great majority [of companies], however, cannot provide protection against the minority. We have had some narrow escapes in the food field.").

26. *See* H.R. RESOL. 323, 81st Cong., 2d Sess., 96 CONG. REC. 8933 (1950) (calling for an investigation into "the nature, extent, and effect of the use of chemicals, compounds, and synthetics in the production, processing, preparation, and packaging of food products to determine the effect of such chemicals, compounds, and synthetics (A) upon the health and welfare of the Nation and (B) upon the stability and well-being of our agricultural economy").

27. *See Chemicals in Foods and Cosmetics: Hearings Before the House Select Comm. to Investigate the Use of Chemicals in Foods and Cosmetics*, 82d Cong., 2d Sess. (1952); *Chemicals in Food Products: Hearings Before the House Select Comm. to Investigate the Use of Chemicals in Food Products*, 82d Cong., 1st Sess. (1951); *Chemicals in Food Products: Hearings Before the House Select Comm. to Investigate the Use of Chemicals in Food Products*, 81st Cong., 2d Sess. (1950).

28. H.R. REP. NO. 2356, 82d Cong., 2d Sess. 4 (1952); *see also* National Academy of Sciences, *The Use of Chemical Additives in Food Processing*, NAS Pub. No. 398 (1956); Report of the Joint FAO/WHO Expert Committee on Food Additives, *General Principles Governing the Use of Food Additives* (1956).

29. H.R. REP. NO. 2356, 82d Cong., 2d Sess. 3-4 (1952); *see also 1957 Hearings, supra* note 25, at 421 (statement of Elliot L. Richardson, Assistant Secretary of HEW) ("The potential danger of food additives, indeed, is more insidious [than untested drugs] because it is a danger from the daily intake of small amounts of chemical substances . . . ."); *cf. id.* at 167 (statement of Hon. Leonor K. Sullivan) ("Seldom do the chemicals add anything of nutritional value. Mostly, they are intended to cut costs, or to cut corners, or to cut spoilage or waste. They are put into the foods mostly for the manufacturer's benefit . . . rather than the consumer's.").

30. H.R. REP. NO. 2356, 82d Cong., 2d Sess. 4 (1952). Subsequent estimates ran much higher. *See, e.g.*, *Food Additives: Competitive, Regulatory, and Safety Problems: Hearings Before the Senate Select Comm. on Small Business*, 95th Cong., 1st Sess. 52 (1977) (statement of Sherwin Gardner, Acting Commissioner of Food and Drugs) ("There are over 400 nonflavor GRAS substances; approximately 1,650 flavors and spices, some of which are GRAS and some regulated additives; about 400 regulated direct food additives and on the order of 10,000 GRAS and regulated indirect additives.").

31. H.R. REP. NO. 2356, 82d Cong., 2d Sess. 27 (1952). Some scientists viewed the Committee's conclusions as largely unsupported and inappropriately alarmist. *See, e.g.*, Maurice H. Seevers, *Perspective Versus Caprice in Evaluating Toxicity of Chemicals in Man*, 153 JAMA 1329, 1331-32 (1953) (Congressman Delaney's "lurid article, a masterpiece of innuendo and fantasy, based principally on conjecture, was designed for the one purpose of frightening the [consumer] into demanding further legislation.").

32. *See, e.g.*, *1957 Hearings, supra* note 25, at 43-49 (reproducing a chart prepared by subcommittee staff comparing the food additive bills introduced in 1957).

33. *See* S. REP. NO. 2422, 85th Cong., 2d Sess. 3-4 (1958) (describing extensive hearings leading up to the consideration of the final bill); *1957 Hearings, supra* note 25, at 50 (statement of Hon. John B. Williams, Subcomm. Chairman) ("[I]t seems to me that a 10-year period is a sufficiently long incubation period even for difficult legislation."); Vincent A. Kleinfeld, *"Chemicals in Foods"—A Legal Viewpoint*, 9 FOOD DRUG COSM. L.J. 115 (1954) (discussing the initial efforts at drafting legislation to regulate food additives).

34. *See* Pub. L. No. 83-518, § 3 (408(a)), 68 Stat. 511 (1954) (codified at 21 U.S.C. § 346a(a) (1994)), repealed and replaced by the Food Quality Protection Act of 1996, Pub. L. No. 104-170, § 405, 110 Stat. 1514.

35. *See* 104 CONG. REC. 19,359 (1958) (statement of Sen. Hill) ("[T]his measure now has the overwhelming support of the major industrial and business concerns which would be affected by it."); *1957 Hearings, supra* note 25, at 247 (statement of Howard O. Hunter, President of the American Institute of Baking); *1956 Hearings, supra* note 19, at 1-2 (statement of Hon. J. Percy Pierce, Committee Chairman) ("The industries concerned—those who manufacture the chemicals in question and those who use them in connection with food products—and the Government agencies are in agreement that an advance determination by the Government as to the acceptability of a chemical in connection with foods is desirable from the point of view both of the industries concerned, the Government, and the consumer.").

36. *See 1957 Hearings, supra* note 25, at 71-73 (statement of Charles W. Dunn, counsel for the Grocery Manufacturers of America) (explaining the industry's grudging acceptance of a system based on licensing through the issuance of regulations); *id.* at 116-17 (statement of Lawrence A. Coleman, appearing on behalf of the Manufacturing Chemists' Association); *1956 Hearings, supra* note 19, at 73 (statement of Glenn G. Paxton, appearing as counsel for various food industry associations) (observing that "the consensus among the food group was that this is a subject that does not require a strict licensing arrangement by the [FDA]"); *id.* at 91 (supporting a "provision to the effect that after an unfavorable opinion by the Secretary the proponent may not use the additive without first giving to the Secretary at least 30 days notice of intended use, which would enable the Secretary to institute any type of legal action which he deems advisable").

37. *1957 Hearings, supra* note 25, at 21 (letter from Marion B. Folsom, Secretary of HEW) ("Moreover, as the bill is drawn, the requirement to notify us of an intended shipment would apply only to the person submitting the pretesting data, and our adverse evaluation would not legally operate to prevent shipment by others.").

38. *See* H.R. 6747, 85th Cong., 1st Sess. § 5 (1957); *1957 Hearings, supra* note 25, at 28-36 (letter and memorandum from Marion B. Folsom, Secretary of HEW).

39. *See 1957 Hearings, supra* note 25, at 447 (statement of George P. Larrick, Commissioner of Food and Drugs) ("When issued, the regulation would give all food manufacturers who might wish to use a new chemical in their foods official assurance that its safety has been established under the precise conditions set out in the regulation; the regulation would be a rule for all to follow, not a license to a single manufacturer."); *id.* at 423 (statement of Elliot L. Richardson, Assistant Secretary of HEW) ("[S]uch determinations should have the maximum possible future value in regulating the use of the substance . . . [by] prescribing conditions for its use by all others in the same segment of the food industry."); *cf. id.* at 141 (testimony of Lawrence A. Coleman, appearing on behalf of the Manufacturing Chemists' Association) (declining

to take a position on the relative merits of licensing for an individual applicant rather than issuing a generally applicable regulation).

40. *See* H.R. 2245, 83rd Cong., 1st Sess. § 6 (407(d)) (1953). Such a passive approval approach resembled that used by the FDA for new drug approvals before passage of the Drug Amendments of 1962.

41. *See* H.R. 10,404, 85th Cong., 2d Sess. § 5 (409(e)) (1958); *see also* H.R. 8390, 85th Cong., 1st Sess. § 5 (409(f)) (1957) (requiring notification 90 days before use); H.R. 7607, 84th Cong., 1st Sess. § 5 (409(e)) (1955).

42. *See 1956 Hearings*, *supra* note 19, at 141 (HEW memorandum) ("We believe that the time limit which the bills would allow for initial action by the Secretary should be extended to 120 days, with authority to the Secretary to extend it to 180 days when found necessary. . . . Consideration of the adequacy of testing of additives will be no less difficult and time consuming than passing on a new-drug application.").

43. Pub. L. No. 85-929, 72 Stat. 1784 (1958) (codified as amended in scattered sections of title 21 U.S.C.). The bill passed unanimously in both the House of Representatives and the Senate. *See, e.g.*, 104 CONG. REC. 19,359 (1958) (statement of Sen. Hill).

44. *See* S. REP. NO. 2422, 85th Cong., 2d Sess. 2 (1958) ("[T]he processor who wants to add a new and unproven additive [must] accept the responsibility now voluntarily borne by all responsible food processors of first proving it to be safe for ingestion by human beings.").

45. *See* H.R. REP. NO. 2284, 85th Cong., 2d Sess. 1 (1958) ("The purpose of the legislation is twofold: (1) To protect the health of consumers . . . ; and (2) to advance food technology by permitting the use of food additives at safe levels."); S. REP. NO. 2422, 85th Cong., 2d Sess. 2 (1958) ("The second flaw in existing law which has proved detrimental to consumers, to processors, and to our national economy and which this bill seeks to remove is a provision which has inadvertently served to unnecessarily proscribe the use of additives that could enable the [consumer] to safely keep food longer, the processor to make it more tasteful and appetizing, and the Nation to make use of advances in technology calculated to increase and improve our food supplies."); *id.* at 3 (noting that the legislation "could materially advance our ability to make more wholesome foods available to more people at all seasons"); *see also id.* at 6 (By requiring reasonable rather than absolute certainty of safety, the legislation "will protect the public health from harm and will permit sound progress in food technology."); Continental Chemiste Corp. v. Ruckelshaus, 461 F.2d 331, 340 (7th Cir. 1972) (describing the "two broad purposes to be accomplished by the food additive legislation").

46. *See 1957 Hearings*, *supra* note 25, at 455 (statement of George P. Larrick, Commissioner of Food and Drugs); *id.* at 499 (testimony of Hon. James J. Delaney) (noting that, in addition to New York, "there are at least a dozen other States that are considering legislation along these lines").

47. 21 U.S.C. § 321(f) (1994); *see also* Nutrilab, Inc. v. Schweiker, 713 F.2d 335, 337 (7th Cir. 1983) ("This definition is not too helpful, but it does emphasize that 'food' is to be defined in terms of its function as food, rather than in terms of its source, biochemical composition or ingestibility."); *id.* ("The statutory definition of 'food' . . . is a term of art and is clearly intended to be broader than the common-sense definition of food, because the statutory definition of 'food' also includes chewing gum and food additives.").

48. *See 1957 Hearings*, *supra* note 25, at 456 (HEW memorandum) ("The purpose of clause (3), of course, is to subject all intentional additives, as soon as offered for introduction into interstate commerce, to all the act's requirements for food. . . ."); *id.* at 219 (testimony of H.T. Austern, appearing on behalf of the National Canners Association) (noting that there is no difference between an "ingredient" and an "additive").

49. 21 U.S.C. § 342(a)(1) (1994).

50. *Id.* § 343(i)(2); *see also id.* § 341 (optional ingredients in standards of identity for fabricated foods).

51. 21 U.S.C. § 321(s) (1994); *see also* 21 C.F.R. § 170.3(e) (1996) (tracking statutory definition). The United States Department of Agriculture (USDA) regulates food additives to the extent that they are used in meat products. 9 C.F.R. § 318.7 (1996). The statutory definition of adulteration largely defers, however, to FDA decisions regarding the safety of such additives. 21 U.S.C. § 601(m)(2)(C) (1994).

52. *See* 21 U.S.C. § 321(s) (1994) (including "any substance intended for use in producing, manufacturing, packing, processing, preparing, treating, packaging, transporting, or holding food; and including any source of radiation intended for any such use").

53. *See id.* § 321(s)(1)-(6). One of the other exceptions covers certain substances approved prior to 1958. *See id.* § 321(s)(4); *see also infra* Part II.C. Many of these exceptions have been modified over the years, most recently by the

Dietary Supplement Health and Education Act of 1994, Pub. L. No. 103-417, 108 Stat. 4325, and the Food Quality Protection Act of 1996, Pub. L. No. 104-170, 110 Stat. 1489.

54. *See* 21 U.S.C. §§ 346a (1994) (tolerances for pesticide residues), 350b (premarket notification for new dietary ingredients), 360b (premarket review of drugs for food-producing animals), 379e (listing of color additives). Recently, Congress substantially amended the provision authorizing tolerances for pesticide residues in or on raw agricultural commodities to also include processed foods. *See* Food Quality Protection Act of 1996, Pub. L. No. 104-170, 110 Stat. 1489.

55. *See* S. REP. No. 493, 73d Cong., 2d Sess. 2-3 (1934) ("The use to which a product is put will determine the category into which it will fall. . . . The manufacturer of the article, through his representations in connection with its sale, can determine the use to which an article is to be put."); United States v. Undetermined Quantities of "Cal-Ban 3000," 776 F. Supp. 249, 253-54 (E.D.N.C. 1991) (holding that guar gum product advertised as interfering with the absorption of food was a drug); *cf. Nutrilab,* 713 F.2d at 337 (noting that the statutory definition of food, unlike other articles subject to FDA regulation, does not explicitly refer to intended use); *see also* Lars Noah & Barbara A. Noah, *Nicotine Withdrawal: Assessing the FDA's Effort to Regulate Tobacco Products*, 48 ALA. L. REV. 1, 9-10 (1996).

56. *See 1957 Hearings, supra* note 25, at 62 (statement of Charles W. Dunn, counsel for the Grocery Manufacturers of America) ("We presume that the FDA gave this amendment a chemical additive name to emphasize that it mainly applies to such industrial additives . . . and to give it a strong congressional and popular appeal.").

57. *See, e.g., 1957 Hearings, supra* note 25, at 209 (statement of H.T. Austern, appearing on behalf of the National Canners Association) ("Although some of these bills are titled as 'chemical additive' proposals, every one of them covers every new food ingredient—animal, vegetable, chemical, biological, natural, or even something not found in nature. . . ."); United States v. An Article of Food . . . FoodScience Labs., 678 F.2d 735, 738 (7th Cir. 1982) ("[H]ad Congress intended the [FDA] and the courts to rely on common parlance it would not have so carefully crafted the foregoing definition of the term ['food additive']."); National Nutritional Foods Ass'n v. Kennedy, 572 F.2d 377, 391 (2d Cir. 1978) (doubting that "a substance gains immunity from this [food additive] criterion merely because it also qualifies as a food"); *see also* 21 U.S.C. § 342(a)(2)(C) (1994) (providing that a food shall be deemed to be adulterated "if *it is*, or it bears or contains, *any food additive* which is unsafe" (emphasis added)); Merrill, *supra* note 10, at 203 ("Popular misconception assumes that 'food additives' are artificial substances used in food production while natural ingredients, such as salt or potatoes, are simply that—ingredients. In fact, not every artificial substance used to make food is a food additive. Moreover, the Act does not distinguish between ingredients produced by chemical synthesis and those produced naturally by agriculture.").

58. *See* 21 U.S.C. § 321(s) (1994) (including "any substance intended for use in producing, manufacturing, packing, processing, preparing, treating, packaging, transporting, or holding food; and including any source of radiation intended for any such use").

59. *See* S. REP. No. 2422, 85th Cong., 2d Sess. 5 (1958) (explaining that the legislation covers both "intentional" and "incidental" additives but not "accidental" additives); *cf.* H.R. 8112, 85th Cong., 1st Sess. § 5 (1957) (proposing a separate review mechanism for incidental additives). Under the FDA's ingredient labeling regulations, "incidental additives" are defined to include processing aids such as "[s]ubstances that are added to a food during processing, are converted into constituents normally present in the food, and do not significantly increase the amount of the constituents naturally found in the food." 21 C.F.R. § 101.100(a)(3)(ii)(*b*) (1996).

60. *See, e.g.*, Gerber Prods. Co. v. Fisher Tank Co., 833 F.2d 505, 508 (4th Cir. 1987) (holding that liner on hot water storage tank used in processing baby foods constituted a food additive); Natick Paperboard Corp. v. Weinberger, 525 F.2d 1103, 1106-07 (1st Cir. 1975) (holding that PCB contamination in paperboard packaging material constituted a food additive if likely to migrate into food), *cert. denied*, 429 U.S. 819 (1976); United States v. Articles of Food Consisting of . . . Pottery, 370 F. Supp. 371, 373 (E.D. Mich. 1974) (holding that lead in pottery dinnerware could constitute a food additive); *see also* Jerome H. Heckman, *Fathoming Food Packaging Regulation: A Guide to Independent Industry Action*, 42 FOOD DRUG COSM. L.J. 38 (1987).

61. *See* Monsanto Co. v. Kennedy, 613 F.2d 947, 955 (D.C. Cir. 1979) ("Congress did not intend that the component requirement of a 'food additive' would be satisfied by a mere recitation of the diffusion principle, a mere finding of any contact whatever with food. . . . [A substance's] presence in food [must] be predicted on the basis of a meaningful projection from reliable data."); 21 C.F.R. § 170.3(e) (1996) ("If there is no migration of a packaging component from the package to the food, it does not become a component of the food and thus is not a food additive.").

62. *See* 49 Fed. Reg. 36,635, 36,635-36 (1984) (summarizing the regulatory history); 42 Fed. Reg. 17,529 (1977) (announcing a formal evidentiary hearing on the matter); 42 Fed. Reg. 13,546 (1977) (staying approval of acrylonitrile in

the production of beverage bottles). Two years earlier, the Agency found that, because of the possibility of significant migration from a food-contact surface, acrylonitrile copolymer was a food additive when used to manufacture beverage containers, and it set tolerances for acceptable levels of migration. *See* 40 Fed. Reg. 6489 (1975).

63. *See* 42 Fed. Reg. 48,528, 48,543 (1977).

64. 613 F.2d 947 (D.C. Cir. 1979).

65. *See id.* at 952 ("[T]he Commissioner had made a projection of migration from 3.3 ppm RAN containers without any actual data showing that migration had occurred from such containers.").

66. *See id.* at 954-56. The court explained that the Commissioner ultimately may determine "that the level of migration into food of a particular chemical is so negligible as to present no public health or safety concerns. . . . This authority derives from the administrative discretion, inherent in the statutory scheme, to deal appropriately with *de minimis* situations." *Id.* at 955 (footnote omitted).

67. *See* 49 Fed. Reg. 36,635, 36,642 (1984) (codified as amended at 21 C.F.R. § 177.1040 (1996)); *see also* 52 Fed. Reg. 33,802, 33,803 (1987) (approving acrylonitrile for use in alcoholic beverage containers).

68. *See* 21 C.F.R. pts. 175-178 (1996) (listing all approved indirect additives); *see also id.* pt. 186 (listing GRAS affirmations for indirect food-use substances).

69. *See 1995 Hearings*, *supra* note 1, at 31 (testimony of Linda A. Suydam, Interim Deputy Commissioner for Operations, FDA) ("[A]bout 75 percent are the indirects."); Hutt, *supra* note 1, at 122 ("It is easy to be misled about the efficiency of FDA regulation of food additives by counting the *Federal Register* food additive notices. . . . More than 80% of these notices relate to obscure indirect food additives that have no possible bearing on the public health.").

70. *See* 60 Fed. Reg. 36,582, 36,595 (1995) (codified at 21 C.F.R. § 170.39 (1996)). This "threshold of regulation" policy is discussed more fully at *infra* notes 530-35 and accompanying text.

71. *See* United States v. 29 Cartons . . . An Article of Food, 987 F.2d 33, 37-39 (1st Cir. 1993); United States v. Two Plastic Drums . . . Black Currant Oil, 984 F.2d 814, 820 (7th Cir. 1993).

72. Evidently, the FDA harbored concerns about the product's safety but was not able to shoulder the burden of proving that the substance was poisonous and deleterious such that it might render the food injurious to health. *See 29 Cartons*, 987 F.2d at 35 ("Although the FDA suspects that BCO may be unhealthful, it is unable at the present time to translate this suspicion into legally competent proof.").

73. *See, e.g.*, NationsBank of North Carolina, N.A. v. Variable Annuity Life Ins. Co., 115 S. Ct. 810, 813-15 (1995); Young v. Community Nutrition Inst., 476 U.S. 974, 981 (1986); Chevron U.S.A. Inc. v. Natural Resources Defense Council, Inc., 467 U.S. 837, 842-43 (1984); *see also* Thomas W. Merrill, *Judicial Deference to Executive Precedent*, 101 YALE L.J. 969, 980-93 (1992); Mark Seidenfeld, *A Syncopated* Chevron*: Emphasizing Reasoned Decisionmaking in Reviewing Agency Interpretations of Statutes*, 73 TEX. L. REV. 83, 94-103 (1994).

74. *See 29 Cartons*, 987 F.2d at 37 ("We are reluctant to believe that Congress traffics in absurdities. . . . [T]he FDA's reading of the Act is nonsensical, and, hence, must be incorrect."); *id.* at 39 (concluding that the Agency's reading "perverts the statutory text, undermines legislative intent, and defenestrates common sense"); *Two Plastic Drums*, 984 F.2d at 819 ("The only justification for this Alice-in-Wonderland approach is to allow the FDA to make an end-run around the statutory scheme and shift to the processors the burden of proving the safety of a substance in all circumstances.").

75. *See 29 Cartons*, 987 F.2d at 37; *Two Plastic Drums*, 984 F.2d at 819-20. Although not discussed in these terms, the courts' interpretation helps make sense of the previously mentioned incongruity between the definitions of "food" (including "components") and "food additive" (including "component[s]"). *See* United States v. 29 Cartons . . . An Article of Food, 792 F. Supp. 139, 141 (D. Mass. 1992), *aff'd*, 987 F.2d 33 (1st Cir. 1993); *cf.* Nutrilab, Inc. v. Schweiker, 713 F.2d 335, 337 (7th Cir. 1983) (concluding that the statutory definition of "food" is broad enough to encompass "food additives").

76. *See 29 Cartons*, 987 F.2d at 35, 37; *Two Plastic Drums*, 984 F.2d at 816-17, 819. In fact, the FDA originally premised its seizure on a claim that the gamma linolenic acid in the BCO constituted an unapproved food additive component of the BCO capsules. *See 29 Cartons*, 987 F.2d at 38-39 n.6 (adding that the Agency's shifting litigation position made judicial deference to its interpretation of the statute even less appropriate).

77. *See, e.g.*, *29 Cartons*, 987 F.2d at 36-37.

78. *See Two Plastic Drums*, 984 F.2d at 817 ("This language is very broad, and thus, the general rule is that a component of an article of food is a food additive, even if the component in question is the 'principal component,' i.e., the ingredient sought when purchasing the food.").

79. *See 29 Cartons*, 987 F.2d at 37 (suggesting that such an interpretation would create "a bizarre paradox"); *Two Plastic Drums*, 984 F.2d at 817 ("[T]o hold that BCO is a component of the dietary supplement would be to find that BCO is a component of itself.").

80. *See 29 Cartons*, 987 F.2d at 38 ("In the final analysis, what counts is the use of an ingredient for its effect on food. Here . . . BCO is not being used for its effect on gelatin and glycerine. . . . [I]f the BCO is removed, one is left with nothing but an empty capsule."); *Two Plastic Drums*, 984 F.2d at 818 ("[E]ven if we were to find that BCO was a component of the BCO dietary supplement capsules, the language of the Act indicates that it is not a food additive because, as the single active ingredient, it does not affect the characteristics of any food.").

81. *Cf. 29 Cartons*, 987 F.2d at 35 (noting that these ingredients "have no independent nutritional value"); *Two Plastic Drums*, 984 F.2d at 816-17 & n.2 (mentioning that gelatin and glycerin are functional insofar as they prevent the black currant oil from becoming rancid, but then explaining that they "do not interact with or change the character of the BCO," and noting that gelatin and glycerin do not qualify as food additives for a different reason, namely, because they are generally recognized as safe); United States v. An Article of Food . . . FoodScience Labs., 678 F.2d 735, 738 (7th Cir. 1982) (rejecting claimant's argument that the definition of "food additive" applied only to minor rather than principal ingredients, and observing that the "term 'component' of course includes large quantities of unsafe substances as well as small").

82. *See 29 Cartons*, 987 F.2d at 38 n.5 ("We do not quarrel with those courts that have held, when confronted with multi-ingredient products containing two or more active ingredients, that each active ingredient is potentially a food additive."); *Two Plastic Drums*, 984 F.2d at 818 ("When two or more active ingredients comprise a food, each component is arguably different from the food in such a way that the addition of each has affected the characteristics of the other components and of the food."); *see also* 21 C.F.R. § 170.3(g) (1996) ("The word *substance* in the definition of the term 'food additive' includes a food component consisting of one or more ingredients.").

83. United States v. 21/180 Kg. Bulk Metal Drums . . . , 761 F. Supp. 180, 182, 185 (D. Me. 1991).

84. United States v. 45/194 Kg. Drums of Pure Vegetable Oil, 961 F.2d 808, 812 & n.3 (9th Cir.), *cert. denied*, 506 U.S. 940 (1992); *see also* Dietary Supplement Coalition, Inc. v. Sullivan, 978 F.2d 560, 563-64 (9th Cir. 1992) (holding that FDA action against the makers of Co-enzyme Q10 was not ripe for judicial review, in part because the distinction between "food" and "food additive" was not a pure legal question but would depend on Agency findings of fact), *cert. denied*, 508 U.S. 906 (1993); United States v. An Article of Food . . . FoodScience Labs., 678 F.2d 735, 738 (7th Cir. 1982) (holding that the "principal ingredient" in a dietary supplement nonetheless constituted a food additive because it was combined with another active ingredient); United States v. 42/30 Tablet Bottles . . . , 779 F. Supp. 253, 255 (E.D.N.Y. 1991) ("[B]oth CoQ10 and Germanium satisfy the plain meaning of the 'component' requirement of the food additive definition because they are one or two of several ingredients in each of the dietary supplements produced by claimants.").

85. *See, e.g.*, Nutrilab, Inc. v. Schweiker, 713 F.2d 335, 338-39 (7th Cir. 1983) (upholding FDA classification of starch blockers, capsules containing a protein derived from raw kidney beans, as drugs rather than food).

86. *See* Dietary Supplement Health and Education Act of 1994, Pub. L. No. 103-417, 108 Stat. 4325 (codified in scattered sections of 21 U.S.C.). Among other things, the Act places on the FDA the burden of proof in an adulteration proceeding against a dietary supplement product, and the Agency must prove that the supplement "presents a significant or unreasonable risk of illness or injury." 21 U.S.C. § 342(f)(1)(A) (1994). In addition, a 75-day premarket notification requirement applies to "new dietary ingredients." *Id.* § 350b(a). Finally, the statute authorizes special labeling claims under certain circumstances. *See id.* §§ 343(r)(6), 343-2; *see also* 60 Fed. Reg. 67,194 (1995) (announcing the FDA's proposed labeling regulations); Robert G. Pinco & Paul D. Rubin, *Ambiguities of the Dietary Supplement Health and Education Act of 1994*, 51 FOOD & DRUG L.J. 383 (1996).

87. *See Food Lawyer Says Current Regulatory Framework Doesn't Work for New Food Ingredients*, FOOD CHEM. NEWS, Sept. 30, 1996, at 4.

88. *See* 21 U.S.C. § 321(s)(6) (1994).

89. *Id.* § 350b(c). A person wishing to use a "new dietary ingredient" would first have to petition the Agency, "proposing the issuance of an order prescribing the conditions under which a new dietary ingredient under its intended

conditions of use will reasonably be expected to be safe." *Id.* § 350b(b) (adding that the Agency "shall make a decision on such petition within 180 days").

90. *See id.* § 350b(a)(2) (the notification would have to demonstrate that "[t]here is a history of use or other evidence of safety"). If the FDA was not persuaded by the notification, it could prevent marketing only by initiating (or threatening) formal enforcement proceedings, and the Agency would shoulder the burden of proving that the product is adulterated.

91. *Id.* § 321(ff)(1).

92. *Id.* § 350(c)(1)(B) (as cross-referenced by § 321(ff)(2)(A)). By "liquid form," the statute means only fluid carriers intended for ingestion in small quantities. *Id.* § 350(c)(2). The definition of "dietary supplement" also requires that the product "is not represented for use as a conventional food or as a sole item of a meal or the diet," *id.* § 321(ff)(2)(B), repeating the requirement of § 350(c)(1)(B)(ii), thereby effectively extending this limitation on conventional foods to products such as tablets or capsules.

93. *Id.* § 321(ff)(2)(C). The statute also specifies how the definition will affect certain dietary supplements previously approved by the FDA as new drugs, antibiotics, or biologics. *See id.* § 321(ff)(3).

94. Unlike GRAS food ingredients, for which no advance notification is required, a person wishing to introduce a previously marketed dietary supplement or ingredient must first alert the FDA. If the dietary ingredient is not safe, the manufacturer faces some risk of an adulteration charge. The primary difference is a more favorable cut-off date for asserting an exception based on prior use—1994 for a dietary ingredient rather than 1958 for GRAS.

95. 21 U.S.C. § 321(s) (1994).

96. *Id.*; *see also* 21 C.F.R. § 170.30(a) (1996) (tracking statutory definition).

97. *See 1957 Hearings*, *supra* note 25, at 94-95 (statement of Robert B. Smith, Jr., President of the Medical College of Virginia).

98. *See 1956 Hearings*, *supra* note 19, at 66 (statement of Glenn G. Paxton, appearing as counsel for various food industry associations) ("[A]ll of the bills that I have seen which have ever been written on this subject have had a general exception for substances generally recognized by the experts to be safe."); Frederick H. Degnan, *Rethinking the Applicability and Usefulness of the GRAS Concept*, 46 FOOD DRUG COSM. L.J. 553, 556-61 (1991).

99. *See* 104 CONG. REC. 17,420 (1958) (letter from John L. Harvey, Deputy Commissioner of Food and Drugs); 104 CONG. REC. 17,415 (1958) (letter from Elliot L. Richardson, Assistant Secretary of HEW) ("The grandfather clause, as proposed in some of the bills before your committee would have exempted substances used in food prior to enactment of the legislation from having to meet its requirements at all. The Department opposed such a provision. . . .").

100. *See, e.g.*, *1956 Hearings*, *supra* note 19, at 40 (statement of Hon. A. L. Miller) ("[L]egislation requiring exhaustive laboratory analysis, pretesting and reporting of the old, recognized, safe additives would serve no useful purpose and would be unduly burdensome upon both industry and Government."); *id.* at 228 (statement of William W. Goodrich, FDA Counsel) (arguing that the GRAS exception was necessary "to make the legislation reasonable"); *see also* GAO, NEW FOOD TECHNOLOGIES, *supra* note 9, at 62 (noting that defenders of the exception "believe that the GRAS provisions give FDA a flexible mechanism to rank-order expenditures of limited resources and to focus its efforts on food additives posing the greatest concern to public health"); Huber, *supra* note 18, at 1038-39 (arguing that the GRAS exception "mandate[d] that old additives should be regulated less strictly than new ones").

101. *See* Pub. L. No. 85-929, § 6, 72 Stat. 1788 (1958). Some members of Congress criticized the transitional provisions and (correctly) feared future extensions. *See* 104 CONG. REC. 17,424 (1958) (statement of Hon. Leonor K. Sullivan) ("[E]xperience has shown us that an extended grace period in any legislation affecting a long overdue reform in existing practices almost always seems to lead to additional moratoriums and delays and there always seems to be a good reason for allowing the industry affected more and more time in which to comply with the law.").

102. *See* Food Additives Transitional Provisions Amendment of 1964, Pub. L. No. 88-625, § 2, 78 Stat. 1002 (extension until December 31, 1965); Food Additives Transitional Provisions Amendment of 1961, Pub. L. No. 87-19, § 2, 75 Stat. 42 (extension until June 30, 1964); *see also* 29 Fed. Reg. 18,496 (1964) (implementing second extension); 29 Fed. Reg. 15,812 (1964) (implementing first extension); Degnan, *supra* note 98, at 561 (explaining that the FDA allowed the marketing of more than 3,000 substances on a transitional basis); Hutt, *supra* note 1, at 120-21 (praising the "heroic effort by FDA" during this transitional period, adding that its productivity "at that time in history stands in stark contrast to the inefficiency and paralysis of today").

103. *See* 21 U.S.C. § 321(p)(1) (1994) (excluding from the definition of "new drug" any drug "generally recognized, among experts qualified by scientific training and experience to evaluate the safety and effectiveness of drugs, as safe and effective for use under the conditions prescribed, recommended, or suggested in the labeling thereof"). Unlike the definition for food additives, a GRAS/GRAE drug also must have "been used to a material extent or for a material time under such conditions." *Id.* § 321(p)(2); *see also* Kenneth C. Baumgartner, *Getting a Grip on Material Time and Extent*, 49 FOOD & DRUG L.J. 433 (1994).

104. *See* Pub. L. No. 83-518, § 3 (408(a)), 68 Stat. 511 (1954) (codified at 21 U.S.C. § 346a(a) (1994)), repealed and replaced by the Food Quality Protection Act of 1996, Pub. L. No. 104-170, § 405, 110 Stat. 1514.

105. *See 1956 Hearings*, *supra* note 19, at 203-05 (testimony of George P. Larrick, Commissioner of Food and Drugs) (describing the FDA's experience in applying the GRAS exception for drugs); *see also 1957 Hearings*, *supra* note 25, at 65 (statement of Charles W. Dunn, counsel for the Grocery Manufacturers of America) (declining to propose alternative GRAS language "because these laws have been practically successful, notwithstanding the obscurity of this clause and because it has been given a reasonable construction of necessity"); *1956 Hearings*, *supra* note 19, at 121 (statement of Charles W. Dunn, counsel for the Grocery Manufacturers of America) (GRAS "does not mean the opinion of the FDA alone, which might perhaps be its administrative construction to a more or less extent. Neither does it mean the opinion of a manufacturer alone. But otherwise its meaning is very obscure."); Degnan, *supra* note 98, at 557-60.

106. *See* Pub. L. No. 86-618, § 101(c), 74 Stat. 397 (1960) (codified at 21 U.S.C. § 321(t) (1994)). Instead, Congress authorized a transitional category, allowing the FDA to include color additives in use in 1960 on a "provisional list" pending further safety testing. *See id.* § 203, 74 Stat. 404; *see also* 21 U.S.C. § 379e(b)(4) (1994) (excluding a color additive if listed by the FDA as a GRAS food substance); 42 Fed. Reg. 6992 (1977) (requiring further testing); McIlwain v. Hayes, 690 F.2d 1041, 1046-49 (D.C. Cir. 1982) (upholding the FDA's authority to continue postponing final action on provisionally listed color additives, especially where made necessary by improvements in safety testing standards); Certified Color Mfrs. Ass'n v. Mathews, 543 F.2d 284, 286-88 (D.C. Cir. 1976) (describing provisional listing system); Hutt, *supra* note 1, at 126-27 (explaining that the FDA repeatedly extended the transitional period as it imposed additional testing requirements, and noting that, over the last 35 years, it has approved for permanent listing only one new coal-tar color additive for broad food use).

107. *See* Degnan, *supra* note 98, at 573-74.

108. *See* Weinberger v. Hynson, Westcott & Dunning, Inc., 412 U.S. 609, 632 (1973) (requiring a consensus "founded upon 'substantial evidence'"); Weinberger v. Bentex Pharmaceuticals, Inc., 412 U.S. 645, 652 (1973) (noting that general recognition should be reflected in published scientific literature).

109. Degnan, *supra* note 98, at 570-80 (describing evolution from a flexible and informal concept to a more rigidly defined category). For instance, the Agency modified its implementing regulations on several occasions. *See, e.g.*, 53 Fed. Reg. 16,544 (1988); 41 Fed. Reg. 53,600 (1976); 36 Fed. Reg. 12,093 (1971).

110. *See* 21 C.F.R. § 170.30(a) (1996) (GRAS "requires common knowledge about the substance throughout the scientific community knowledgeable about the safety of substances directly or indirectly added to food."); *see also* United States v. An Article of Food . . . FoodScience Labs., 678 F.2d 735, 740 (7th Cir. 1982) (holding that the trial judge "was entitled to credit the testimony of the government's five doctors that DMG is not" GRAS as against the claimant's single expert who testified to the contrary); United States v. Articles of Food & Drug . . . , 518 F.2d 743, 746 (5th Cir. 1975) ("What is required is not unanimous recognition but general recognition."); United States v. 41 Cases, More or Less, 420 F.2d 1126, 1130 (5th Cir. 1970) ("The absence of scientific knowledge on the part of an expert and his colleagues is sufficient to show lack of general recognition of safety."). *But cf.* United States v. An Article of Food . . . , 622 F.2d 768, 772-73 (5th Cir. 1980) (reversing order granting the government's motion for summary judgment in an action for seizure of gentian violet pre-mix, finding a genuine issue of material fact concerning this substance's GRAS status because the claimant countered the FDA's two experts with references to 23 studies and 40 scientists or veterinarians who purportedly recognized its safety).

111. *See* 21 C.F.R. § 170.30(b) (1996); *see also id.* § 170.3(h) ("*Scientific procedures* include those human, animal, analytical, and other scientific studies, whether published or unpublished, appropriate to establish the safety of a substance."); United States v. 45/194 Kg. Drums of Pure Vegetable Oil, 961 F.2d 808, 813 (9th Cir.) (rejecting claimant's expert testimony asserting that evening primrose oil was GRAS because the data relied upon concerned its use in drugs rather than dietary supplements and the "[o]ther data was based on unpublished materials, which were not subjected to peer evaluation"), *cert. denied*, 506 U.S. 940 (1992); *cf.* Daubert v. Merrell Dow Pharmaceuticals, Inc., 509 U.S. 579, 587-95 (1993) (rejecting the general acceptance standard as the sole test for the admissibility of scientific evidence, but suggesting

additional factors such as peer review and publication as bases for ensuring reliability); *1957 Hearings, supra* note 25, at 343 (statement of Dr. Henry F. Smith, Jr., Mellon Institute) (calling for publication and peer review of toxicology studies).

112. *See, e.g.*, United States v. An Article of Food, 752 F.2d 11, 15 (1st Cir. 1985); United States v. Naremco, Inc., 553 F.2d 1138, 1143 (8th Cir. 1977) (holding that the definition "refers to experience based on common use as a food additive or under conditions producing long-term ingestion," and, therefore, that "the pre-1958 use of gentian violet as an animal drug cannot be considered probative"); National Nutritional Foods Ass'n v. Kennedy, 572 F.2d 377, 392 (2d Cir. 1978) ("[W]e see no reason why [the Commissioner] cannot determine that too much of even a good thing [i.e., use of high potency vitamins and minerals with a history of common use at lower levels] may come within the definition of a 'food additive.'"); United States v. Articles of Food . . . Buffalo Jerky, 456 F. Supp. 207, 209 (D. Neb. 1978) ("While the claimant points to other uses of sodium nitrate and sodium nitrite which have been recognized as being safe, these examples are not comparable to the use in this case . . . ."), *aff'd*, 594 F.2d 869 (8th Cir. 1979) (per curiam); *cf.* 21 C.F.R. § 170.30(c)(1) (1996) (Prior use GRAS "shall be based solely on food use of the substance prior to January 1, 1958, and shall ordinarily be based upon generally available data and information.").

113. *See, e.g.*, United States v. An Article of Food, 752 F.2d 11, 15 (1st Cir. 1985).

114. *See* 21 C.F.R. § 170.30(c)(1) (1996) ("General recognition of safety through experience based on common use in food prior to January 1, 1958, may be determined without the quantity or quality of scientific procedures required for approval of a food additive regulation."); *see also* 41 Fed. Reg. 53,600, 53,600 (1976) ("[F]or those substances that were widely used before 1958, under the terms of the statute FDA must consider available data and may not prohibit use of a substance merely because tests that would be required for new food additives have not been performed."). *But cf. 1957 Hearings, supra* note 25, at 388 (statement of Dr. W.C. Hueper, National Cancer Institute) ("[A]bsence of incriminating evidence [from prolonged prior use] is not an adequate guaranty for the carcinogenic innocuousness of a chemical.").

115. *See, e.g.*, 21 C.F.R. § 170.3(f) (1996) ("*Common use in food* means a substantial history of consumption of a substance for food use by a significant number of consumers."); United States v. An Article of Food, 752 F.2d 11, 15 n.7 (1st Cir. 1985) ("Use in one manufacturer's product does not constitute 'common use' in that food."); *Naremco*, 553 F.2d at 1143 n.7 ("Testimony that prior to 1958 one particular gentian violet drug was recommended for continuous use . . . is patently insufficient. . . ."); *cf. 1957 Hearings, supra* note 25, at 497 (statement of Hon. James J. Delaney) ("Just how long is 'prolonged use'? Two years? Five years? Ten years? And if adequate tests have not been made, how can a criterion be established for safety through 'prolonged use'? In the case of some chemicals, it might take as long as 20 years for their accumulative effect to be felt.").

116. *See* 21 C.F.R. § 170.3(f) (1982) ("'Common use in food' means a substantial history of consumption of a substance by a significant number of consumers in the United States."); 39 Fed. Reg. 34,194, 34,195 (1974) (explaining that "use in foreign countries often cannot be verified, and in any event the experience based upon such use cannot be monitored or evaluated"). At least one of the food additives bills would have defined GRAS by reference to prior use only in the United States. *See* H.R. 7764, 84th Cong., 1st Sess. § 1 (1955).

117. *See* Fmali Herb, Inc. v. Heckler, 715 F.2d 1385, 1390 (9th Cir. 1983) ("[I]t is an illogical and, we think, unwarranted constriction of the statute to rule that evidence of long use of a substance in food outside the United States can *never* provide probative evidence of safety. . . . The statute provides no basis for a purely ethnocentric distinction of this kind, divorced from demographic considerations.").

118. 21 C.F.R. § 170.30(c)(2) (1996); *see also* 53 Fed. Reg. 16,544, 16,544-45 (1988) (defending the revised regulation as consistent with the court's holding in *Fmali Herb*); 50 Fed. Reg. 27,294, 27,295 (1985) (explaining the need to require ready availability of information concerning the foreign use). The FDA suggests that pre-1958 approval by a foreign government might provide overwhelming evidence of safety. *See* 53 Fed. Reg. at 16,545.

119. *See* 21 C.F.R. § 170.30(c)(2) (1996) (requiring that "the information about the [foreign] experience establish[] that the use of the substance is safe within the meaning of the act"); *see also* 50 Fed. Reg. at 27,296 ("The review needs to be performed to assure that the substance has been shown to be safe, as that term is understood in this country."); *id.* at 27,295-96 (explaining that different societies have different conceptions of safety).

120. *See* 21 C.F.R. § 170.30(c)(2) (1996); *see also* 60 Fed. Reg. 48,890, 48,891 (1995) (affirming GRAS status of maltodextrin derived from potato starch based in part on consumption in Europe prior to 1958); 54 Fed. Reg. 38,219, 38,220, 38,223 (1989) (codified at 21 C.F.R. § 184.1472 (1996)) (affirming GRAS status of menhaden oil based on extensive consumption in Europe prior to 1958); 53 Fed. Reg. at 16,545-46 (emphasizing that FDA concurrence is not mandatory, but justifying this suggestion by reference to the Agency's power to detain imports of adulterated food and the special difficulties of resolving GRAS status during a detention hearing).

121. *See, e.g.*, 21 C.F.R. § 170.30(d) (1996) ("A food ingredient of natural biological origin that has been widely consumed for its nutrient properties in the United States prior to January 1, 1958 . . . will ordinarily be regarded as GRAS without specific inclusion" in one of the GRAS lists.).

122. *1957 Hearings*, *supra* note 25, at 461-62 (statement of George P. Larrick, Commissioner of Food and Drugs); *see also id.* at 464 ("There are literally thousands of substances in that category."). One witness read the GRAS exception to mean that "this amendment would not apply to normally safe food additives of agricultural and farm origin; it would principally apply to food chemical additives in an industrial sense." *Id.* at 64 (statement of Charles W. Dunn, counsel for the Grocery Manufacturers of America).

123. *See, e.g.*, 26 Fed. Reg. 938 (1961); 24 Fed. Reg. 9368 (1959); *see also* Arthur A. Checchi, *Food-Additives Amendment—Requirements and Proposed Regulations*, 13 FOOD DRUG COSM. L.J. 765, 767 (1958); William W. Goodrich, *The Beginning Point Under the Food-Additives Amendment—What Substances Do Qualified Experts Generally Recognize as Safe?*, 14 FOOD DRUG COSM. L.J. 584, 587 (1959); George P. Larrick, *Status of Food-Additives Control*, 15 FOOD DRUG COSM. L.J. 268, 270 (1960). One of the earlier bills would have required the issuance and periodic revision of a GRAS list. *See* H.R. 366, 85th Cong., 1st Sess. § 5 (409(h)) (1957).

124. 21 C.F.R. § 121.101(d) (1965).

125. *See* 34 Fed. Reg. 17,063 (1969); *see also* H.R. REP. NO. 1585, 91st Cong., 2d Sess. (1970). Most scientists now conclude that cyclamates pose no carcinogenic risk. *See* Malcolm Gladwell, *FDA Confirms Cyclamate Ban May End*, WASH. POST, May 17, 1989, at A5.

126. *See* 21 C.F.R. § 170.30(e) (1996); *see also id.* § 182.1(d) ("When the status of a substance has been reevaluated, it will be deleted from [the original GRAS list], and will be issued as a new regulation under the appropriate part . . . ."); 36 Fed. Reg. 12,093, 12,093 (1971) ("A current review of GRAS substances is necessary because of new scientific knowledge, the development of modern toxicological techniques, and the expanded usage of some GRAS substances beyond the exposure patterns considered when the GRAS list was originally promulgated."); 35 Fed. Reg. 18,623 (1970) (announcing prior GRAS criteria for the comprehensive review). President Nixon ordered the FDA to undertake this review. *Consumer Protection*, 5 Weekly Comp. Pres. Doc. 1516, 1522 (1969) ("I have asked the Secretary of [HEW] to initiate a full review of food additives . . . , re-examining the safety of [GRAS] substances. . . .").

127. 21 C.F.R. § 170.30(f) (1996); *see also* Roger D. Middlekauff, *Food Safety Review—New Concepts for GRAS*, 30 FOOD DRUG COSM. L.J. 288, 291 (1975) (commenting that "the FDA believed that some GRAS substances are more GRAS than others").

128. *See* 36 Fed. Reg. 20,546 (1971); NAS, *A Comprehensive Survey of Industry on the Use of Food Chemicals Generally Recognized as Safe* (1972); *see also* 42 Fed. Reg. 30,894 (1977) (announcing follow up NAS survey).

129. *See* 38 Fed. Reg. 20,054, 20,055 (1973). The FDA initiated similar reviews in the drug area. *See* Kenneth C. Baumgartner, *A Historical Examination of the FDA's Review of the Safety and Effectiveness of Over-the-Counter Drugs*, 43 FOOD DRUG COSM. L.J. 463 (1988); Gary L. Yingling, *Are We on the Road to a Single Drug Approval Process?*, 45 FOOD DRUG COSM. L.J. 235 (1990).

130. *See 1995 Hearings*, *supra* note 1, at 114 (statement of Kenneth D. Fisher, Former Director of LSRO, FASEB); *see also* SCOGS, *Evaluation of Health Aspects of GRAS Food Ingredients: Lessons Learned and Questions Unanswered*, 36 FEDERATION PROCEEDINGS 2519 (1977); STEPHEN BREYER, REGULATION AND ITS REFORM 142-47 (1982) (discussing difficulties encountered in the FASEB GRAS review); SHEILA JASONOFF, THE FIFTH BRANCH: SCIENCE ADVISORS AS POLICYMAKERS 218-22 (1990) (praising FASEB's review).

131. *See 1995 Hearings*, *supra* note 1, at 115 (statement of Kenneth D. Fisher, Former Director of LSRO, FASEB) (describing the advantages of using this approach).

132. *See id.* at 117. In addition, SCOGS concluded that 15% should remain GRAS but with use limitations because of the need for additional safety information for new uses; that 7% should lose GRAS status unless data is submitted for review; and that 5% should become subject to an interim food additive regulation to resolve uncertainties. *See id.*; *see also* H.R. REP. NO. 436, 104th Cong., 1st Sess. 5 (1995) (summarizing FASEB's GRAS list review).

133. *See* Hutt, *supra* note 1, at 121 ("In spite of the fact that FASEB completed its work several years ago, not only has FDA failed to complete its much more limited role in this process, but the end is not even in sight.").

134. *See* 21 C.F.R. §§ 184.1005-.1985 (1996). In addition, numerous substances remain on the original GRAS list pending the completion of the Agency's review of each substance. *See id.* §§ 182.10-.8997.

135. *Id.* § 170.30(d).

136. *Id.*; *see also id.* § 170.30(k) ("In addition to the use(s) specified in [a GRAS affirmation] regulation, other uses of such an ingredient may also be GRAS."); GAO, NEW FOOD TECHNOLOGIES, *supra* note 9, at 28 ("FDA estimates that approximately 1,450 of about 2,700 substances that it knows are added directly to food are GRAS and prior sanctioned substances. The majority of these substances have not been reviewed by FDA."); Merrill, *supra* note 10, at 214 n.160 (noting that the FDA "has been unable to devise a procedure to force users of unlisted ingredients to seek review and confirmation of their safety").

137. 21 C.F.R. § 182.1(a) (1996). This language first appeared in the FDA's original notice of proposed rulemaking. *See* 23 Fed. Reg. 9511, 9516 (1958).

138. 21 C.F.R. § 170.30(h)(1) (1996) (incorporating the second edition, published in 1972). If specifically indicated by a GRAS affirmation regulation, the third edition (published in 1981) may apply instead. *Id.* The FOOD CHEMICALS CODEX represents a compilation of monographs published by the NAS and is now in its fourth edition (published in 1996).

139. 21 C.F.R. § 170.30(h)(2) & (3) (1996).

140. *Id.* § 170.30(j) ("Any use of such an ingredient not in full compliance with each such established limitation shall require a food additive regulation."); *see also id.* § 184.1(b)(2); 48 Fed. Reg. 48,457, 48,458 (1983) ("The agency has determined that a GRAS affirmation regulation should only include those CGMP conditions of use that are necessary to ensure the continued safe use of the ingredient . . . and to discourage any potentially unsafe proliferation in the use of these substances.").

141. 21 C.F.R. § 170.30(i) (1996) ("In such a case a manufacturer may not rely on the regulation as authorizing the use but must independently establish that the use is GRAS or must use the substance in accordance with a food additive regulation."); *see also id.* § 184.1(b)(1) & (3); *id.* § 184.1(a) (providing that substances affirmed as GRAS as direct ingredients also are GRAS as indirect ingredients); 48 Fed. Reg. at 48,458 ("[T]he existence of a GRAS affirmation regulation that contains conditions of use does not bar a manufacturer from expanding the use of a GRAS ingredient beyond the conditions described in the regulation if the manufacturer makes its own GRAS determination."); 41 Fed. Reg. 53,600, 53,601 (1976) (noting that a substance may be GRAS for some uses and also be covered by a food additive regulation for other uses).

142. 21 C.F.R. § 170.30(*l*) (1996) (cross-referencing 21 C.F.R. § 170.38); *see, e.g.*, 36 Fed. Reg. 12,109, 12,110 (1971) (proposing to revoke saccharin's GRAS status and substitute a provisional food additive regulation); 34 Fed. Reg. 17,063 (1969) (revoking cyclamate's GRAS status); Jane E. Henney, *Food Safety Challenges and the New Center*, 48 FOOD & DRUG L.J. 473, 477 (1993) (describing on-going safety reviews of BHA and MSG).

143. *See* 21 C.F.R. § 171.130(a) (1996) (cross-referencing the procedures specified in 21 C.F.R. pt. 10); *id.* § 10.50(c)(5) (providing for an opportunity for a formal evidentiary hearing to the extent required for the issuance, amendment or repeal of food additive regulations under the statute); *see also infra* Part III.C (describing the use of "interim" food additive status when the safety of a food-use substance is brought into question).

144. *See, e.g.*, 53 Fed. Reg. 16,544, 16,545 (1988) ("acknowledg[ing] that persons have the right to make independent GRAS determinations"); Eugene P. Grisanti, *Legal Aspects of Technical Problems and Chemical Additives*, 26 FOOD DRUG COSM. L.J. 588, 590-92 (1971).

145. *See 1995 Hearings*, *supra* note 1, at 116 (statement of Kenneth D. Fisher, Former Director of LSRO, FASEB); *id.* at 170 (estimating that FASEB had conducted five or six private GRAS reviews). A company may also choose to sponsor studies of a substance for eventual publication. *See, e.g.*, *Safety Evaluation of Erythritol*, 24 REG. TOXICOL. & PHARMACOL. S191 (1996) (a special issue assembling 15 studies of one substance).

146. *See* 56 Fed. Reg. 37,712 (1991); *FASEB Panel Finds New Fat Substitute GRAS*, FOOD CHEM. NEWS, Feb. 3, 1992, at 50; Joel G. Brenner, *New Ingredient Enables Mars to Unveil a Leaner Milky Way*, WASH. POST, Jan. 16, 1992, at D11; *P&G Disputes Liver Damage Implication in Caprenin Study*, FOOD CHEM. NEWS, Mar. 13, 1995, at 17.

147. *See Salatrim Should Receive GRAS Status, FASEB Ad Hoc Panel Says*, FOOD CHEM. NEWS, July 25, 1994, at 19; *see also* 59 Fed. Reg. 33,774 (1994) (announcing the filing of a GRAS affirmation petition for salatrim).

148. *See Industry-Funded Food Additive Panels May Begin This Year*, FOOD CHEM. NEWS, Mar. 6, 1995, at 3.

149. *See 1995 Hearings*, *supra* note 1, at 113-14 (statement of Kenneth D. Fisher, Former Director of LSRO, FASEB).

150. *Id.* at 114. "Where appropriate, reports include new research opportunities, specific recommendations, a comprehensive literature review, and reflect the knowledge and experience of the scientists who participate in the study and those of the LSRO staff." *Id.*

151. *See, e.g., id.* at 114-15, 118 (describing SCOGS); Food Chem. News, Inc. v. Young, 900 F.2d 328, 329-30 (D.C. Cir. 1990) (describing the creation and operations of another ad hoc FASEB panel under a contract with the FDA).

152. *See MSG Adverse Effect on Subgroups Demonstrated: Final FASEB Report*, FOOD CHEM. NEWS, Sept. 4, 1995, at 51; *BHA Poses No Human Risk at Current Exposure Levels: FASEB*, FOOD CHEM. NEWS, July 25, 1994, at 3; *FASEB to Study MSG, BHA Under New Contracts with FDA*, FOOD CHEM. NEWS, Nov. 2, 1992, at 3.

153. *See, e.g.*, GAO, NEW FOOD TECHNOLOGIES, *supra* note 9, at 28 ("For example, the expert panel of the Flavor and Extract Manufacturers' Association has asserted the GRAS status of hundreds of synthetic flavoring chemicals."); Degnan, *supra* note 98, at 566-67 (describing the FEMA GRAS review and the FDA's reaction); Robert S. McCaleb, *Food Ingredient Safety Evaluation*, 47 FOOD & DRUG L.J. 657, 661-63 (1992) (describing GRAS "self-affirmation" project undertaken by the Herb Research Foundation).

154. *See* Degnan, *supra* note 98, at 567; John B. Hallagan & Richard L. Hall, *FEMA GRAS—A GRAS Assessment Program for Flavor Ingredients*, 21 REG. TOXICOL. & PHARMACOL. 422, 423 & 425 (1995); Bernard L. Oser & Richard A. Ford, *FEMA Expert Panel: 30 Years of Safety Evaluation for the Flavor Industry*, FOOD TECH., Nov. 1991, at 84, 86.

155. *See, e.g.*, Robert L. Smith et al., *GRAS Flavoring Substances 17*, FOOD TECH., Oct. 1996, at 72; Richard L. Hall & Bernard L. Oser, *Recent Progress in the Consideration of Flavoring Ingredients under the Food Additives Amendment*, FOOD TECH., Feb. 1965, at 151.

156. *See* Hallagan & Hall, *supra* note 154, at 423 & 425.

157. *See* Lauren A. Woods & John Doull, *GRAS Evaluation of Flavoring Substances by the Expert Panel of FEMA*, 14 REG. TOXICOL. & PHARMACOL. 48, 51 (1991).

158. *See id.*; Bernard L. Oser & Richard L. Hall, *Criteria Employed by the Expert Panel of FEMA for the GRAS Evaluation of Flavoring Substances*, 15 FOOD & CHEM. TOXICOL. 457 (1977); *see also GRAS Private Determinations to Be Discouraged by FEMA*, FOOD CHEM. NEWS, Nov. 16, 1992, at 40, 41 ("Citing a need for increased 'transparency' in the Expert Panel's operations, . . . the FEMA board had decided to review the role and operation of the Panel and publish more widely the criteria and procedures followed in GRAS determinations.").

159. Lawrence J. Lin, *Interpretation of GRAS Criteria*, 46 FOOD DRUG COSM. L.J. 877, 881-82 (1991).

160. *See id.* at 882; 26 Fed. Reg. 5222 (1961) (finalizing the GRAS list of natural flavors); 26 Fed. Reg. 3991 (1961) (finalizing the GRAS list of synthetic flavors). Notably, the GRAS list review initiated in 1969 explicitly excluded flavors, spices and essential oils. The GRAS lists of natural and synthetic flavoring substances now appear at 21 C.F.R. §§ 182.10, 182.60 (1996).

161. *See, e.g.*, 29 Fed. Reg. 6957 (1964) (proposing to approve numerous synthetic flavors based on prior use in food but not deemed eligible for GRAS status because the evidence of safety was not readily available to the scientific community); Lin, *supra* note 159, at 882. The lists of approved natural and synthetic flavoring substances now appear at 21 C.F.R. §§ 172.510, 172.515 (1996).

162. *See* Woods & Doull, *supra* note 157, at 56.

163. *See* Hallagan & Hall, *supra* note 154, at 428 & 430; *see also* Smith, *supra* note 155, at 74 ("By 1994, the Panel completed th[is] process for approximately 400 aliphatic acyclic substances used as flavor ingredients. . . . The Panel plans to publish the results of th[is] program in a series of publications in the peer-reviewed literature. . . .").

164. *See* Degnan, *supra* note 98, at 567; Hallagan & Hall, *supra* note 154, at 429; Lin, *supra* note 159, at 882.

165. *See, e.g.*, 44 Fed. Reg. 71,460, 71,461 (1979); 41 Fed. Reg. 4954 (1976).

166. *See, e.g.*, 48 Fed. Reg. 4486, 4486 (1983) (stearic acid); 47 Fed. Reg. 47,438, 47,439 (1982) (thiamine hydrochloride).

167. *See* SUMMARY OF EVALUATIONS PERFORMED BY THE JOINT FAO/WHO EXPERT COMMITTEE ON FOOD ADDITIVES (1994).

168. *See infra* Part VI.B.5. Under the regulations promulgated in 1971, "no substance will be eligible for GRAS status if it has no history of food use." 36 Fed. Reg. 12,093, 12,094 (1971) (codified at 21 C.F.R. § 121.3(c) (1972)). Just five

years later, the FDA deleted this restriction. *See* 41 Fed. Reg. 53,600, 53,605 (1976) (codified at 21 C.F.R. § 170.30 (1996)); *see also* 39 Fed. Reg. 34,194, 34,194 (1974) ("GRAS status may be achieved for post-1958 food ingredients on the basis of scientific procedures even prior to any significant history of marketing and use. Unlike the definition of 'new drug' . . . , section 201(s) does not require that a food ingredient be used 'to a material extent or for a material time' before it may become GRAS.").

169. *See supra* note 110-15 (citing cases).

170. PETER BARTON HUTT & RICHARD A. MERRILL, FOOD AND DRUG LAW 332-33 (2d ed. 1991).

171. *See id.* at 333 ("In such an action, however, the agency would have to prove that the ingredient was not GRAS. Neither the ingredient's absence from FDA's GRAS lists nor the manufacturer's failure to consult the agency in advance would be relevant."); *1957 Hearings*, *supra* note 25, at 455 (HEW memorandum) ("[T]he burden would be on the Government, in an enforcement proceeding, to prove that a substance is not [GRAS] and is therefore within the scope of the bill."); *1956 Hearings*, *supra* note 19, at 226 (statement of William W. Goodrich, FDA Counsel) ("We have the burden . . . of proving that a product is not [GRAS] in the courts."); *see also* Director, Office of Workers' Compensation Programs v. Greenwich Collieries, 114 S. Ct. 2251, 2255-59 (1994) (discussing the Administrative Procedure Act's allocation of the burden of proof in agency proceedings).

172. *See* 41 Fed. Reg. 53,600, 53,604 (1976) ("The burden of proof is always on the manufacturer to demonstrate that the ingredient he is using is GRAS."); United States v. An Article of Food, 752 F.2d 11, 15 (1st Cir. 1985) (upholding FDA seizure of product that manufacturer had thought was GRAS: "The burden of proving general recognition of safe use is placed on the proponent of the food substance in question."); GAO, NEW FOOD TECHNOLOGIES, *supra* note 9, at 29 ("When challenged, a manufacturer must prove that its food substance is, in fact, GRAS."); *cf.* United States v. Vital Health Prods., Ltd., 786 F. Supp. 761, 774 (E.D. Wis. 1992) (In applying the GRAS exception for drugs, "the moving party bears the burden of proof as to each element. Moreover, because the clause is an exception to a comprehensive regulatory scheme which protects public safety, it must be strictly construed.").

173. *See* 41 Fed. Reg. 53,600, 53,604 (1976) ("The manufacturer may solicit an advisory opinion from the agency," for instance, "if there is a question whether the ingredient he is using differs from the ingredient identified" in a GRAS affirmation regulation); GAO, FOOD AND DRUG ADMINISTRATION: CARRAGEENAN FOOD ADDITIVE FROM THE PHILIPPINES CONFORMS TO REGULATIONS, No. HEHS-94-141 (1994).

174. *See infra* Part III.B; *see also* 38 Fed. Reg. 20,054, 20,056 (1973) ("[A]ll future [advisory] opinions relating to GRAS or prior-sanctioned status will be issued in the form of FEDERAL REGISTER notices proposing appropriate new regulations.").

175. *See* Degnan, *supra* note 98, at 572 (adding that food processors may be willing to use a substance in their products on this basis); Heckman, *supra* note 60, at 45 (explaining that, because the "FDA's acceptance of the petition amounts to a prima facie finding that GRAS status is probable, the substance may be marketed while the petition is pending").

176. *See* Hutt, *supra* note 1, at 126 ("For new food substances, the GRAS exclusion has turned out to be the single most important statutory provision.").

177. Pub. L. No. 85-929, § 2, 72 Stat. 1784 (1958) (codified at 21 U.S.C. § 321(s)(4) (1994)); *see also* Poliquin, *supra* note 10, at 122-35, 153 & n.170. The Poultry Products Inspection Act (PPIA) was enacted in 1957. *See* Pub. L. No. 85-172, 71 Stat. 441 (1957) (codified as amended at 21 U.S.C. §§ 451-470 (1994)). The Federal Meat Inspection Act (FMIA) originally was enacted in 1907. *See* Meat Inspection Act, ch. 2907, tit. I, 34 Stat. 1260 (1907) (codified as amended at 21 U.S.C. §§ 601-680 (1994)).

178. 21 C.F.R. §§ 170.3(*l*), 181.5(a) (1996).

179. 52 Fed. Reg. 18,923, 18,923 (1987) ("In the event that a formal approval, such as a food standard regulation promulgated under the act before 1958, does not exist, the agency recognizes the correspondence issued by authorized agency officials can constitute an informal prior sanction."); *see also* 58 Fed. Reg. 33,860, 33,861 (1993) ("FDA has accepted several kinds of evidence of approval as evidence of a prior sanction, including correspondence dealing with a specific substance issued before 1958 by authorized agency officials, scientific articles authored by FDA officials, or other official FDA records in which the agency approved the use of the substance at issue."); 41 Fed. Reg. 23,940, 23,941-42 (1976) (canvassing various evidence of prior sanctions for use of acrylonitrile in food packaging); *1957 Hearings*, *supra* note 25, at 63 (statement of Charles W. Dunn, counsel for the Grocery Manufacturers of America) ("That exception would apply to additives sanctioned by food identity standards administratively established under this act, and those administratively approved by informal advisory opinions."); *id.* at 458 (HEW memorandum) ("Orderly administration and

reasonable consumer protection both demand that chemicals not be exempted from the provisions of the bill because of alleged prior approval unless there is a written record of the approval."); Merrill, *supra* note 10, at 215 ("Though a continuing source of controversy, the kind of documentation needed to establish a 'prior sanction' is principally a matter of interest for archivists. . . .").

180. *See* United States v. An Article of Food, 752 F.2d 11, 16 (1st Cir. 1985) ("The sanction permitting very limited use of potassium nitrate in meats cannot be construed to sanction use of the same substance for an altogether different purpose in beverages."); Public Citizen v. Foreman, 631 F.2d 969, 975-77 (D.C. Cir. 1980) (rejecting request for declaratory judgment that nitrites used as preservatives in cured meats were unsafe food additives, finding that prior sanction from USDA was not limited to their use as a color-fixative); United States v. Articles of Food . . . Buffalo Jerky, 456 F. Supp. 207, 209-10 (D. Neb. 1978) (holding that prior sanctions for use of sodium nitrate and sodium nitrite with other meats did not apply to their use with bison meat), *aff'd*, 594 F.2d 869 (8th Cir. 1979) (per curiam).

181. *See* 21 C.F.R. §§ 181.33-.34 (1996); *see also* 48 Fed. Reg. 9299, 9299-300 (1983) (summarizing the convoluted regulatory history of nitrites, including subsequently withdrawn proposals to restrict nonessential uses and to find no prior sanction for use in poultry, reflecting Agency concerns about the formation of carcinogenic nitrosamines); *supra* note 180 (collecting cases). The USDA gradually has increased restrictions on the use of nitrites. *See, e.g.*, 54 Fed. Reg. 43,041, 43,045 (1989) (codified at 9 C.F.R. § 318.7(b) (1996)).

182. *See* 21 C.F.R. §§ 181.22-.32 (1996). The original list appeared in 25 Fed. Reg. 866 (1960); *see also 1957 Hearings*, *supra* note 25, at 461-62 (statement of George P. Larrick, Commissioner of Food and Drugs) (submitting a partial list of chemicals previously accepted by the FDA or the USDA for use in foods).

183. *See* 37 Fed. Reg. 16,407, 16,407 (1972) ("Not all of these sanctions and approvals can be ascertained because of the destruction of old records and the retirement of personnel involved in these matters."); 35 Fed. Reg. 5810, 5810-11 (1970) (codified as amended at 21 C.F.R. § 170.6 (1996)) (revoking certain informal opinions and requesting the submission of opinion letters for possible reissuance); Merrill, *supra* note 10, at 215 n.169 ("Because of the diverse evidence of approval accepted by the FDA, estimates of the number of [prior sanctioned] ingredients . . . are mere speculation, but persons familiar with the matter doubt the number exceeds 200.").

184. *See* 21 C.F.R. § 181.5(d) (1996) ("[T]he failure of any person to come forward with proof of such an applicable prior sanction in response to a proposal will constitute a waiver of the right to assert or rely on such sanction at any later time."); *see also id.* § 170.35(c)(6) (a notice proposing affirmation of GRAS status will call for the submission of any applicable prior sanctions); *id.* § 170.38(d) (same in the case of a determination of food additive status). In response to objections, the FDA explained that fairness among processors, efficient enforcement and opportunities for the full airing of safety questions justified this disclosure requirement. *See* 41 Fed. Reg. 53,600, 53,603 (1976).

185. *Compare* 52 Fed. Reg. 18,923 (1987) (proposing to recognize a prior sanction for caffeine in nonalcoholic carbonated beverages) *with* 45 Fed. Reg. 69,816, 69,830-31 (1980) (proposing to revoke caffeine's GRAS status and to require additional safety studies pursuant to an interim food additive regulation). Both proposals are still pending, and caffeine remains on the GRAS list, 21 C.F.R. § 182.1180 (1996), in part because of continuing ambiguity in the safety data. *See, e.g.*, Jane E. Brody, *The Latest on Coffee? Don't Worry. Drink Up*, N.Y. TIMES, Sept. 13, 1995, at C1 ("A substantial amount of research, including several large studies done in the last few years, has turned up very little solid scientific evidence to indict a moderate intake of coffee or caffeine as a serious or even minor health threat."); 46 Fed. Reg. 32,453 (1981) (reviewing available teratogenicity studies).

186. *See* Merrill, *supra* note 10, at 216 ("The FDA has historically assumed that a prior sanctioned ingredient is permanently grandfathered, i.e., that it may never become a food additive so long as it is used for its sanctioned purpose, even if new evidence casts doubt on its safety."); *id.* at 244 (commenting that the prior sanction exception "provides apparently indefinite protection for ingredients once approved, however casually, by the FDA or the USDA"); Gary A. Sunshine, *Regulatory Aspects of Food Additives—Yesterday, Today and Tomorrow*, 31 FOOD DRUG COSM. L.J. 264, 269 (1976) ("It would seem logical that, if Congress said a substance was not a food additive if a particular act had occurred prior to the enactment of the Food Additives Amendment, nothing could be done 15 years later to change the previously occurring exempting act.").

187. *See, e.g.*, *1957 Hearings*, *supra* note 25, at 35 (HEW memorandum) ("This, of course, would not prevent rescission of such a sanction or approval, and consequent inclusion of the additive under the bill, if the particular use of the additive is subsequently found to be toxic or of doubtful safety."); Timothy Larkin, *Exploring Food Additives*, FDA CONSUMER, June 1976, at 4 ("[T]hese are probationary squatter's rights, since the FDA can act, and has acted, to remove a prior

sanctioned substance from foods if evidence shows it to be in any way harmful."); Poliquin, *supra* note 10, at 130 (describing the discussion of this issue during congressional consideration of the Color Additive Amendments of 1960).

188. For instance, the FDA rescinded its pre-1958 sanctions for glycine in human food and for nitrites and nitrates to the extent that they were being used in curing premixes containing secondary or tertiary amines, 21 C.F.R. §§ 170.50, 170.60 (1996), but, notwithstanding the associated calls for food additive petitions, these actions should only render the sanctions inoperative as to the statute's adulteration provisions.

189. 21 U.S.C. § 342(a)(1) (1994) (providing that a food containing such a poisonous or deleterious substance shall be deemed to be adulterated).

190. *See* 21 C.F.R. §§ 181.1(b)-(c), 181.5(b)-(c) (1996); 38 Fed. Reg. 12,737 (1973); *see also* 60 Fed. Reg. 33,106, 33,109 (1995) ("FDA finds that a prior sanction exists for the use of lead solder in food cans. However, the available toxicological and exposure data on lead demonstrate that this use of lead solder may be injurious . . . ."); 58 Fed. Reg. 33,860, 33,865 (1993) (Because of its prior sanction, "lead solder used in food containers is not a food additive . . . [but it] may be subject to regulation as an added poisonous or deleterious substance. . . ."). A list of such prohibited substances identified by the FDA appears in 21 C.F.R. pt. 189 (1996).

191. *See* 60 Fed. Reg. at 33,107 ("[One] comment stated that a prior sanction for the use of a food ingredient is based solely on its recognized use prior to enactment of the Food Additives Amendment of 1958. . . . FDA considers the comment to be making a semantic point that ultimately has no effect on the agency's action. . . . If the agency prohibits use of a prior-sanctioned food ingredient [under the basic adulteration provision], this action has the effect of revoking the prior sanction for that use of the ingredient.").

192. *See* Michael R. Taylor, *Food Safety Regulation*, *in* FOOD AND DRUG LAW 182, 196 (RICHARD M. COOPER ed., 1991) (There is a "kind of hierarchy of food substances, ranging from foods to 'food additives,' with various subcategories of GRAS and prior-sanctioned substances in between. This hierarchy has great practical importance because a substance's place in it determines the basis upon which the substance may enter and remain on the market.").

193. *See* 21 U.S.C. §§ 331(a)-(c) (1994) (designating the adulteration of food, or its delivery or receipt, in interstate commerce as a prohibited act), 332(a) (authorizing injunctions to restrain violations of the Act), 333(a) (authorizing the imposition of criminal penalties for violations of the Act), 334(a) (authorizing seizure of products in violation of the Act); *see also* United States v. Park, 421 U.S. 658, 671-74 (1975) (affirming the imposition of strict criminal liability under the FD&C Act in a case involving food adulteration); Sherry Schnell & Susan M. Swafford, Survey, *Federal Food and Drug Act Violations*, 32 AM. CRIM. L. REV. 407, 415-21 (1995). In practice, the FDA typically sends a warning letter first, threatening to pursue formal enforcement action only if the company fails to bring itself into prompt compliance.

194. 21 U.S.C. § 342(a)(2)(C) (1994), as amended by the Food Quality Protection Act of 1996, Pub. L. No. 104-170, § 404, 110 Stat. 1514.

195. 21 U.S.C. § 348(a) (1994). If a food contains an approved food additive, then it may not be regarded as adulterated under the statute's broader prohibition against bearing or containing any added poisonous or deleterious substance which may render it injurious to health. *See id.* (cross-referencing 21 U.S.C. § 342(a)(1)).

196. *See, e.g.*, GAO, NEED FOR MORE EFFECTIVE REGULATION OF DIRECT ADDITIVES TO FOOD, No. HRD-80-90 (1980), at v (recommending the elimination of the GRAS and prior sanction exceptions); *see also* GAO, NEW FOOD TECHNOLOGIES, *supra* note 9, at 10 ("[B]ecause new food products may incorporate GRAS substances—such as oat fiber, beta carotene, or egg white—in previously untested quantities, concentrations, or forms, some . . . have questioned whether the laws leaving GRAS determinations up to industry adequately protect public health.").

197. *See, e.g.*, Degnan, *supra* note 98, at 553, 580-82. Mr. Degnan suggested, for instance, that new uses of previously approved and widely used food additives could be treated as falling within the GRAS exception rather than requiring the submission of a new food additive petition. *Id.* at 581; *see also* Hutt, *supra* note 1, at 124 (observing that the GRAS exception has been "a resounding success from the standpoint of public policy, precisely because FDA involvement is not needed to make it work").

198. *See* 21 U.S.C. § 348(b) (1994). The Agency also may issue a food additive regulation on its own initiative. *See id.* § 348(d); 21 C.F.R. § 170.15 (1996). The amendment or repeal of regulations must abide by the same procedures required for initial promulgation. *See* 21 U.S.C. § 348(h) (1994).

199. *See* 21 U.S.C. § 348(b)(2) (1994). The FDA's implementing regulations describe in greater detail the required format and content of a petition. *See* 21 C.F.R. § 171.1 (1996).

200. *See* 21 U.S.C. § 348(b)(3) & (4) (1994); 21 C.F.R. § 171.1(j) (1996).

201. *See, e.g.*, 21 U.S.C. § 331(j) (1994) (prohibiting the disclosure of trade secret information acquired under, inter alia, the provision governing food additive petitions); 21 C.F.R. §§ 171.1(h)(1)(iii) (1996) (prohibiting the disclosure of identifying information in adverse reaction reports and consumer complaints), 171.1(h)(2) (prohibiting the disclosure of manufacturing methods, sales data, and quantitative formulas).

202. The FDA promulgated these regulations one year after enactment of the Food Additives Amendment. *See* 24 Fed. Reg. 2434 (1959) (originally codified at 21 C.F.R. pt. 121 (1965)); 23 Fed. Reg. 9511 (1958) (notice of proposed rulemaking). The EPA also implements this provision of the FD&C Act insofar as it must set finished food tolerances for pesticides used on raw agricultural commodities. *See* 55 Fed. Reg. 50,282 (1990) (codified at 40 C.F.R. pt. 180 (1996)); 53 Fed. Reg. 41,126 (1988). The EPA's procedures for revocation parallel those used for the establishment of food additive regulations. 40 C.F.R. pts. 177-178 (1996).

203. *See* 21 C.F.R. § 171.1(i)(1) (1996).

204. *Id.* § 171.1(d) & (i)(1); *see also id.* § 171.1(g) ("A petition shall be retained but shall not be filed if any of the data prescribed by . . . the act are lacking or are not set forth so as to be readily understood."). If the food additive petition is not accepted for filing, the petitioner may either supplement it to address any identified deficiencies or demand that it be filed as originally submitted. *Id.* § 171.1(i)(1).

205. 21 U.S.C. § 348(b)(5) (1994); 21 C.F.R. § 171.1(i)(2) (1996).

206. 21 C.F.R. § 171.7 (1996). Even after the rejection of a food additive petition, nothing prevents a resubmission based on additional safety data. *See, e.g.*, 47 Fed. Reg. 51,227 (1982) (announcing the filing of a second food additive petition for cyclamate more than six years after the FDA originally rejected the first petition).

207. *See* 61 Fed. Reg. 33,654, 33,655 (1996) ("Although public notice of a petition is required, the act is silent with respect to public comment on a petition."). This contrasts with the procedure used for GRAS affirmation petitions, described *infra* Part III.B, which expressly provides for a 60-day public comment period. 21 C.F.R. § 170.35(c)(3) (1996). The statute does, however, require that at least 30 days elapse before the Agency finalizes a food additive regulation proposed on its own initiative. *See* 21 U.S.C. § 348(d) (1994).

208. *See* S. Rep. No. 2422, 85th Cong., 2d Sess. 7-9 (1958) (describing the exhaustive consideration of the judicial review question).

209. *See 1957 Hearings*, *supra* note 25, at 459-60 (HEW memorandum) (concluding that such an added procedure "would complicate materially the efficient administration of the act without giving any genuine benefit either to the Government or the petitioner."). The statutory procedure for action on food additive petitions contrasts with the two-stage process contained in Section 701(e) of the Act which involves a notice-and-comment period followed by a formal rulemaking hearing if necessary. *See* Pharmaceutical Manufacturers Ass'n v. Gardner, 381 F.2d 271, 278 (D.C. Cir. 1967). The drafters of Section 409 were aware of this more formal procedure and could have easily covered food additive petitions through a cross-reference in that section, but instead they chose a procedure which only contemplates public objections after a food additive order is published. The FDA's general procedures for notice-and-comment rulemaking specifically exempt food additive petitions from the regulation. 21 C.F.R. § 10.40(e)(2) (1996).

210. *See* Merrill, *supra* note 10, at 248 (The FDA "ordinarily approves food additives simply by publishing in the Federal Register a regulation specifying the terms of the approval and reciting that the additive has been found safe. The supporting safety data are evaluated privately, except on those rare occasions when a member of the public comes to the agency to evaluate the petition.").

211. *See* 40 Fed. Reg. 40,682, 40,699 (1975) ("[T]he Commissioner will make available for public disclosure all safety and functionality data relating to any color additive or food additive at the time of filing of the petition, so that public comment can be prepared meaningfully and submitted prior to publication of the final regulations.").

212. The procedures used by the EPA for pesticide residue petitions under Section 409 of the FD&C Act are similar in tacitly allowing prepublication comment. *See* 53 Fed. Reg. 41,126, 41,128 (1988) (observing that, because "section 409(b) does not require publication of a proposed version of a food additive regulation for notice and comment by the public, the section 409(b)(5) notice of filing may be the only opportunity for members of the public to submit any comments they wish to make"). The EPA regulations differ from the FDA's in one respect, however: the Administrator may respond to a petition by "publish[ing] a proposed food additive regulation and request[ing] public comment thereon." 40 C.F.R. § 177.125(b) (1996). "This could occur because of the complexity or controversiality of the issues raised by a petition or because of a need to gather information from members of the public." 53 Fed. Reg. at 41,128.

213. *See* 60 Fed. Reg. 57,586, 57,587 (1995) (conceding that the FD&C Act "is silent with respect to public comment on a [food additive] petition," but viewing this as a difficulty only in choosing a proper deadline). Indeed, the Agency went to some lengths in justifying its decision to impose any deadline on comments in this case, *see id.*, even though the food additive petition under review had been filed more than eight years earlier and been the subject of a week-long advisory committee meeting, *see infra* Part V.C.

214. *See* 21 U.S.C. § 348(c)(1) & (2) (1994); 21 C.F.R. § 171.100 (1996). Apparently, an order denying a petition need only be made available to the petitioner. *See* 21 C.F.R. § 171.100(a) (1996) (calling for publication in the Federal Register only in the case of approvals).

215. *See* Alan M. Rulis & Laura M. Tarantino, *The Food Additive Petition Process: Recent Data*, 48 FOOD & DRUG L.J. 137, 138-39 & 145 (1993).

216. *See infra* Part VI.A.

217. *See* 21 C.F.R. § 171.1(j) (1996) ("The date used for computing the 90-day limit . . . shall be moved forward 1 day for each day after the mailing date of the [FDA] request taken by the petitioner to submit the sample."); *id.* § 171.6 ("[I]f the Commissioner determines that the additional information or data amount to a substantive amendment, the petition as amended will be given a new filing date, and the time limitation will begin to run anew."); *id.* § 171.7 (If a petition is withdrawn and then refiled, "the time limitation will begin to run anew.").

218. Alan M. Rulis, *The Food and Drug Administration's Food Additive Petition Review Process*, 45 FOOD DRUG COSM. L.J. 533, 535 (1990). The FDA uses a similar 180-day review clock for new drug applications. *See* 21 C.F.R. §§ 314.60, 314.100-.101 (1996).

219. 21 U.S.C. § 348(e) (1994); *see also* 21 C.F.R. § 171.102 (1996). By contrast, the filing of objections and requests for an evidentiary hearing automatically stays a final FDA order terminating the listing of a color additive. *See* 21 U.S.C. § 371(e)(2) (1994).

220. 21 U.S.C. § 348(f)(1) (1994); 21 C.F.R. § 171.110 (1996) (cross-referencing 21 C.F.R. pt. 12). The Agency's original implementing regulations contained detailed procedures for conducting a formal hearing on any objections to an order on a food additive petition, 24 Fed. Reg. 2434 (1959) (previously codified at 21 C.F.R. §§ 121.55-.69 (1965)), but these became unnecessary after the FDA promulgated generic procedural regulations, *see* 41 Fed. Reg. 51,706 (1976).

221. 21 U.S.C. § 348(f)(1) & (2) (1994).

222. *See* 21 C.F.R. § 12.24(b) (1995); Community Nutrition Inst. (CNI) v. Young, 773 F.2d 1356, 1363 (D.C. Cir. 1985) ("If the agency determines that no hearing is necessary, the regulation approving the food additive becomes final."), *cert. denied*, 475 U.S. 1123 (1986); Marshall Minerals, Inc. v. FDA, 661 F.2d 409, 417, 425 (5th Cir. 1981).

223. *See* Merrill, *supra* note 10, at 209 & n.139 (describing hearings on the denial of a food additive petition for cyclamates and the approval of one for aspartame). Since 1980, the FDA consistently has denied hearing requests. *See, e.g.*, 57 Fed. Reg. 6667 (1992) (acesulfame potassium); 49 Fed. Reg. 6672 (1984) (aspartame). The Agency has held formal hearings on decisions concerning other food-use substances. *See, e.g.*, 48 Fed. Reg. 48,533 (1983) (Red No. 4); 42 Fed. Reg. 17,529 (1977) (acrylonitrile copolymer); 41 Fed. Reg. 29,896 (1976) (Red No. 2).

224. *See 1957 Hearings*, *supra* note 25, at 211 (statement of H.T. Austern, appearing on behalf of the National Canners Association) (noting the risk of delays at this stage because the bill failed to specify any deadlines). An earlier bill would have established a deadline of 120 days for final action on objections. *See* H.R. 7606, 84th Cong., 1st Sess. § 5 (409(d)) (1955).

225. *See, e.g.*, Abbott Laboratories v. Harris, Food Drug Cosm. L. Rep. (CCH) ¶ 38,046 (N.D. Ill. June 12, 1980) (refusing to compel final agency action in response to the manufacturer's objections to the FDA's denial of a food additive petition for cyclamate, though noting that "over six-and-one-half years is just not, by any view, compatible with the prompt determination intended by Congress"); *cf. CNI*, 773 F.2d at 1361-62 (noting that a five-month delay in ruling on objections to the approval of aspartame in carbonated beverages was not excessive).

226. *See* 21 U.S.C. § 348(f)(3) & (g) (1994) (though the filing of a petition for review does not automatically stay the effective date of the order). A petition for review may be filed in a federal appellate court within sixty days after entry of an order responding to objections. *Id.* § 348(g)(1); *see also CNI*, 773 F.2d at 1360-62 (holding that the federal district court lacked jurisdiction). Once the Agency transmits to the court the record of proceedings, the order may no longer be modified, and the court then has exclusive jurisdiction over the matter. 21 U.S.C. § 348(g)(2) (1994). The court may, however, order the Commissioner to take additional evidence under limited circumstances. *Id.* § 348(g)(4).

227. *See, e.g.*, Nader v. EPA, 859 F.2d 747, 751 (9th Cir. 1988), *cert. denied*, 490 U.S. 1034 (1989).

228. 21 U.S.C. § 348(g)(2) (1994); *see also* S. REP. NO. 2422, 85th Cong., 2d Sess. 8 (1958) (explaining that this "represents a new standard of judicial review, which differs from the standard of 'substantial evidence on the record as a whole' that has heretofore been the criterion."); 104 CONG. REC. 17,418 (1958) (statement of Hon. John B. Williams) ("The Committee has endeavored to prescribe a new statutory criterion requiring that a high standard of fairness be observed in administrative rulemaking under this bill. Personal attitudes or preferences of administrative officials could not prevail on the basis of being supported by substantial evidence picked from the record without regard to other evidence of probative value in the record.").

229. 21 C.F.R. § 171.130 (1996). "Any such petition shall include an assertion of facts, supported by data, showing that new information exists with respect to the food additive or that new uses have been developed or old uses abandoned, that new data are available as to toxicity of the chemical, or that experience with the existing regulation or exemption may justify its amendment or repeal." *Id.* § 171.130(b).

230. *See 1995 Hearings*, *supra* note 1, at 88 (testimony of Rhona S. Applebaum, Executive Vice President, National Food Processors Association) ("The average cost for a food additive application typically ranges between $15 million and $25 million. However, there have been applications whose total costs have exceeded $200 million."); *see also* 49 Fed. Reg. 50,856, 50,859 (1984) (estimating that it takes 5-7 years from the time that safety testing on a direct food additive starts to FDA approval); *cf.* 60 Fed. Reg. 36,582, 36,593 (1995) (estimating that an indirect food additive petition "can require on average 2,600 hours to prepare and cost anywhere from $85,000 to $100,000").

231. *See* GAO, NEW FOOD TECHNOLOGIES, *supra* note 9, at 27 ("Unlike approvals for new drugs, food additives regulations are not licenses. Once FDA has issued a regulation specifying the uses and conditions of use for a food additive, any company is free to market the additive as long as the additive is in compliance with the regulation and is not patented."); Rulis, *supra* note 218, at 534; *1957 Hearings*, *supra* note 25, at 67 (statement of Charles W. Dunn, counsel for the Grocery Manufacturers of America) (explaining that the food additive bill "radically differs from the new drug law of the FDC Act, because its administrative regulation has a general industry force; whereas an effective application under the latter law is an individual one"). In the case of unpatented products or processes, the FDA's confidential treatment of "trade secrets" such as manufacturing methods and formulas, 21 C.F.R. § 171.1(h)(2) (1996), may provide a limited substitute for market exclusivity, but only if such information could not be discovered independently by a competitor. *See, e.g.*, David D. Friedman et al., *Some Economics of Trade Secret Law*, 5 J. ECON. PERSPECTIVES 61 (1991).

232. *See* 21 C.F.R. pt. 330 (1996); *see also* 21 U.S.C. § 357 (1994) (antibiotics are approved through published regulations rather than private licenses).

233. 21 C.F.R. pt. 60 (1996); *see, e.g.*, 54 Fed. Reg. 38,289, 38,290 (1989) (determining that the FDA's regulatory review period for an indirect food additive exceeded 11 years for purposes of possibly granting patent term restoration of up to five years). To date, the FDA has advised the Patent and Trademark Office (PTO) of the regulatory review times for only three direct food additives in response to requests for patent term extensions. 62 Fed. Reg. 763 (1997) (olestra) *See* 56 Fed. Reg. 3110 (1991) (gellan gum); 53 Fed. Reg. 48,727 (1988) (acesulfame potassium).

234. *See* Hutt, *supra* note 1, at 125; *see also* 21 U.S.C. § 355(j)(4)(D) (1994); Suzan Kucukarslan & Jacqueline Cole, *Patent Extension Under the Drug Price Competition and Patent Term Restoration Act of 1984*, 49 FOOD & DRUG L.J. 511 (1994).

235. *See* Hutt, *supra* note 1, at 125-26 ("[T]here is no incentive to innovate in the field of new direct human food additives, however valuable those additives might be to the health of the American public.").

236. 21 U.S.C. § 348(i) (1994).

237. *See id.* §§ 355(i), 360j(g) (1994); *see also* Donald O. Beers, *Emergency Use INDs and IDEs: What Is Required? What Are the Risks?*, 43 FOOD DRUG COSM. L.J. 759 (1988).

238. *See* Stephen H. McNamara, *Can You Taste It Without FDA Approval? What to Do When You Need to Taste-Test a New Food Additive Before FDA Approval*, 46 FOOD DRUG COSM. L.J. 869, 870-75 (1991) (describing the limited scope of the investigational use exemption and possible alternative bases for lawful testing of an unapproved additive in humans).

239. 21 C.F.R. § 170.17(a) (1996) (The label must include the following language: "*Caution*: Contains a new food additive for investigational use only in laboratory research animals or for tests in vitro. Not for use in humans."). Nonetheless, investigational substances may be utilized in clinical trials, perhaps under an investigational new drug (IND) exemption, *id.* pt. 312, and any results from such trials included in a food additive petition must be accompanied by a statement concerning compliance with institutional review requirements. *See id.* § 171.1(m); *see also infra* note 442

(discussing the use of an IND for clinical trials of olestra); GAO, NEW FOOD TECHNOLOGIES, *supra* note 9, at 59-61 (noting that the FDA has the authority and has considered promulgating regulations to govern human clinical trials of novel food additives).

240. *See* 21 C.F.R. § 170.17(b)-(c) (1996).

241. *Cf.* 21 C.F.R. § 170.6(d) (1996) (revoking informal opinions issued in the decade after enactment of the Food Additives Amendment concerning the GRAS or other status of substances added to food).

242. *See* 37 Fed. Reg. 25,706 (1972) (originally codified at 21 C.F.R. § 121.40 (1975)); 37 Fed. Reg. 6207 (1972) (notice of proposed rulemaking); *see also* Degnan, *supra* note 98, at 572.

243. Congress did not adopt an explicit GRAS affirmation procedure, though it had been recommended by some industry representatives. *See 1957 Hearings*, *supra* note 25, at 251 (statement of George Faunce, Jr., appearing on behalf of the American Bakers Association); *id.* at 64 (statement of Charles W. Dunn, counsel for the Grocery Manufacturers of America).

244. The FDA rejected numerous objections to the mandatory inclusion of information about the manufacturing process in its revised GRAS criteria. *See* 41 Fed. Reg. 53,600, 53,603-04 (1976).

245. *See* 21 C.F.R. §§ 170.35(c)(1)(i)-(iv) (1996). In addition, the petitioner must certify that "to the best of his knowledge [the petition] is a representative and balanced submission that includes unfavorable information, as well as favorable information, known to him pertinent to the evaluation of the safety and functionality of the substance," that any nonclinical studies complied with good laboratory practice requirements, and, unless categorically exempt, include an environmental assessment. *Id.* §§ 170.35(c)(1)(v)-(viii). Similar rules apply to food additive petitions. *See id.* §§ 171.1(c), (k) & (m).

246. *See* 21 C.F.R. § 170.35(c)(1)(i)(*h*) (1996) (permitting the exclusion of any trade secrets concerning manufacturing processes); 41 Fed. Reg. 53,600, 53,604 (1976); 37 Fed. Reg. 25,705, 25,705 (1972) ("None of the data and information to be submitted in support of a petition requesting affirmation of GRAS status may properly be regarded as trade secrets requiring confidential handling. All safety and functionality data must be generally available to the public for there to be any conclusion that the substance is GRAS.").

247. 21 C.F.R. § 170.35(c)(1)(iv) (1996). Although GRAS "based upon scientific procedures shall require the same quantity and quality of scientific evidence as is required to obtain approval of a food additive," *id.* § 170.30(b), a GAO review concluded that the FDA initially did not strictly abide by this rule. *See* GAO, *supra* note 196, at v ("GAO reviewed 15 of these [GRAS affirmed] substances and found that only 2 had been subjected to the same type of scientific tests FDA considers necessary for a food additive."). As described below, "functionality" refers only to a substance's effectiveness in accomplishing an intended physical or other technical effect, not to the utility of that effect. *See infra* notes 310-13 and accompanying text.

248. 21 C.F.R. §§ 170.35(c)(2)-(3) (1996). If the Agency proposes GRAS affirmation on its own initiative, it also must provide an opportunity for public comment. *Id.* § 170.35(b).

249. *Id.* §§ 170.35(c)(4) & (5); *see also id.* § 170.38(a) (authorizing the FDA to publish a notice that a substance is not GRAS). Even if not the product of an unsuccessful GRAS affirmation petition, the FDA may, either on its own initiative or at the prompting of a citizen petition, propose to determine that a substance is not GRAS and invite public comment before issuing any final notice to that effect. *See id.* § 170.38(b); *see also* Heterochemical Corp. v. FDA, 741 F. Supp. 382, 384-85 (E.D.N.Y. 1990) (discussing the application of parallel procedures for food additives intended for consumption by animals).

250. In the preamble to the final regulation, the FDA rejected suggestions of a self-imposed deadline for final action on GRAS affirmation petitions, though it did promise to "make every effort to act upon such petitions within 90 days." 37 Fed. Reg. 25,705, 25,706 (1972) ("[A] specific time period should not be included in the regulation because it is entirely possible that extraneous circumstances [such as the need to consult with outside experts or the volume of petitions] will preclude meeting any time limit established.").

251. *See, e.g.*, 61 Fed. Reg. 43,447, 43,450 (1996) (affirming the GRAS status of high fructose corn syrup more than 22 years after the first petition was filed and more than 13 years after the substance was listed as GRAS); 55 Fed. Reg. 6384 (1990) (affirming the GRAS status of a microparticulated egg white and milk protein product as a fat-replacer in frozen desserts, more than 15 months after receiving the petition); *see also* GAO, *supra* note 196, at iii ("As of October 1979, FDA had received 39 petitions for GRAS substances . . . and had completed its review of 18. Only 4 of the 18 contained sufficient scientific evidence to support a GRAS affirmation."); Hutt, *supra* note 1, at 124 (The "FDA has become simply a

dumping ground for GRAS affirmation petitions. The current backlog is more than 50 GRAS affirmation petitions for direct human food substances, in various stages of consideration, and it has been growing every year.").

252. *See infra* text accompanying note 508.

253. *See infra* Part VI.A (comparing delays in FDA action on food additive and GRAS affirmation petitions). As one FDA officially presciently warned at the outset: "I shudder to think of the difficulty in securing general agreement on each specification and each usage. . . . [W]e may be so hopelessly tied up with trying to figure out what is not subject to the amendment that we won't be able to deal effectively with that which is." Arthur A. Checchi, *Food-Additives Procedures and Policies*, 14 FOOD DRUG COSM. L.J. 591, 592 (1959).

254. *See* Hutt, *supra* note 1, at 124 ("Nonetheless, the program is still a resounding success from the standpoint of public policy, precisely because FDA involvement is not needed to make it work. Self-determination of GRAS permits immediate marketing, whether or not a GRAS affirmation petition is filed, and whether or not FDA ever acts on it."). Shortly after the completion of this paper, the FDA proposed, and invited submissions under, a simplified GRAS notification procedure that would replace the affirmation petition procedure. *See* 62 Fed. 18,938 (1997). A discussion of some of its implications appears in the proceedings of this workshop.

255. *See* 37 Fed. Reg. 25,705 (1972) (codified as amended at 21 C.F.R. pt. 180 (1996)); 37 Fed. Reg. 6207, 6208 (1972) ("The conclusion that an interim food additive order is or is not justified will depend upon the nature of the question raised, the reliability of the other scientific data pertinent to the additive, the purpose for which the additive is used, and the availability of alternative ingredients.").

256. *See* 35 Fed. Reg. 12,062 (1970), *aff'd*, Jacobson v. Edwards, Food Drug Cosm. L. Rep. (CCH) ¶ 40,817 (D.D.C. July 6, 1971) ("I think it is, within the letter and the spirit of the Statute, permissible for the agency to issue interim orders of this kind."), *aff'd mem.*, No. 71-2046 (D.C. Cir. Dec. 15, 1972); *see also* Federation of Homemakers, Inc. v. Harris, Food Drug Cosm. L. Rep. (CCH) ¶ 38,100 (D.D.C. Mar. 25, 1981) (refusing to compel the FDA to remove caffeine from the GRAS list, and recognizing the Agency's authority to propose an interim food additive regulation instead). Because the preliminary data from the additional studies on brominated vegetable oil did not suggest any safety concerns, the FDA concluded in 1974 that the ongoing studies could continue. *See* 39 Fed. Reg. 36,113 (1974).

257. 37 Fed. Reg. at 25,706; *see also* Merrill, *supra* note 10, at 213 n.155 ("The Act makes no provision for the transition between the loss of GRAS status and the approval as a food additive. To bridge this gap, the FDA has established procedures for the issuance of interim food additive regulations."); Richard A. Merrill & Michael R. Taylor, *Saccharin: A Case Study of Government Regulation of Environmental Carcinogens*, 5 VA. J. NAT. RESOURCE L. 1, 23-24 (1985) (suggesting that the procedure grew out of the Agency's experience with cyclamate). In contrast to its silence with regard to food additives whose safety is later brought into question, Congress created a transitional category for existing color additives. *See supra* note 105.

258. 21 C.F.R. § 180.1(a) (1996). "No interim food additive regulation may be promulgated if the new information is conclusive with respect to the question raised or if there is a reasonable likelihood that the substance is harmful or that continued use of the substance will result in harm to the public health." *Id.* § 180.1(b); *see also* 37 Fed. Reg. 25,705 (1972) ("The purpose of an interim food additive regulation is not to permit the continued use of a substance in food for which there is no reasonable certainty of safety . . . .").

259. *See* 21 C.F.R. § 180.1(c) (1996) (cross-referencing the procedures specified in 21 C.F.R. pt. 10); *see also id.* § 10.50(c)(5) (providing for an opportunity for a formal evidentiary public hearing to the extent required for the issuance, amendment or repeal of food additive regulations under the statute); *see also* 37 Fed. Reg. at 25,706 (explaining that § 121.74, the regulation governing the procedures for amending or repealing a food additive regulation or exemption but not GRAS status (now codified at § 170.38), was revised to state that it is "applicable to a petition for determination of food additive status and for an interim food additive regulation").

260. 21 C.F.R. § 180.1(c)(1) (1996).

261. *See* 37 Fed. Reg. at 25,706 (explaining that "these regulations will encourage additional testing").

262. 21 C.F.R. § 180.1(c)(2) (1996). Any nonclinical laboratory studies and clinical investigations must comply with applicable good laboratory practice and institutional review regulations. *See id.* §§ 180.1(c)(4) & (6). The regulation also suggests that the FDA may decide to undertake such studies itself, *id.* § 180.1(c)(2), but "this will occur only in very rare instances, if at all." 38 Fed. Reg. 20,054, 20,056 (1973) ("As a general rule, the [FDA] intends to institute little or no testing for the purpose of providing data necessary to justify continued marketing of food ingredients, because of its conclusion that this is properly the function of private industry.").

263. 37 Fed. Reg. at 25,706 (adding that "[t]his requires that studies be instituted as rapidly as possible"); *see also* 45 Fed. Reg. 69,817, 69,830 (1980) ("A primary advantage of interim regulation is that it permits FDA to require the sponsor of a substance about which questions have been raised to perform the studies necessary to resolve the questions.").

264. 21 C.F.R. § 180.1(c)(3) (1996) ("If the progress report is inadequate or if the Commissioner concludes that the studies are not being pursued promptly and diligently or if interim results indicate a reasonable likelihood that a health hazard exists, [a revocation] order will promptly be published. . . .").

265. *Id.* § 180.1(d). The Commissioner may communicate with experts outside of the Agency to assess the available evidence. *See id.* § 180.1(e). The procedures governing interim food additive regulations parallel those applicable to provisionally listed color additives. *See* Color Additive Amendments of 1960, Pub. L. No. 86-618, § 203, 74 Stat. 404; 41 Fed. Reg. 41,852, 41,853 (1976) (summarily terminating provisional listing for Red No. 4 because the manufacturers had failed to undertake the toxicological studies necessary to resolve safety questions); Certified Color Mfrs. Ass'n v. Mathews, 543 F.2d 284, 296-98 (D.C. Cir. 1976) (upholding summary termination of provisional listing of Red No. 2).

266. *See* 21 C.F.R. §§ 180.22-.37 (1996). Two other interim food additive regulations were proposed but not finalized. *See* 45 Fed. Reg. 69,817 (1980) (caffeine); 42 Fed. Reg. 27,603 (1977) (BHT).

267. In the case of saccharin, the FDA awaited conclusion of ongoing studies in Canada. 21 C.F.R. § 180.37(c) (1996). In the case of mannitol, the FDA simply demanded "timely and adequate progress reports" of feeding studies. *Id.* § 180.25(f). Although it did not explicitly require progress reports in the case of acrylonitrile, the Agency enumerated six elements necessary for the toxicity review and called for the prior submission of study protocols. *Id.* § 180.22(e).

268. *See* 37 Fed. Reg. 2437 (1972) (to be codified at 21 C.F.R. § 121.4001(c)).

269. *See* 38 Fed. Reg. 13,733, 13,734 (1973); *see also* Merrill & Taylor, *supra* note 257, at 84 ("Despite the Agency's efforts to create a legal middle ground . . . , this territory could only be occupied temporarily.").

270. *See* 38 Fed. Reg. 19,218 (1973) (to be codified at 21 C.F.R. § 121.4002), *revoked*, 38 Fed. Reg. 31,679, 31,680 (1973) (noting that preliminary studies detected nitrosamines even in buffered curing premixes).

271. *See* 61 Fed. Reg. 7990, 7991 (1996). The 1994 notice of filing did explain that the Agency was still reviewing a 1986 FASEB report which found that mannitol and other sugar alcohols caused a statistically significant increased incidence of adrenal medullary hyperplasia and pheochromocytoma at high doses in rats. *See* 59 Fed. Reg. 64,207, 64,208 (1994).

272. *See* Saccharin Study and Labeling Act, Pub. L. No. 95-203, 91 Stat. 1451 (1977) (codified at 21 U.S.C. § 343(o)(1) (1994)). The Act prohibits the Agency from revoking or amending any interim food additive regulations applicable to saccharin. *Id.* § 3; *see also* Pub. L. No. 102-142, 105 Stat. 910 (1991) (extending moratorium until May 1, 1997).

273. *See* Heterochemical Corp. v. FDA, 741 F. Supp. 382, 385-86 (E.D.N.Y. 1990) (holding that, pursuant to its regulations, the FDA could not find a lack of evidence to support GRAS status but then fail to demand a food additive petition or to take some other appropriate action). For example, the litigation concerning the use of acrylonitrile copolymers in beverage containers concluded in 1979. *See* 42 Fed. Reg. 48,528, 48,543 (1977) (staying food additive regulations pending the completion of further safety studies pursuant to an interim food additive order), *rev'd*, Monsanto Co. v. Kennedy, 613 F.2d 947, 954-56 (D.C. Cir. 1979) (remanding final order so that the FDA could determine whether any migration actually was detectable and, even if it was, whether the Agency would regard it as de minimis). The Agency has amended the applicable food additive regulations to allow certain uses in beverage containers, *e.g.*, 49 Fed. Reg. 36,635 (1984) (codified at 21 C.F.R. § 177.1040 (1996)), but its interim food additive regulation for acrylonitrile copolymers remains in effect. *See* 41 Fed. Reg. 23,940, 23,946 (1976) (codified as amended at 21 C.F.R. § 180.22 (1996)).

274. *See* Cutler v. Kennedy, 475 F. Supp. 838, 853-55 (D.D.C. 1979) (invalidating the FDA's original scheme for the review of OTC drugs which allowed for the continued marketing of products designated as Category III in a final monograph on the condition that additional testing be undertaken); *cf.* Cutler v. Hayes, 818 F.2d 879, 899-901 (D.C. Cir. 1987) (upholding the FDA's revised Category III regulations because they only authorized continued marketing during testing before the completion of a final monograph); McIlwain v. Hayes, 690 F.2d 1041, 1046 (D.C. Cir. 1982) (upholding the FDA's authority to continue postponing final action on provisionally listed color additives, noting that the statute "sets no time limit on provisional listings, a fact that is particularly significant since Congress has set such time limits in analogous statutes").

275. 21 U.S.C. § 348(c)(3)(A) (1994). A discussion of the special proviso in this subsection which governs potential carcinogens is reserved for Part IV.B.

276. 21 U.S.C. § 348(c)(5) (1994). Lack of effectiveness alone would not justify the denial of a food additive petition. *See* Marshall Minerals, Inc. v. FDA, 661 F.2d 409, 423 (5th Cir. 1981). Lack of effectiveness may, however, still be relevant insofar as such an additive may promote consumer deception or otherwise result in a misbranding violation. *Id.* at 423 n.18; *see also* 21 U.S.C. § 348(c)(3)(B) (1994) (providing that a food additive shall not be approved if "the proposed use of the additive would promote deception of the consumer in violation of this chapter").

277. H.R. REP. NO. 2284, 85th Cong., 2d Sess. 4-5 (1958) (emphasis added); *accord* S. REP. NO. 2422, 85th Cong., 2d Sess. 6 (1958); *1957 Hearings, supra* note 25, at 87-88 (statement of Robert B. Smith, Jr., President of the Medical College of Virginia); *see also* Food Quality Protection Act of 1996, Pub. L. No. 104-170, § 405 (408(b)(2)(A)(ii)), 110 Stat. 1516 ("[T]he term 'safe,' with respect to a tolerance for a pesticide chemical residue, means that the Administrator has determined that there is a reasonable certainty that no harm will result. . . .").

278. *See* S. REP. NO. 2422, 85th Cong., 2d Sess. 2 (1958) ("[I]nstead of insisting on proof beyond any possible doubt that no harm will result under any conceivable circumstances from the use of a particular additive—which could, of course, occur if an individual decided to eat a pound of salt or drink 4 gallons of pure water in an hour—the test" is reasonable certainty.).

279. *See* 21 C.F.R. § 170.30(b), (c)(1) (1996).

280. *See supra* notes 14-19 and accompanying text; *see also* David D. Doniger, *Federal Regulation of Vinyl Chloride: A Short Course in the Law and Policy of Toxic Substances Control*, 7 ECOLOGY L.Q. 497, 593 (1978) (arguing that the safety standards are identical).

281. *See 1957 Hearings, supra* note 25, at 456 (HEW memorandum) (preferring a more stringent "without hazard" standard, even while conceding an inability to be "absolutely sure"). The initial version of the bill that Congress ultimately enacted included a separate definition of the term "safe" as meaning "without hazard," *see* H.R. 13,254, 85th Cong., 2d Sess. § 2 (201(t)) (1958), but this did not appear in the final version.

282. 104 CONG. REC. 17,418 (1958).

283. *See* H.R. REP. NO. 2284, 85th Cong., 2d Sess. 4 (1958) ("The concept of safety used in this legislation involves the question of whether a substance is hazardous to the health of man or animal."); S. REP. NO. 2422, 85th Cong., 2d Sess. 11 (1958) (explaining that the intent of the bill was "to assure our people that nothing shall be added to the foods they eat which can reasonably be expected to produce any type of illness").

284. 21 C.F.R. § 121.1(i) (1970) (emphasis added); *see also 1957 Hearings, supra* note 25, at 456 (HEW memorandum) ("We do not want to feed chemically treated food to our children if the only assurance we have is that it is reasonably probable that the added chemicals will not cause harm. We want to know that it has been established convincingly. . . .").

285. 36 Fed. Reg. 12,093 (1971) (codified at 21 C.F.R. § 121.1(i) (1972)).

286. 41 Fed. Reg. 53,600, 53,604 (1976) (codified at 21 C.F.R. § 170.3(i) (1996)); *see also* 45 Fed. Reg. 61,474, 61,477 (1980) (discussing the general safety standard in the course of affirming the decision to reject the food additive petition for cyclamate); Marshall Minerals, Inc. v. FDA, 661 F.2d 409, 419 (5th Cir. 1981) (noting that the FDA "assert[ed] that this later definition is taken from the legislative history of the Act," but resolving the dispute concerning gentian violet without regard to which of the two standards applied).

287. 21 C.F.R. § 170.3(i) (1996) ("It is impossible in the present state of scientific knowledge to establish with complete certainty the absolute harmlessness of the use of any substance."). The 1974 proposal that led to the current regulation differed from the final rule in two respects: (1) it included a reference to the consideration of benefits, and (2) it failed to limit the safety evaluation only to intended uses. 39 Fed. Reg. 34,194, 34,195 (1974).

288. 21 C.F.R. § 70.3(i) (1996). In *Scott v. FDA*, 728 F.2d 322, 325 (6th Cir. 1984), the petitioners claimed that the FDA's "constituents" policy was inconsistent with both the Delaney clause and the general safety clause applicable to color additives, and the court's discussion suggests that the general safety clause (with the "reasonable certainty that no harm will result" interpretation in the FDA's regulation) is less stringent than the Delaney clause.

289. Courts accord heightened deference to contemporaneous agency interpretations of a statute and require that any subsequent modifications in the original interpretation be well explained. *See, e.g.*, General Elec. Co. v. Gilbert, 429 U.S. 125, 142 (1976); NLRB v. Bell Aerospace Co., 416 U.S. 267, 274-75 (1974); Les v. Reilly, 968 F.2d 985, 989-90 (9th Cir. 1992), *cert. denied*, 507 U.S. 950 (1993); Rhodia, Inc. v. FDA, 608 F.2d 1376, 1379 (D.C. Cir. 1979); United States v. Undetermined Quantities . . . Exachol, 716 F. Supp. 787, 795 (S.D.N.Y. 1989).

290. *See* Community Nutrition Inst. v. Young, 773 F.2d 1356, 1363 (D.C. Cir. 1985) (aspartame); *cf.* Simpson v. Young, 854 F.2d 1429, 1431 (D.C. Cir. 1988) (FD&C Blue No. 2); *Scott*, 728 F.2d at 324 (D&C Green No. 5); Daryl M. Freedman, *Reasonable Certainty of No Harm: Reviving the Safety Standard for Food Additives, Color Additives, and Animal Drugs*, 7 ECOLOGY L.Q. 245, 255-73 (1978) (concluding that FDA and judicial interpretations of the food additive safety standard are overly permissive).

291. 21 C.F.R. § 170.3(i) (1996); *see also id.* § 170.20(a) ("[T]he Commissioner will give due weight to the anticipated levels and patterns of consumption of the additive specified or reasonably inferrable."). This interpretation of the safety standard comports with the legislative history. *See* H.R. REP. NO. 2284, 85th Cong., 2d Sess. 5 (1958) ("In determining the 'safety' of an additive, scientists must take into consideration the cumulative effect of such additive in the diet of man or animals over their respective life spans together with any chemically or pharmacologically related substances in such diet."). The FDA typically uses the estimated 90th percentile chronic intake as the proper measure of consumption. *See, e.g.*, 53 Fed. Reg. 6595, 6597-98 (1988).

292. 21 C.F.R. § 170.20(a) (1996).

293. *Id.* § 170.22.

294. *See* Rulis, *supra* note 218, at 537; *see also* 60 Fed. Reg. 36,582, 36,583 n.1 (1995). Efforts have been made to disaggregate the different uncertainty factors imbedded in this margin of safety. *See* WHO, *Principles for the Safety Assessment of Food Additives and Contaminants in Food*, ENVTL. HEALTH CRITERIA No. 70 (1987) (suggesting 10-fold uncertainty factors for both interspecies differences and interindividual variations); A.G. Renwick, *Data-Derived Safety Factors for the Evaluation of Food Additives and Environmental Contaminants*, 10 FOOD ADDITIVES & CONTAMINANTS 275 (1993) (suggesting further subdivision of each 10-fold uncertainty factor to account for individual differences in sensitivity and pharmacokinetic differences).

295. *See* Rulis & Tarantino, *supra* note 215, at 138; Rulis, *supra* note 218, at 536-38. Dr. Rulis, then the Chief of the FDA's Regulatory Food Chemistry Branch and the manager of the food additives program, concluded that the "inquiry must not be so stringent as to make it impossible for additives to be approved; it must be finite in scope. Yet, it must be rigorous enough to ensure with reasonable certainty that additives are safe for consumption by the consumers." *Id.* at 544; *see also id.* at 536 ("If the FDA's scientists approached this problem as some of their counterparts in academia might, they would be prepared to ask an infinite range of questions.").

296. Taylor, *supra* note 192, at 204.

297. *See infra* note 504.

298. *See* Rulis & Tarantino, *supra* note 215, at 138; *see also 1995 Hearings*, *supra* note 1, at 184 (statement of Michael F. Jacobson, Executive Director, CSPI) ("Efforts to accelerate the review process must take into account the complexity of this post-filing review, and must acknowledge that clearing up unresolved issues can take years."); Rulis, *supra* note 218, at 536 ("The scientific aspects of the evaluation are conducted simultaneously within several separate scientific disciplines. . . . This parallel review procedure decentralizes petition review and makes it possible for scientific questions to be resolved under a type of consensus system. . . .").

299. *See 1957 Hearings*, *supra* note 25, at 459 (HEW memorandum) ("The [FDA] agrees that a fixed set of uniform test procedures which are prescribed and obligatory would serve effectively to slow down progress in the development of more effective procedures and methods. . . . [T]he scientist working in this field and utilizing his training and experience should be able to design for each proposed additive the research program which will be most likely to yield helpful information."); *cf. id.* at 67 (statement of Charles W. Dunn, counsel for the Grocery Manufacturers of America) (urging that the statute specify the appropriate testing procedures). For a description of the FDA's early guidelines on this subject, see Arnold J. Lehman et al., *Procedures for the Appraisal of the Toxicity of Chemicals in Foods*, 4 FOOD DRUG COSM. L.J. 412 (1949); *see also* NRC, *Principles and Procedures for Evaluating the Safety of Intentional Chemical Additives in Foods* (1954).

300. 21 C.F.R. § 170.20(a) (1996).

301. *Id.* § 170.20(b); *see also id.* § 10.90(b)(1)(i) (Although persons are free to use procedures other than those identified as acceptable in guidelines, the FDA encourages such persons to "discuss the matter in advance with FDA to prevent the expenditure of money and effort on activity that may later be determined to be unacceptable.").

302. *See Food Additives: Competitive, Regulatory, and Safety Problems: Hearings Before the Senate Select Comm. on Small Business*, 95th Cong., 1st Sess. 57-60 (1977) (statement of Sherwin Gardner, Acting Commissioner of Food and Drugs); *see also* Howard R. Roberts, *Food Additives—A Study in the Evolution of Safety*, 31 FOOD DRUG COSM. L.J. 404,

409 (1976); Alan M. Rulis & Richard J. Ronk, *Cyclic Review—Looking Backward or Looking Forward?*, 36 FOOD DRUG COSM. L.J. 156, 157-59 (1981).

303. *See* Hutt, *supra* note 1, at 122 (explaining that the process "died a natural death by the mid-1980s" because the Agency's goal "was clearly unachievable"); *see also 1995 Hearings*, *supra* note 1, at 41 (statement of Richard L. Hall, Chairman, NAS Food Forum) ("Due partly to the progress of toxicology, but even more to the phenomenal advances in analytical chemistry, we are now aware of possible hazards, often remote or simply theoretical, of which, 20 or 40 years ago, we were blissfully unaware.").

304. *See* 47 Fed. Reg. 46,141 (1982). The notice explains that the principles will not apply to the review of indirect additives. *Id.* at 46,142; *see also* Edward F. Bouchard, *The Food and Drug Administration's Redbook: The Practical Implications for Business Practices*, 39 FOOD DRUG COSM. L.J. 211 (1984); Hutt, *supra* note 1, at 124 (criticizing the evolution of the Redbook into a "rigid compendium of required tests designed more to protect an FDA reviewer from criticism than to protect the consuming public"). For a description of international efforts on this subject, see 60 Fed. Reg. 53,078, 53,083-84 (1995) (announcing the FDA's policy on harmonization efforts and explaining that Redbook II will take into account existing OECD guidelines); Charles Feldberg, *The Food and Drug Administration's* Redbook*: International Implications*, 38 FOOD DRUG COSM. L.J. 368 (1983).

305. 58 Fed. Reg. 16,536 (1993). Some of the important changes include recommendations for routine neurotoxicity and immunotoxicity screening assays.

306. *See Food Additive Approvals to Halt if Redbook II Adopted*, FOOD CHEM. NEWS, Jan. 3, 1994, at 41. The notice of availability of the original Redbook, 47 Fed. Reg. at 46,141-42, nowhere suggested that the FDA would apply its guidelines to GRAS determinations.

307. *See* 21 C.F.R. § 10.90(b) (1996); *see also* United States v. Bioclinical Systems, Inc., 666 F. Supp. 82, 83-84 (D. Md. 1987) (rebuffing the FDA's effort to impose new requirements announced in a guideline rather than a duly promulgated regulation).

308. *See* 57 Fed. Reg. 6667, 6669 & n.2 (1992); *see also* Simpson v. Young, 854 F.2d 1429, 1435 (D.C. Cir. 1988) (holding that the FDA need not demand adherence to the guidelines set out in the Redbook given the "permissive language in the manual").

309. *See* 57 Fed. Reg. 47,314 (1992).

310. *See, e.g.*, H.R. 6747, 85th Cong., 1st Sess. § 5 (409(c)(3)) (1957); *see also 1957 Hearings*, *supra* note 25, at 22 (HEW memorandum) ("[T]he law should make certain that no active poison be allowed in the food supply in any case where its use, or the particular level of use, is not clearly shown to result in a definite benefit to the producer or consumer."); *id.* at 257 (statement of Hon. John D. Dingell) (suggesting that "for many centuries the human race has gotten along without these things, and if these things serve no useful purpose, there is no reason for adding them"); *id.* at 448-53 (statement of George P. Larrick, Commissioner of Food and Drugs).

311. *See, e.g.*, *1957 Hearings*, *supra* note 25, at 68-69 (statement of Charles W. Dunn, counsel for the Grocery Manufacturers of America); *id.* at 117 (statement of Lawrence A. Coleman, appearing on behalf of the Manufacturing Chemists' Association) (joining "the overwhelming consensus of food manufacturers" in opposition of any consideration of functional value); *1956 Hearings*, *supra* note 19, at 74 (statement of Glenn G. Paxton, appearing as counsel for various food industry associations) ("[I]t would be a mistake to inject into legislation dealing with questions of safety or toxicity of foods questions as to the functional value of a given ingredient.").

312. *See* Food Additives Amendment of 1958, Pub. L. No. 85-929, § 4, 72 Stat. 1786 (codified at 21 U.S.C. § 348(c)(4) (1994)); H.R. REP. NO. 2284, 85th Cong., 2d Sess. 6 (1958) (This standard "does not involve any judgment on the part of the Secretary of whether such effect results in any added 'value' to the consumer of such food or enhances the marketability from a merchandising point of view."); *1957 Hearings*, *supra* note 25, at 503 (statement of Charles W. Dunn, counsel for the Grocery Manufacturers of America); Bernard L. Oser, *The Functional Value of Food Additives*, 13 FOOD DRUG COSM. L.J. 131 (1958); *see also* H.R. REP. NO. 1338, 92d Cong., 2d Sess. 6 (1972).

313. *See* 41 Fed. Reg. 53,600, 53,601 (1976) ("The ordinary understanding of the term 'safe' would require some benefit-to-risk analysis in such circumstances."). The Agency suggested that it might tolerate chronic risks posed by a major food source but not the same risk if posed by a minor additive. *See id.* Nonetheless, the FDA deleted from the regulations a separate reference to benefits because they will only occasionally be relevant and are sufficiently subsumed within the safety determination. *See id.*; *see also* Merrill, *supra* note 10, at 246 (noting that the statute "does not state whether other considerations may enter into [the FDA's] judgment"). Similarly, the EPA "has interpreted the general safety clause in

section 409 as allowing the balancing of risks and benefits," 55 Fed. Reg. 17,560, 17,561 (1990), though it previously had noted that the FDA applies a risk-only interpretation. 53 Fed. Reg. 41,126, 41,127 (1988).

314. *See* 44 Fed. Reg. 54,852, 54,882 (1979) ("This language . . . has never been the basis for an agency decision. . . . [T]here is no justification for such a statement either in the statute itself or in its legislative history."). The controversy over saccharin had peaked two years earlier.

315. 21 U.S.C. § 348(c)(3)(A) (1994). Substantially similar clauses appear in provisions governing animal drugs and color additives. *See id.* §§ 360b(d)(1)(H), 379e(b)(5)(B).

316. Merrill, *supra* note 10, at 178; *see also* Frederick H. Degnan & W. Gary Flamm, *Living with and Reforming the Delaney Clause*, 50 FOOD & DRUG L.J. 235, 244-56 (1995). Most of the commentary on this subject has been critical. *See, e.g.*, Charles H. Blank, *The Delaney Clause: Technical Naïveté and Scientific Advocacy in the Formulation of Public Health Policies*, 62 CAL. L. REV. 1084, 1116-20 (1974); Margaret Gilhooley, *Plain Meaning, Absurd Results and the Legislative Purpose: The Interpretation of the Delaney Clause*, 40 ADMIN. L. REV. 267, 296-301 (1988); Richard A. Merrill, *FDA's Implementation of the Delaney Clause: Repudiation of Congressional Choice or Reasoned Adaptation to Scientific Progress?*, 5 YALE J. ON REG. 1, 74-88 (1988).

317. *See, e.g.*, Timothy Noah, *Congress Eases Rules for Pesticides in Processed Foods*, WALL ST. J., July 25, 1996, at A22 ("Ending two decades of fighting between consumer groups and the food industry, Congress voted to eliminate the Delaney Clause, a 1958 law that prohibits even minute traces of carcinogens in processed foods.").

318. *See* 21 U.S.C. § 342(a)(2) (1994), repealed and replaced by the Food Quality Protection Act of 1996, Pub. L. No. 104-170, §§ 404, 405, 110 Stat. 1514; *see also* Edward Dunkelberger & Richard A. Merrill, *The Delaney Paradox Reexamined: Regulating Pesticides in Processed Foods*, 48 FOOD & DRUG L.J. 411, 430-37 (1993).

319. *See* 104 CONG. REC. 17,414 (1958) (statement of Hon. Oren Harris); 104 CONG. REC. 17,420 (1958) (statement of Hon. James J. Delaney). The subject was, however, discussed at some length during the Subcommittee's earlier hearings. *See, e.g., 1957 Hearings*, *supra* note 25, at 168-69 (statement of Hon. James J. Delaney) (explaining his introduction of a new bill revised only to add the anti-cancer clause); *id.* at 383 (letter from James S. Adams, American Cancer Society) (recommending the inclusion of such a clause).

320. S. REP. NO. 2422, 85th Cong., 2d Sess. 10-11 (1958); *see also* 104 CONG. REC. 17,414 (1958) (statement of Hon. Oren Harris) ("While the Committee felt that the bill as reported by the committee includes the matter covered by the Delaney amendment in the general language contained in the bill, there was no objection to the addition of the amendment suggested by Mr. Delaney."); 104 Cong. Rec. 17,415 (1958) (letter from Elliot L. Richardson, Assistant Secretary of HEW) ("To single out one class of diseases for special mention would be anomalous and could be misinterpreted. . . . At the same time, if it would serve to allay any lingering apprehension on the part of those who desire an explicit statutory mandate on this point, the Department would interpose no objection to appropriate mention of cancer in food additives legislation."); *cf.* H.R. REP. NO. 2284, 85th Cong., 2d Sess. 5 (1958) ("Since the scientific investigation and the other relevant data to be taken into consideration by the Secretary include information with respect to possible cancer causing characteristics of a proposed additive, the public will be protected from possible harm on this count."). The Delaney clause prompted some minor debate on the floor of the House. *See* 104 CONG. REC. 17,421-22 (1958).

321. *See 1957 Hearings*, *supra* note 25, at 170 (statement of Dr. William E. Smith) (explaining that the proposed clause "enables the Secretary to exercise judgment in evaluating claims for carcinogenicity of chemicals"); *see also Color Additives: Hearings Before the House Comm. on Interstate and Foreign Commerce*, 86th Cong., 2d Sess. 501 (1960) (statement of Arthur S. Flemming, Secretary of HEW) ("[T]he opposition to the inclusion of an anticancer clause arises largely out of a misunderstanding of how this provision works. It allows the Department and its scientific people full discretion and judgment in deciding whether a substance has been shown to cause cancer. . . ."); Merrill, *supra* note 10, at 182 ("[S]cientific judgment has played, and apparently was intended to play, an important role in the policy's application.").

322. *See, e.g.*, 42 Fed. Reg. 48,528, 48,543 (1977) (explaining that "a carcinogenic substance *per se* cannot be considered [GRAS]," and also that a "substance that is the subject of testing whose preliminary results strongly indicate that it will be shown to be carcinogenic cannot be considered [GRAS]"); 34 Fed. Reg. 17,063 (1969) (deleting cyclamate from the GRAS list because of evidence of carcinogenicity in laboratory animals); *cf.* Public Citizen v. Young, 831 F.2d 1108, 1119-20 (D.C. Cir. 1987) (noting in dicta that the GRAS exception "may permit a *de minimis* exception at a stage that logically precedes the FDA's ever reaching the food additive Delaney Clause").

323. 44 Fed. Reg. 39,858 (1979).

324. 50 Fed. Reg. 10,372 (1985). The FDA has on a number of occasions explicitly endorsed the OSTP guidelines. *See, e.g.*, 52 Fed. Reg. 49,572, 49,577-78 (1987).

325. The IRLG report summarized the role of judgment in evaluating evidence from animal tests in the following terms:

> Determination that a causal relationship exists between a test treatment and the responses observed in a bioassay is a complex judgmental activity that includes evaluation of the identity of the test agent and the biologic test system, the conditions of exposure, the methods of observation, and the qualitative and quantitative nature of the pathologic response. The assessment of carcinogenicity therefore relies upon the judgment and expertise of professionals.

44 Fed. Reg. at 39,862-63. The detailed discussions concerning bioassay design, pathological evaluation of the test animals, and the statistical analysis of study results demonstrate that scientific judgment pervades any assessment of a substance's carcinogenicity. The OSTP digest of principles for evaluating chemical carcinogens makes the same points. 50 Fed. Reg. at 10,414-19; *cf.* 61 Fed. Reg. 17,960 (1996) (proposing revisions to the EPA's cancer assessment guidelines).

326. 52 Fed. Reg. at 49,577 (quoting with approval from a report of the Interdisciplinary Panel on Carcinogenicity entitled *Criteria for Evidence of Chemical Carcinogenicity*, 225 SCIENCE 682, 683 (1984)); *see also* 50 Fed. Reg. at 10,415 (OSTP guidelines emphasizing the need for biological as well as statistical significance); 45 Fed. Reg. 61,474, 61,478 (1980) (The Commissioner's final decision denying the food additive petition for cyclamate explained that "there is an interrelationship between statistical significance and biological significance. Scientists view the statistical and the biological data together to determine what, if any, conclusions can be drawn from the results of the study.").

327. 50 Fed. Reg. at 10,417.

328. *See, e.g.*, 51 Fed. Reg. 41,765, 41,767-71 (1986) (Yellow No. 6); 48 Fed. Reg. 5252, 5254-57 (1983) (Blue No. 2); 47 Fed. Reg. 24,278, 24,281-83 (1982) (Green No. 5).

329. 48 Fed. Reg. at 5257 ("[B]iological factors must be brought to bear and may be determinative when evaluating the results of a carcinogenesis bioassay.").

330. 47 Fed. Reg. at 24,283. "Thus, in acceptable carcinogenicity bioassays in two species where numerous tissues were examined in both sexes, a slightly higher [though by some measures statistically significant] number of neoplasms was observed in only one site (the liver), one dose group of one sex and in one species." *Id.* (adding that "all other evidence indicates that the effect was unlikely to be related to treatment with D&C Green No. 5").

331. 47 Fed. Reg. 49,629 (1982).

332. 57 Fed. Reg. 6667, 6675 (1992). "The evidence can reasonably include a dose response or a lack of a dose response, consideration of historical controls, associated pathological data, the time to induction [of] tumors, and the multiplicity of tumors." 53 Fed. Reg. 28,379, 28,381 (1988).

333. 57 Fed. Reg. at 6674-75; *see also* 61 Fed. Reg. 3118, 3128-30 (1996) (disregarding various effects observed in chronic rodent studies in the course of approving the new food additive olestra).

334. 38 Fed. Reg. 10,458, 10,460 (1973).

> [E]ven some human nutrients—such as selenium, chromium, and nickel—when isolated and administered to laboratory animals in the enormous quantities represented by the maximum tolerated dose, have been found to be carcinogenic. In short, without interposing an evaluation of genuine risk of causing cancer, a regulatory assumption that any chemical that has a carcinogenic effect of any kind is unsafe could require that a significant portion of the food supply be banned.

52 Fed. Reg. 5081, 5083 (1987); *see also* 58 Fed. Reg. 33,690, 33,694 (1993) (same); Richard A. Merrill et al., *The FDA's Authority Under the Delaney Clause to Consider Mechanisms of Action in Determining Whether Additives "Induce Cancer,"* 47 FOOD & DRUG L.J. 77 (1992); Bruce N. Ames et al., *Ranking Possible Carcinogenic Hazards*, 236 SCIENCE 271, 277 (1987); *Indirect Mechanisms of Carcinogenesis Discussed at FDA Workshop*, FOOD CHEM. NEWS, Mar. 11, 1996, at 24.

335. *See* 39 Fed. Reg. 1355 (1974); 38 Fed. Reg. 10,458 (1973). In addition to selenium, the Agency has permitted the continuing use of suspected secondary carcinogens such as the antioxidant butylated hydroxyanisole (BHA), 21 C.F.R. § 172.110 (1996), and the indirect food additive melamine, *id.* § 175.105; 49 Fed. Reg. 18,120, 18,121 (1984) (proposed EPA tolerance citing FDA conclusions).

336. *See, e.g., Indirect Mechanisms of Carcinogenesis Discussed at FDA Workshop*, FOOD CHEM. NEWS, Mar. 11, 1996, at 24.

337. 47 Fed. Reg. 14,464, 14,466-68 (1982); *see also Agriculture, Rural Development and Related Agencies Appropriations for 1984 (Part 4): Hearing Before a Subcomm. of the House Comm. on Appropriations*, 98th Cong., 1st Sess. 472-77 (1983) (testimony of Arthur H. Hayes, Commissioner of Food and Drugs). Thus, the FDA approved D&C Green No. 5 even though it contained D&C Green No. 6 which was manufactured with and contained trace levels of p-toluidine, a suspect carcinogen. 47 Fed. Reg. 24,278 (1978); *see also* 60 Fed. Reg. 36,582, 36,589 (1995) (clarifying that references to carcinogenicity in the "threshold of regulation" policy referred only to the food-contact substance and not to any of its impurities); 51 Fed. Reg. 4177, 4180 (1986) (applying constiuents policy to vinyl chloride polymers, an indirect food additive); 49 Fed. Reg. 36,635, 36,636-37 (1984) (same, for acrylonitrile copolymers).

338. *See* Scott v. FDA, 728 F.2d 322, 325 (6th Cir. 1984) (holding that the Delaney clause is satisfied if the color additive as a whole did not cause cancer in animals, irrespective of whether constituents or impurities present in the additive may be carcinogenic).

339. 21 C.F.R. § 173.255(c) (1996).

340. 50 Fed. Reg. 51,551, 51,557 (1985).

341. *See* 47 Fed. Reg. 14,464, 14,466 (1982) ("As the number of chemicals that are found to cause cancer in animals has grown, and as scientists' ability to detect the components of a substance has become more acute, the chances that a food additive or color additive will be found to contain a carcinogenic chemical entity increase."); 44 Fed. Reg. 17,070, 17,075 (1979) (noting that detection limits have improved by several orders of magnitude).

342. 21 U.S.C. § 348(c)(1)(A) (1994); *see also* 21 C.F.R. § 171.100(a) (1996) (tracking statutory language). Another subsection authorizes the FDA to fix tolerances if necessary to assure safe use at a level no higher than reasonably required to achieve the additive's effect. *See* 21 U.S.C. § 348(c)(4) (1994); 21 C.F.R. § 170.18 (1996).

343. For instance, in approving the food additive olestra, the FDA required special labeling, vitamin fortification and postmarketing studies. *See* 61 Fed. Reg. 3118, 3172-73 (1996) (codified at 21 C.F.R. § 172.867(d)-(f) (1996)), discussed *infra* Part V.C. The Agency properly conceded that its misbranding rather than food additive authority provided the legal foundation for this special labeling requirement. *See* 61 Fed. Reg. at 3160-61 & n.83.

344. *See* 21 C.F.R. § 170.30(j) (1996); *id.* § 184.1(b)(1) ("[W]hen the safety of an ingredient has been evaluated on the basis of limited conditions of use, the agency will describe in the regulation that affirms the GRAS status of the ingredient, one or more of these limited conditions of use, which may include the category of food(s), the technical effect(s) or functional use(s) of the ingredient, and the level(s) of use.").

345. *See generally* Lars Noah, *The Imperative to Warn: Disentangling the "Right to Know" from the "Need to Know" About Consumer Product Hazards*, 11 YALE J. ON REG. 293 (1994).

346. 58 Fed. Reg. 24,314, 24,314 (1993); *see also* 56 Fed. Reg. 28,592, 28,615 (1991) ("[T]he information present in the ingredient list is adequate to enable the consumer to avoid ingredients of concern."). Allergic responses to proteins in common foods can be quite serious. *See* Hugh A. Sampson et al., *Fatal and Near-Fatal Anaphylactic Reactions to Food in Children and Adolescents*, 327 NEW ENGL. J. MED. 380 (1992).

347. *See* 21 C.F.R. § 74.705(d)(2) (1996). A comparable requirement applies to drugs containing Yellow No. 5. *See id.* §§ 74.1705(c)(3), 201.20(a).

348. *See id.* §§ 101.100(a)(4), 130.9. By comparison, prescription drugs must include a "warning" statement about sulfiting agents in labeling. *Id.* § 201.22(b).

349. *See id.* §§ 172.110(c)(2) (BHA), 172.170(b)(1) (sodium nitrate), 172.175(b)(1) (sodium nitrite), 172.375(b)(2) (potassium iodide).

350. *Id.* §§ 172.170(b)(3), 172.175(b)(3).

351. *See id.* § 172.804(e)(2).

352. *See id.* § 172.841(e) ("The label and labeling of food a single serving of which would be expected to exceed 15 grams of [polydextrose] shall bear the statement: 'Sensitive individuals may experience a laxative effect from excessive consumption of this product.'"); *id.* § 172.867(e) (olestra); *id.* § 184.1835(e) ("The label and labeling of food whose reasonably foreseeable consumption may result in a daily ingestion of 50 grams of sorbitol shall bear the statement: 'Excess consumption may have a laxative effect.'"); *id.* § 180.25(e) (same requirement for mannitol).

353. 42 Fed. Reg. 6835, 6836 (1977).

354. *See* 44 Fed. Reg. 37,212, 37,214 (1979) (adding, however, that it would reconsider proposals for a ban if the labeling requirements prove to be inadequate).

355. 51 Fed. Reg. 25,012, 25,012-13 (1986) (noting that "labeling alone will not always provide adequate protection for sulfite-sensitive individuals"); *see also* 55 Fed. Reg. 9826 (1990) (revoking the GRAS status of sulfiting agents used on "fresh" potatoes), *withdrawn,* 59 Fed. Reg. 65,938 (1994) (withdrawing revocation after it was invalidated by a court on procedural grounds).

356. 51 Fed. Reg. at 25,013; *see also* 50 Fed. Reg. 13,306, 13,306 (1985) (in proposing the regulation, the FDA explained that "a label declaration of sulfites in food will enable persons intolerant to sulfites to minimize their exposure to these ingredients"). In extending this ingredient declaration requirement to standardized foods, the Agency repeated its earlier conclusion that, notwithstanding the fact that sulfites "are one of the few food ingredients known to cause anaphylactic shock and death," it is "[un]necessary to require a warning statement on food labels or to ban all uses of sulfites." 58 Fed. Reg. 2850, 2855-56 (1993).

357. *See, e.g.*, 21 C.F.R. § 101.4(d) (1996) (when used in food products represented as "nondairy," caseinate will have to be described as "(a milk derivative)"); *see also id.* § 184.1498(b)(3) (GRAS affirmation of microparticulated protein conditioned on disclosure of protein source for the benefit of consumers allergic to milk or eggs).

358. 58 Fed. Reg. 2850, 2872 (1993); *see also* 56 Fed. Reg. 28,592, 28,615 (1991) (declining "to require warnings for ingredients that only cause mild idiosyncratic responses").

359. 56 Fed. Reg. 28,592, 28,615 (1991). The Agency recently reiterated that it "does not intend to require warning statements [on food labels] except in specific instances where there is scientifically based evidence of a potential health hazard." 58 Fed. Reg. at 2872.

360. 44 Fed. Reg. 59,509, 59,513 (1979).

361. *See* 42 Fed. Reg. 19,996, 20,002 (1977); *see also* Curtis C. Travis et al., *Cancer Risk Management: A Review of 132 Federal Regulatory Decisions*, 21 ENVTL. SCI. TECH. 415, 417 (1987) (noting that the lifetime human cancer risk extrapolated from the animal data then available was one-in-2500).

362. *See* 42 Fed. Reg. 52,814, 52,814 (1977) (rejecting a suggestion that the labels of contaminated food products bear a warning because, "[i]f any food is found to be hazardous to health, FDA will not permit it to be distributed"); *see also* Richard M. Cooper, *Freedom of Choice in the Real World*, 34 FOOD DRUG COSM. L.J. 612, 622-23 (1979) (defending FDA policy of regulating hazards in food through prohibitions rather than warnings).

363. *See* Peter Barton Hutt, *Public Policy Issues in Regulating Carcinogens in Food*, 33 FOOD DRUG COSM. L.J. 541, 556 (1978); Peter Barton Hutt, *The Basis and Purpose of Government Regulation of Adulteration and Misbranding of Food*, 33 FOOD DRUG COSM. L.J. 505, 537-39 (1978) (arguing that risk labeling may be appropriate whenever an outright prohibition would restrict consumer freedom of choice); Note, *Health Regulation of Naturally Hazardous Foods: The FDA Ban on Swordfish*, 85 HARV. L. REV. 1025, 1041, 1044-46 (1972) (arguing that a labeling requirement would have been more appropriate than the strict limits on mercury contamination of fish adopted by the FDA).

364. *See* 56 Fed. Reg. 28,592, 28,615 (1991) (expressing concern that such a requirement "would overexpose consumers to warnings," and that then "consumers may ignore, and become inattentive to, all such statements"). In the final regulations, the Agency affirmed its tentative conclusion, citing comments "that an overabundance of warning statements may desensitize the general public to safety concerns and subsequently cause warning statements to lose some of their value as a means of informing the consumer about potential health hazards." 58 Fed. Reg. 2850, 2872 (1993).

365. *See* Richard M. Cooper, *A Time to Warn and a Time to Ban*, *in* PRODUCT LABELING AND HEALTH RISKS 299, 302 (Louis A. Morris et al. eds., 1980). *See generally* Richard Zeckhauser, *Measuring Risks and Benefits of Food Safety Decisions*, 38 VAND. L. REV. 539 (1985).

366. *See* David McCallum, *Risk Factors for Cardiovascular Disease: Cholesterol, Salt, and High Blood Pressure*, *in* RISK COMMUNICATION 67, 69 (J. CLARENCE DAVIES et al. eds., 1987) (Risk communication "campaigns must recognize

overall nutrition and the interaction of dietary factors. (For example, not drinking milk to avoid fat rather than drinking low-fat milk can lead to calcium deficiencies.)"). *See generally* NRC, DIET AND HEALTH: IMPLICATIONS FOR REDUCING CHRONIC DISEASE RISK (1989).

367. *See* Merrill, *supra* note 10, at 206 (suggesting that the statute only covers the labeling of bulk quantities of an additive sold to food processors and other commercial users).

368. *See* 61 Fed. Reg. 3118, 3160 & n.83 (1996) (approving olestra). This question is discussed more fully in Part V.C *infra*.

369. *Compare* 21 U.S.C. § 348(c)(3)(B) (1994) (listing grounds for denial) *with id.* § 348(c)(1) (listing conditions "under which such additive may be safely used").

370. *See* Rulis, *supra* note 218, at 540-41; Taylor, *supra* note 192, at 210.

371. *See* 38 Fed. Reg. 5921 (1973).

372. *See* 39 Fed. Reg. 27,317, 27,320 (1974) (codified as amended at 21 C.F.R. § 172.804(c) (1996)) (approving the use of aspartame as a tabletop sweetener and in cold breakfast cereals, powdered beverages, desserts, dessert toppings and chewing gum). Technically, aspartame is a nutritive rather than non-nutritive sweetener, but its caloric contribution is trivial because this substance is almost 200 times sweeter than an equal quantity of sugar. *See* 46 Fed. Reg. 38,284, 38,285 (1981).

373. *See* 39 Fed. Reg. 27,317, 27,320 (1974) (codified at 21 C.F.R. § 172.804(e)(2) (1996)). In addition, labeling of tabletop sweeteners containing aspartame must advise consumers not to use it in cooking or baking. *See id.* (§ 172.804(e)(3)). This latter requirement exists for functional rather than safety reasons. *See id.* at 27,318 (explaining that, under prolonged heating, aspartame breaks down to diketopiperazine (DKP) and loses sweetness, adding that the safety of DKP remains under investigation).

374. *See* 40 Fed. Reg. 56,907 (1975); *see also* GAO, REGULATION OF THE FOOD ADDITIVE ASPARTAME, No. MWD-76-111 (1976). An independent audit eventually validated the study results. *See* 44 Fed. Reg. 31,716, 31,717 (1979).

375. *See* 45 Fed. Reg. 2908 (1980); 44 Fed. Reg. at 31,717. Normally, an Administrative Law Judge (ALJ) would conduct such a hearing, but the objectors agreed to the modified procedure and submitted a slate of names from which Board members would be selected.

376. *See In re* Aspartame, Food Drug Cosm. L. Rep. (CCH) ¶ 38,072 (Sept. 30, 1980); *see also* 45 Fed. Reg. 69,558 (1980) (announcing the availability of the Board's decision); Sidney A. Shapiro, *Scientific Issues and the Function of Hearing Procedures: Evaluating the FDA's Public Board of Inquiry*, 1986 DUKE L.J. 288, 307-13; Todd R. Smyth, Note, *The FDA's Public Board of Inquiry and the Aspartame Decision*, 58 IND. L.J. 627 (1983).

377. *See* 46 Fed. Reg. 50,947 (1981) (vacating stay); 46 Fed. Reg. 38,284, 38,287-89 (1981) (Commissioner's final decision) (commenting that "[f]ew compounds have withstood such detailed testing and repeated, close scrutiny").

378. 46 Fed. Reg. at 38,303. "One assumption in this proceeding is that extremely high amounts of aspartame's component amino acids may cause brain damage. Aspartame is being approved only because the available data establish that the maximum projected consumption of aspartame is still far, far below any level even suspected of being toxic. Nevertheless, prudence dictates that these estimated use levels be compared to actual use levels to ensure the validity of the safety assessment." *Id.* The FDA did not require additional safety information.

379. *See* Pub. L. No. 97-414, § 11, 96 Stat. 2049, 2065 (1983) (codified at 35 U.S.C. § 155 (1994)). The patent term extension represented a floor amendment to a bill amending the Orphan Drug Act and triggered little debate. *See* 128 CONG. REC. 26,979 (1982) (amendment introduced by Sen. Byrd); 128 CONG. REC. 30,451 (1982) (statement by Hon. Henry Waxman) (explaining simply that "the Senate amendment extends the patent for a food additive").

380. *See* 47 Fed. Reg. 46,140 (1982).

381. *See* 48 Fed. Reg. 31,376, 31,382 (1983) (codified at 21 C.F.R. § 172.804(c)(6) (1996)). In the preamble, the Agency reiterated its previous conclusions concerning the safety of aspartame, and it reviewed new information including studies on DKP and other degradation/reaction products. *See id.* at 31,378-81.

382. *See* 49 Fed. Reg. 6672 (1984); *see also* 48 Fed. Reg. 52,899 (1983) (rejecting requests for a stay).

383. *See* Community Nutrition Inst. v. Young, 773 F.2d 1356, 1362 (D.C. Cir. 1985) (holding that "the FDA properly denied a hearing after finding that petitioners have raised no material issue regarding the safety of the wet use of aspartame"), *cert. denied*, 475 U.S. 1123 (1986).

384. *See id.* at 1362-63 ("The agency's conclusions concerning the safety of the dry use of aspartame, except to the extent that new evidence suggests that the FDA may not rely on these prior findings in its deliberations on wet use, may not be raised again in this proceeding in the interests of administrative finality and judicial economy.").

385. *See id.* at 1364-67 (deferring to the FDA's expert judgment on these matters). The court also found no basis for arguments urging revised labeling requirements. *Id.* at 1366.

386. *See* 21 C.F.R. § 172.804(c)(7)-(23) (1996); *see also id.* § 172.800(c) (acesulfame potassium). The citations to the numerous Federal Register notices announcing amendments for new uses appear at the end of these sections in the regulations.

387. *See* 53 Fed. Reg. 6595, 6600 (1988).

388. *See* 61 Fed. Reg. 33,654, 33,656 (1996) (to be codified at 21 C.F.R. § 172.804).

389. *See, e.g.*, *"NutraSweet"—Health and Safety Concerns: Hearing Before the Senate Comm. on Labor and Human Resources*, 100th Cong., 1st Sess. 1-3 (1987) (statement of Sen. Metzenbaum); GAO, FOOD AND DRUG ADMINISTRATION: FOOD ADDITIVE APPROVAL PROCESS FOLLOWED FOR ASPARTAME, No. HRD-87-46 (1987) (investigating allegations that the FDA had mischaracterized the available safety data); GAO, FOOD AND DRUG ADMINISTRATION: SIX FORMER HHS EMPLOYEES' INVOLVEMENT IN ASPARTAME'S APPROVAL, No. HRD-86-109BR (1986) (investigating allegations of a conflict of interest by several former FDA officials involved in the review of aspartame who later took positions in the private sector); Robert Frank, *Aspartame Critic Seeks More Research on Possibility of Links to Brain Tumors*, WALL ST. J., Nov. 8, 1996, at B5B.

390. *See NutraSweet Hearing*, *supra* note 389, at 209-12 (statement of Frank E. Young, Commissioner of Food and Drugs) (describing the adverse experience monitoring system established by the FDA in light of consumer complaints about aspartame); *see also id.* at 222 (noting that the "FDA does not require the petitioner of an approved food additive to provide safety studies after the additive has been approved unless questions of safety arise"); *id.* at 293-95 (estimating that the FDA already had expended several millions of dollars on aspartame). The FDA created the Adverse Reaction Monitoring System (ARMS) in 1985. *See* Linda Tollefson, *Monitoring Adverse Reactions to Food Additives in the U.S. Food and Drug Administration*, 8 REG. TOXICOL. & PHARMACOL. 438, 441-44 (1988) (noting that the majority of initial reports concerned aspartame and sulfiting agents); Judy Folkenberg, *Reporting Reactions to Additives*, FDA CONSUMER, Oct. 1988, at 16 (same).

391. *See, e.g.*, 57 Fed. Reg. 6667 (1992) (rejecting objections to the approval of acesulfame potassium); Robert Frank, *Sweetener Ace K Faces Challenge Before Approval*, WALL ST. J., July 30, 1996, at B14 (describing CSPI's plans to protest the anticipated approval of acesulfame potassium for wet use); *CSPI Steps Up Pressure on FDA to Deny Artificial Sweetener Petition*, FOOD CHEM. NEWS, Aug. 5, 1996, at 7; *infra* notes 577-81 and accompanying text (discussing pending food additive petition for sucralose).

392. *See* 59 Fed. Reg. 26,647 (1994).

393. *See* 59 Fed. Reg. 26,700, 26,702 (1994).

394. *See* 57 Fed. Reg. 47,608 (1992) (ruling that Calgene's tomato would no longer be considered a regulated article under the Federal Plant Pest Act). Calgene subsequently received similar rulings on several other tomato lines. *See, e.g.*, 60 Fed. Reg. 38,788 (1995). The USDA's regulatory requirements governing agricultural biotechnology, which are implemented by the Animal and Plant Health Inspection Service (APHIS) and appear at 7 C.F.R. pt. 340 (1996), are beyond the scope of this paper.

395. *See* 56 Fed. Reg. 20,004 (1991).

396. *See* 57 Fed. Reg. 22,772, 22,773 (1992) (noting that Calgene's primary interest in the choice of regulatory classification was whether the company would have to prepare an environmental assessment).

397. *See* 57 Fed. Reg. 22,984 (1992). This policy is discussed more fully below.

398. *See* 58 Fed. Reg. 38,429 (1993).

399. *See* 59 Fed. Reg. 26,647, 26,648 (1994) (announcing the availability of the Agency's correspondence with Calgene).

400. *See id.* at 26,648 (citing 21 C.F.R. § 170.30(f)(2), the provision in the regulations which provides that substances of natural biological origin widely consumed prior to 1958 but then significantly altered through selective breeding will be reviewed for possible GRAS affirmation). Of course, as previously explained in Part II, the tomato itself would not be subject to regulation as a "food additive" when sold as produce, even if not GRAS.

401. *See* 55 Fed. Reg. 10,932, 10,935 (1990) (codified at 21 C.F.R. § 184.1685 (1996)); *see also* 53 Fed. Reg. 16,191 (1988) (notice of filing of GRAS affirmation petition for rDNA alpha-amylase enzyme); 51 Fed. Reg. 10,571 (1986) (same); GAO, NEW FOOD TECHNOLOGIES, *supra* note 9, at 42 (noting that the FDA's review of the GRAS affirmation petition for chymosin took 2.5 years and represented "a learning experience for the agency"); Degnan, *supra* note 98, at 580-81 (urging greater reliance on the GRAS exception for bioengineered foods); *cf.* 60 Fed. Reg. 32,904 (1995) (affirming the GRAS status of several enzyme preparations from animal and plant sources).

402. *See* 59 Fed. Reg. 26,700, 26,711 (codified at 21 C.F.R. §§ 173.170, 573.130 (1996)) (approving APH(3')II encoded by the kan^r gene for use in the development of genetically modified cotton, oilseed rape and tomatoes). In the preamble, the FDA emphasized that "[o]nly the translation product of the kan^r gene, APH(3')II, and not the gene itself, is being regulated as a food additive." *Id.* at 26,701 ("[T]he DNA that makes up the kan^r gene does not differ from any other DNA and does not itself pose a safety concern as a component of food.").

403. *See id.* at 26,702-03.

404. *See id.* at 26,703-04.

405. *See id.* at 26,704-06.

406. *See, e.g.*, CFSAN, *Bioengineered Foods Derived from New Plant Varieties* (last modified Aug. 1, 1996) <http://vm.cfsan.fda.gov/~lrd/biocon.txt> (listing 22 final consultations conducted with various companies since the 1994 Calgene approval); BIOTECHNOLOGY AND FOOD INGREDIENTS (ISRAEL GOLDBERG & RICHARD WILLIAMS eds. 1991); Alan Goldhammer, *The Regulation of Agricultural Biotechnology: An Industrial Perspective*, 48 FOOD & DRUG L.J. 501, 509-10 (1993); Rhonda L. Rundle, *Bright Future Is Predicted For Pest-Resistant Seeds*, WALL ST. J., Aug. 31, 1995, at B4.

407. *See* 57 Fed. Reg. 22,984 (1992); *see also* GAO, NEW FOOD TECHNOLOGIES, *supra* note 9, at 9-10, 31-56 (describing the FDA's approach to the regulation of biotechnology as applied to food, and framing the terms of the debate over the proper regulatory approach); Robert A. Bohrer, *Food Products Affected by Biotechnology*, 55 U. PITT. L. REV. 653, 659-66 (1994) (summarizing the FDA's 1992 policy statement).

408. *See* 51 Fed. Reg. 23,309, 23,312-13 (1986) (discussing the GRAS or food additive status of bioengineered food substances); 49 Fed. Reg. 50,878, 50,878 (1984) (same); *see also* 57 Fed. Reg. 6753 (1992) (announcing supplemental OSTP principles); 53 Fed. Reg. 33,182 (1988) (announcing that FASEB would undertake "a study of which scientific concepts and considerations are most appropriately used to determine the regulatory status of foods and food ingredients that are produced by new technologies"); Jeffrey N. Gibbs & Jonathan S. Kahan, *Federal Regulation of Food and Food Additive Biotechnology*, 38 ADMIN. L. REV. 1, 16-26 (1986); Stephen H. McNamara, *FDA Regulation of Food Substances Produced by New Techniques of Biotechnology*, 42 FOOD DRUG COSM. L.J. 50 (1987); Michele J. Brace, Comment, *Regulation of Genetically Engineered Foods Under the Federal Food, Drug, and Cosmetic Act*, 33 AM. U. L. REV. 899 (1984).

409. *See* 61 Fed. Reg. 8291 (1996) (announcing that FASEB will undertake a comprehensive review of the appropriate scientific criteria and principles for the assessment of the safety of food ingredients, noting that recent innovations such as bioengineering may "present new situations for which an alternative approach to safety assessment may be needed"). The 1992 policy statement suggested that "many of the scientific considerations for evaluating the safety and nutritional aspects of food from new plant varieties . . . are similar regardless of the [traditional or new] technology used." 57 Fed. Reg. at 22,991; *see also* International Food Biotechnology Council, *Biotechnologies and Food: Assuring the Safety of Foods Produced by Genetic Modification*, 12 REG. TOXICOL. & PHARMACOL. S1 (1990).

410. *See* 58 Fed. Reg. 25,837 (1993); 57 Fed. Reg. at 22,991. Furthermore, the policy statement lacks any real binding effect. *See supra* note 309 and accompanying text.

411. 57 Fed. Reg. at 22,984. The Agency recognizes that "[m]ost, if not all, cultivated food crops have been genetically modified" by traditional breeding techniques. *Id.* at 22,984 n.3; *see also id.* at 22,985 ("The genetic modification techniques used to develop new plant varieties constitute a continuum."). The policy statement does not address food uses of biotechnology other than in the development of new plant varieties. *See id.* at 22,985; *cf.* Steven W. Frank, *Food Additive Models for the Regulation of Recombinant DNA Technology Under the Federal Food, Drug, and Cosmetic Act*, 45 FOOD DRUG COSM. L.J. 169, 173-79 (1990) (describing the range of potential agricultural applications).

412. 57 Fed. Reg. at 22,986 (describing various genetic modification techniques); *see also* Charles S. Gasser & Robert T. Fraley, *Transgenic Crops*, SCI. AM., June 1992, at 62.

413. 57 Fed. Reg. at 22,985.

414. *See id.* at 22,986-88 (adding that some of these concerns are magnified with regard to plants used in animal feed because of animals' different consumption patterns); *see also* Ron Winslow, *Allergen Is Inadvertently Transferred to Soybean in Bioengineering Test*, WALL ST. J., Mar. 14, 1996, at B6. In its earlier statements, the FDA called for a food additive petition in every case where a substance added to animal feed was produced with recombinant DNA technology. *See* 51 Fed. Reg. 23,302, 23,311 (1986).

415. 57 Fed. Reg. at 22,984. "The method by which food is produced or developed may in some cases help to understand the safety or nutritional characteristics of the finished food. However, the key factors in reviewing safety concerns should be the characteristics of the food product, rather than the fact that the new methods are used." *Id.* at 22,984-85; *see also* OECD, SAFETY EVALUATION OF FOODS DERIVED BY MODERN BIOTECHNOLOGY (1993); David A. Kessler et al., *The Safety of Foods Developed by Biotechnology*, 256 SCIENCE 1747 (1992).

416. 57 Fed. Reg. at 22,990.

417. *See id.*

418. *Id.*

419. *Id.* ("For example, if a food derived from a new plant variety contains a novel protein sweetener as a result of the genetic modification of the plant, that sweetener would likely require submission of a food additive petition. . . ."). The policy does not further define what might constitute a significant modification, though similar language appears in the GRAS regulations. *See* 21 C.F.R. § 170.30(f)(2) (1996); *see also* Gibbs & Kahan, *supra* note 408, at 16 n.80 (noting that, "[a]t one point, FDA had proposed that a 'significant alteration' would be a 10% or greater increase in a toxicant or a 20% or greater reduction in a nutrient . . . [but] [t]hese numerical criteria were not adopted"); Frank, *supra* note 411, at 193. The flow charts make reference to "macroconstituents" as necessitating possible review, but again the Agency fails to define the term. *See* 57 Fed. Reg. at 22,998-23,004.

420. *Id.* at 22,990.

421. *See id.* at 22,991-23,004 (including several flow charts but emphasizing that they do not impose any new regulatory requirements).

422. *Id.* at 22,991. "This guidance section provides a basis for determining whether new plant varieties are as safe and nutritious as their parental varieties." *Id.* at 22,992. This sounds like the test of "substantial equivalence" for medical devices under Section 510(k) of the FD&C Act to determine the need for premarket review. *See* 21 U.S.C. §§ 360(k), 360c(i)(1) (1994); *see also* Lars Noah, *Amplification of Federal Preemption in Medical Device Cases*, 49 FOOD & DRUG L.J. 183, 207-09 (1994). Indeed, the Agency cites international organizations that have proposed a "substantial equivalence" test for new foods. 57 Fed. Reg. at 22,992.

423. *See id.* at 22,985. As a consequence, a petitioner may avoid the need to submit an environmental assessment, a potentially significant matter for biotechnology products even though an assessment may have been submitted at an earlier stage to the USDA or EPA. Food additive and GRAS affirmation petitions must either include an environmental assessment or claim a categorical exclusion. *See* 21 C.F.R. §§ 25.22(a)(10)&(12), 25.24(b) (1996); *see also* Foundation on Economic Trends v. Heckler, 756 F.2d 143, 153-55 (D.C. Cir. 1985) (enjoining deliberate release experiment of genetically engineered organism until the National Institutes of Health completes an environmental assessment). The FDA recently proposed expanding the list of categorical exclusions. *See* 61 Fed. Reg. 14,922, 14,927-29 (1996).

424. *See* Background Material, FDA Joint CFSAN/CVM Advisory Committee Meeting, *Procedures for Industry-FDA Interaction Prior to Commercial Distribution of Foods Derived from New Plant Varieties Developed Using Recombinant DNA Techniques* (last modified Nov. 1994) <http://vm.cfsan.fda.gov/~lrd/biopro.txt>. Previously, FDA officials had expressed concerns that it lacked the statutory authority to create such a premarket notification system. *See* GAO, NEW FOOD TECHNOLOGIES, *supra* note 9, at 12.

425. *See, e.g.*, CFSAN, *Bioengineered Foods Derived from New Plant Varieties* (last modified Aug. 1, 1996) <http://vm.cfsan.fda.gov/~lrd/biocon.txt> (listing 22 final consultations conducted with various companies since the 1994 Calgene approval); *1995 Hearings*, *supra* note 1, at 13 (statement of Linda A. Suydam, Interim Deputy Commissioner of Operations, FDA); *FDA Sets New Procedures for Consulting with Biotech Firms on Safety Issues*, FOOD CHEM. NEWS, July 15, 1996, at 3.

426. *See* 58 Fed. Reg. 25,837, 25,840 (1993) ("Under FDA's policy, such foods will be required to be labeled to alert consumers to potential allergenic substances derived from commonly allergenic foods, unless the developer can demonstrate scientifically that the introduced substance is not allergenic in the new food."); 57 Fed. Reg. at 22,991 ("For example, if a tomato has had a peanut protein introduced into it and there is insufficient information to demonstrate that the introduced protein could not cause an allergic reaction in a susceptible population, a label declaration would be required to alert consumers who are allergic to peanuts so they could avoid that tomato. . . ."); *cf.* H.R. 5401, 102d Cong., 2d Sess. (1992) (proposing to require disclosure in labeling).

427. *See* 58 Fed. Reg. 59,946, 59,947 (1993) (codified at 21 C.F.R. § 522.2112 (1996)).

428. *See* 59 Fed. Reg. 6279 (1994); *see also* Anne Miller, Comment, *Time for Government to Get Mooo-ving: Facing Up to the rBST Labeling Problem*, 18 HAMLINE L. REV. 503 (1995). Producers recently challenged Vermont's rBST disclosure requirement as an abridgement of their First Amendment rights, and the court granted them a preliminary injunction. *See* International Dairy Foods Ass'n v. Amestoy, 92 F.3d 67 (2d Cir. 1996).

429. *See First Biotech Tomato Marketed*, FDA CONSUMER, Sept. 1994, at 3, 4. The tomato has not been a commercial success, however, thanks in part to problems with distribution. *See* Lee Gomes, *Calgene's CEO Quits as Monsanto Co. Acquires Control*, WALL ST. J., Aug. 1, 1996, at B9.

430. *See, e.g.*, GAO, NEW FOOD TECHNOLOGIES, *supra* note 9, at 45-48.

431. *Id.* at 50 (adding that the FDA's policy statement "did not require premarket notification of food developed through new biotechnology"); *see also id.* at 51-52 (canvassing competing arguments and noting uncertainty about the FDA's power to impose a premarket notification system under its existing statutory authority).

432. *Id.* at 48.

433. 61 Fed. Reg. 3118, 3172 (1996) (codified at 21 C.F.R. § 172.867(c) (1996)) (approving the use of olestra in "savory snacks," which are defined as "snacks that are salty or piquant but not sweet").

434. *See* Marian Burros, *Intensifying Debate on a Fat Substitute*, N.Y. TIMES, Jan. 17, 1996, at C1 ("Procter & Gamble has spent $200 million to $300 million on tests of olestra in the last 25 years."). This investment rivals the average R&D costs for new drugs. *See* Joseph A. DiMasi, *Cost of Innovation in the Pharmaceutical Industry*, 10 J. HEALTH ECON. 107, 125-26 (1991) (estimating that, on average, drug research and development costs $231 million and requires twelve years before a new chemical may be introduced in the United States); F-D-C REP. ("The Pink Sheet"), Dec. 18, 1995, at 11 (quoting the latest estimate as approaching $400 million).

435. The term "macroingredient" usually encompasses substances that make up a significant portion of the diet, such as carbohydrates, proteins, and fats, while "micronutrients" generally refer to vitamins and minerals, and "microingredients" might further encompass direct additives such as emulsifiers and preservatives. Other fat substitutes, though less versatile, were already on the market. *See, e.g.*, 21 C.F.R. § 184.1498 (1996) (affirming the GRAS status of a microparticulated egg white and milk protein product as a fat-replacer in frozen desserts).

436. *See* 21 C.F.R. § 172.867(d)-(f) (1996).

437. *See* H.R. 2805, 102d Cong., 1st Sess. § 1 (1991) (requesting a ten-year extension to start running after FDA approval); S. 1506, 102d Cong., 1st Sess. § 1 (1991). One patent already had expired (and three others were likely to expire prior to FDA approval), so the bills technically would revive rather than extend expired patents. Once the patents expired, patent term restoration would not be available, and food additives do not benefit from the market exclusivity alternative available to drugs irrespective of patent status. *See supra* note 234. Because Congress failed to enact the proposed legislation, though both houses had acted favorably on the bills, a new bill was introduced in the next session. *See* S. 409, 103d Cong., 1st Sess. (1993). Ultimately, Congress enacted a provision authorizing interim patent term extensions when the regulatory review period continues beyond the original patent term. *See* Pub. L. No. 103-179, § 5, 107 Stat. 2040 (1993) (codified at 35 U.S.C. § 156(d)(5) (1994)). The FDA approved olestra just one day before the expiration of this interim extension, thereby allowing the company to seek a further two-year patent term extension. *See* Sally Squires, *FDA Decision Nears on Fat Substitute*, WASH. POST, Jan. 23, 1996, at Z8.

438. *See Interim Patent Extensions: Hearing Before the Subcomm. on Intellectual Property and Judicial Administration of the House Comm. on the Judiciary*, 103d Cong., 1st Sess. 19 (1993) (statement of Walker J. Wallace, Vice President of Procter & Gamble) (summarizing olestra's regulatory history); *Patent Term Extension Legislation: Hearing Before the Subcomm. on Intellectual Property and Judicial Administration of the House Comm. on the Judiciary*, 102d Cong., 1st Sess. 369-74 (1991) [hereinafter *House Patent Extension Hearing*] (Procter & Gamble's regulatory chronology); *Patent Extension Hearing: Hearing Before the Subcomm. on Patents, Copyrights and Trademarks of the Sen. Comm. on the*

Judiciary, 102d Cong., 1st Sess. (1991) [hereinafter *Senate Patent Extension Hearing*]; *see also* Richard M. Cooper, *Legislative Patent Extensions*, 48 FOOD & DRUG L.J. 59 (1993).

439. *See* 21 C.F.R. § 172.867(a) (1996). The original patent term extension legislation would have defined "olestra" as "sucrose esterified with four or more fatty acid groups." H.R. 2805, 102d Cong., 1st Sess. § 3(a) (1991).

440. *See* 61 Fed. Reg., at 3130-52 (reviewing drug and nutrient absorption studies).

441. *See id.* at 3152-59 (reviewing gastrointestinal tract studies, concluding that diarrhea-like symptoms reflect a disruption in the fecal matrix and did not cause any adverse health effects such as dehydration or an electrolyte imbalance).

442. Evidently, the company was told that, under then existing FDA policy, a food could make no claims about fatty acid or cholesterol content. *See Senate Patent Extension Hearing*, *supra* note 438, at 455-56, 459 (written responses from Edwin L. Artzt, Chairman and CEO of the Procter & Gamble Co.); GAO, FDA PREMARKET APPROVAL: PROCESS OF APPROVING OLESTRA AS A FOOD ADDITIVE, No. HRD-92-86 (1992), at 5. Also, the investigational exemption for food additives could not be utilized for purposes of undertaking clinical (as opposed to animal) testing. *See* 138 CONG. REC. E2371 (daily ed. Aug. 4, 1992) (memorandum from Richard M. Cooper, counsel for Unilever) (explaining the use of the investigational new drug exemption for this purpose); *supra* notes 236-40 and accompanying text.

443. *See* 52 Fed. Reg. 23,606 (1987) (notice of filing).

444. *See* S. REP. NO. 64, 103d Cong., 1st Sess. 5 & n.16 (1993); H.R. REP. NO. 775, 102d Cong., 2d Sess. 6, 15-17 (1992); *id.* at 23 (dissenting views of Hon. George E. Sangmeister and Hon. Romano L. Mazzoli) ("In fact, that ambiguities persist—despite the GAO's report—only contributes to the case against these patent extensions."); Jennifer Lawrence, *Whatever Happened to Olestra? How P&G's Hopes for Food Division's Future Got Mired in FDA Quicksand*, ADVERTISING AGE, May 2, 1994, at 16. Competitors testified at the hearings in opposition to patent term extension, arguing that any delays in approval resulted from Procter & Gamble's poor business decisions rather than regulatory tardiness. *See, e.g.*, *House Patent Extension Hearing*, *supra* note 438, at 224-51 (statement of Richard A. Goldstein, President and CEO of Unilever United States, Inc.); *see also* 138 CONG. REC. E2369 (daily ed. Aug. 4, 1992) (remarks by Hon. Terry L. Bruce).

445. *See* 61 Fed. Reg. at 3121 (noting "the novel issues raised by the review of the olestra data").

> The difficulty presented by the olestra food additive petition results from a relatively unique intersection of a number of factors, including the following. First, the volume of available safety evidence for olestra is enormous, all of which FDA was obligated to review, evaluate, and synthesize. Second, as a macro-ingredient, olestra is intended to replace a sizeable portion of the diet, and thus, will likely be consumed in relatively large amounts; this alone sets olestra apart from almost all food additives previously reviewed by FDA. Third, olestra presents a number of questions regarding nutritional effects, most of which have not been presented previously to FDA. . . . [B]ecause of the challenge presented by olestra, the agency used an expanded approach to its evaluation. . . .

Id. at 3167; *see also id.* at 3169 (adding that olestra is "a macro-ingredient that is not metabolized, one of the first of its type to be subject to FDA review").

446. *See* 61 Fed. Reg. at 3119; *Senate Patent Extension Hearing*, *supra* note 438, at 302 (statement of Edwin L. Artzt, Chairman and CEO of the Procter & Gamble Co.). In response to comments fearing that the use of olestra would spread to other fatty foods, the FDA explained that its approval was limited and that other uses would require the filing and review of additional food additive petitions. *See* 61 Fed. Reg. at 3166, 3168.

447. *See* 61 Fed. Reg. at 3121.

448. *See* 60 Fed. Reg. 53,790 (1995) (notice of meeting).

449. *See Food Advisory Committee Meeting: Working Group on Olestra*, Nov. 14-17, 1995; *Vitamin Addition, Labeling for Olestra Foods Recommended by Advisory Group*, FOOD CHEM. NEWS, Nov. 20, 1995, at 31 (summarizing what transpired at the meeting); *see also* Henry Blackburn, *Olestra and the FDA*, 334 NEW ENG. J. MED. 984, 985 (1996) (criticizing the FDA's consultation process, as a member of the olestra working group).

450. *See* 60 Fed. Reg. 57,586 (1995) (announcing a deadline of December 1, later extended to December 21, 1995). The FDA then responded to criticisms that it provided insufficient time for comment. *See* 61 Fed. Reg. at 3163; *see also CSPI*

Charges P&G with Deceptively Publicizing Olestra Study, FOOD CHEM. NEWS, Mar. 4, 1996, at 11 (describing letter filed one month after the close of the comment period and one day before approval).

451. *See* 61 Fed. Reg. at 3162 (noting that it had received approximately 2,300 comments, though roughly 2,000 of those were part of a CSPI letter writing campaign urging rejection of the petition).

452. *See CSPI Files Objections to Olestra Decision; P&G Responds to Charges*, FOOD CHEM. NEWS, Mar. 11, 1996, at 15; *see also* 61 Fed. Reg. at 3162-64 (recounting CSPI's aggressive participation during and after the working group meeting to express its opposition); Marian Burros, *Consumer Group Cites Illnesses in Urging Ban of Fat Substitute*, N.Y. TIMES, July 2, 1996, at C8; Henry I. Miller, *The Naderites' Big Fat Problem*, WALL ST. J., July 11, 1996, at A14; Raju Narisetti, *Anatomy of a Food Fight: The Olestra Debate*, WALL ST. J., July 31, 1996, at B1.

453. *See* Marian Burros, *Question at Olestra's Debut: Is the "Fake Fat" Truly Safe?*, N.Y. TIMES, May 20, 1996, at A1. Procter & Gamble sold an exclusive license for olestra (under the tradename Olean) to Frito-Lay. *See Deal Gives Frito-Lay Head Start in Use of P.&G.'s Fat Substitute*, N.Y. TIMES, June 1, 1996, at 35.

454. *See* 61 Fed. Reg. 8291 (1996) (announcing that FASEB will undertake a comprehensive review of the appropriate scientific criteria and principles for the assessment of the safety of food ingredients, especially novel foods); *see also* 58 Fed. Reg. 16,536 (1993) (announcing the availability of a revised draft of the Redbook, which now addresses some of these issues).

455. *See, e.g.*, *Proceedings of the Workshop on Safety and Regulatory Aspects of Macronutrient Substitutes*, 23 REG. TOXICOL. & PHARMACOL. S1-S62 (1996); Joseph F. Borzelleca, *Macronutrient Substitutes: Safety Evaluation*, 16 REG. TOXICOL. & PHARMACOL. 253 (1992).

456. *See* 61 Fed. Reg. at 3120 ("The fact that olestra is not absorbed also means, however, that . . . the safety issues for olestra are focused on effects in the intestine, including potential interference with absorption of nutrients.").

457. *See, e.g.*, *id.* at 3120 (noting that "it is difficult, if not impossible, to feed olestra to laboratory animals in amounts sufficiently high to allow use of the 100-fold safety factor that is commonly used"); Ian C. Munro et al., *Alternative Approaches to the Safety Assessment of Macronutrient Substitutes*, 23 REG. TOXICOL. & PHARMACOL. S6, S7 (1996).

458. *See* Margaret Cheney, *Postmarket Surveillance to Determine Nutritional Impact of Macronutrient Substitutes*, 23 REG. TOXICOL. & PHARMACOL. S22, S23-S24 (1996); Joseph F. Borzelleca, *A Proposed Model for Safety Assessment of Macronutrient Substitutes*, 23 REG. TOXICOL. & PHARMACOL. S15, S17-S18 (1996). In announcing the FASEB review of safety criteria, the Agency posed the following question: "Can postmarketing surveillance (such as monitoring of use or monitoring of adverse reaction reports by consumers and physicians) be used to ensure safety?" 61 Fed. Reg. 8291, 8292 (1996) ("For example, can such surveillance be used without compromising safety to verify exposure estimates or to eliminate the need for specific data prior to marketing . . . ?").

459. *See* 61 Fed. Reg. at 3120-21, 3125-59. All told, the Agency reviewed more than 150,000 pages of data submitted by Procter & Gamble in the original food additive petition and its subsequent amendments. *Olestra Approved with Special Labeling*, FDA CONSUMER, Apr. 1996, at 11.

460. *See* 61 Fed. Reg. at 3119-20. Several comments supporting approval emphasized problems with obesity and "that the health benefits from lower fat intake far outweigh the perceived adverse side effects," *id.* at 3163, but the Agency again noted that such health benefits were not relevant to its decision. *Id.* at 3166.

461. H.R. REP. NO. 775, 102d Cong., 2d Sess. 16 (1992); *see also* GAO, NEW FOOD TECHNOLOGIES, *supra* note 9, at 11 ("New food technologies, such as functional foods, that incorporate specific food components to lower the risk of disease may not fit the existing categories for food and food ingredients. FDA officials and others believe that these products may blur, if not erase, the legal boundary line between foods and drugs. . . . Some advocates of functional foods believe that neither classification provides manufacturers with sufficient incentive to develop these new products and that a new system is needed for regulating these products.").

462. 21 C.F.R. § 172.867(d) (1996); *see also* 61 Fed. Reg. at 3162 ("The agency has not previously approved an additive which interferes with the absorption of vitamins to a degree that necessitates requiring that foods containing the additive be compensated with such vitamins to mitigate the effect of olestra."). In addition, data indicated that olestra would reduce serum levels of carotenoids, substances from fruits and vegetables believed to prevent certain diseases (such as macular degeneration and prostate cancer), but the FDA dismissed these supposed protective effects as unsupported. *See id.* at 3147-49.

463. 21 C.F.R. § 172.867(e) (1996) (specifying the precise placement and format of the required disclosure statement).

464. *See* 61 Fed. Reg. at 3160 n.83 ("FDA is not requiring the labeling of olestra-containing foods in order to ensure the safe use of olestra.").

465. *See* 21 U.S.C. § 343(a)(1) (1994) (providing that a food shall be deemed to be misbranded if "its labeling is false or misleading in any particular"); *id.* § 321(n) ("[I]n determining whether the labeling or advertising is misleading there shall be taken into account (among other things) . . . the extent to which the labeling or advertising fails to reveal facts material in light of such representations or material with respect to consequences which may result from use. . . .").

466. *See id.* § 348(c)(3)(B) ("No such regulation shall issue if a fair evaluation of the data . . . shows that the proposed use of the additive would promote deception of the consumer in violation of this chapter or would otherwise result in adulteration or misbranding of food within the meaning of this chapter.").

467. *See* 61 Fed. Reg. at 3160-61, 3162. In regard to the gastrointestinal side effect information, the FDA explains that these facts are material with respect to the consequences of use even though not a safety concern. *Id.* at 3161 ("[P]roviding this information to consumers would preclude unnecessary concerns about the origin of GI effects, were they to be observed, and also may prevent unnecessary or inappropriate medical treatment of those symptoms."). In regard to the vitamin fortification aspect of the required statement, the Agency explains that ingredient disclosure elsewhere on the label amounts to a representation that could mislead consumers if it omitted the material facts concerning the need for vitamin replacement. *Id.* ("FDA is requiring a statement indicating that olestra inhibits the absorption of vitamins and other nutrients to set the context for why they are added.").

468. *See* 61 Fed. Reg. at 3160 (providing a 60-day comment period).

469. *See* Raju Narisetti, *P&G Seeks Less-Explicit Labeling Rules from FDA for Products with Olestra*, WALL ST. J., Apr. 9, 1996, at A2; *CSPI Protests Olestra Labeling; NFPA and GMA also Object*, FOOD CHEM. NEWS, Apr. 8, 1996, at 34.

470. 21 C.F.R. § 172.867(f) (1996) (adding that the FDA "will present such data, information, and evaluation to the agency's Food Advisory Committee within 30 months of the effective date of this regulation," and then "will initiate any appropriate regulatory proceedings"). In the preamble, the FDA pointed out that, by using the term "will" in the regulation, it "legally bound itself to institute this review and evaluation." 61 Fed. Reg. at 3168.

471. 61 Fed. Reg. at 3168 ("Procter and Gamble has notified FDA that the company will be conducting additional studies of olestra exposure (both amounts consumed and patterns of consumption) and the effects of olestra consumption. . . . Only with data from the broader marketing of olestra can the agency be in the position to evaluate in the future whether there continues to be reasonable certainty of no harm from the use of olestra."); *see also* GAO, NEW FOOD TECHNOLOGIES, *supra* note 9, at 61 (According to one official, the "FDA may try to negotiate requirements for firms to conduct postmarket surveillance, including the collection and reporting of data on dietary use and on any adverse effects, as a condition for approving novel macroingredients as food additives.").

472. 61 Fed. Reg. at 3169.

473. *Cf. supra* note 231 and accompanying text. The FDA's threat also seemingly ignores the procedures imposed by Congress for withdrawing an approval. *See* 21 U.S.C. § 348(h) (1994); 21 C.F.R. § 171.130 (1996).

474. 61 Fed. Reg. at 3169 (citing 46 Fed. Reg. 38,284, 38,303 (1981)); *cf.* GAO, NEW FOOD TECHNOLOGIES, *supra* note 9, at 61 ("In at least one instance, FDA has been able to obtain *voluntary* postmarket surveillance for a food additive (Aspartame, an artificial sweetener) as part of the approval process for this substance. However, FDA does not have the statutory authority to *require* surveillance for food products, as it does for human drugs, according to the [CFSAN Branch] Director."); *supra* note 378 (discussing condition in aspartame approval).

475. 61 Fed. Reg. at 3169; *see also supra* Part III.C (discussing data collection requirements for interim food additives).

476. *See Olestra Gets Fewer Gripes than Expected, P&G Says*, WALL ST. J., July 25, 1996, at B10 (noting that P&G reported to the FDA an adverse health effect rate of one per 3,000 bags sold). This contrasts with CSPI's claim that 20% of consumers experienced GI problems (3% of them severe). *See* Burros, *supra* note 452, at C8.

477. *See 1995 Hearings*, *supra* note 1, at 35 (statement of Sanford A. Miller, University of Texas Health Science Center) ("[F]or the last two decades, the Center has suffered from substantial reductions in personnel. . . . This occurred at a time when not only the process of safety evaluation had become more complex but the Center, by legislative mandate, had received several new responsibilities."); *id.* at 54 (statement of Stephen A. Ziller, Vice President, Grocery Manufacturers of America) (noting that "CFSAN staffing has remained essentially constant for the last 12 years (ranging from about 800 to 900 [FTEs]) while that for drugs and biologics increased steadily").

478. *See supra* notes 214-18 and accompanying text.

479. *See* Rulis & Tarantino, *supra* note 215, at 140 ("The long review time for these petitions is consistent with the fact that there is no statutory time limit governing FDA review of GRAS petitions, which results in a lower overall review priority allocated to these petitions by the FDA."); *supra* notes 250-51. As the manager of the FDA's food additive program has written, the Agency "is aware that an evaluation delayed can be an evaluation denied because of the competitive pressure of the marketplace." Rulis, *supra* note 218, at 538. Smaller companies may be especially susceptible because they lack the resources to endure lengthy regulatory delays. *See 1995 Hearings*, *supra* note 1, at 88 (statement of Hon. Edolphus Towns); *id.* at 101 (statement of C. Wayne Callaway, George Washington University Medical Center).

480. *See* 37 Fed. Reg. 25,356 (1972) (codified as amended at 21 C.F.R. § 172.185 (1996)). The food additive petition had been filed one year earlier. *See* 36 Fed. Reg. 22,617 (1971). An earlier petition had been withdrawn the previous year. *See* 35 Fed. Reg. 440 (1970).

481. *See* 46 Fed. Reg. 30,080, 30,081 (1981) (codified as amended at 21 C.F.R. § 172.841 (1996)). The food additive petition had been filed more than two years earlier. *See* 44 Fed. Reg. 22,816 (1979).

482. *See* 53 Fed. Reg. 28,379 (1988) (codified at 21 C.F.R. § 172.800 (1996)). The food additive petition had been filed almost six years earlier. *See* 47 Fed. Reg. 46,139 (1982); *see also* 53 Fed. Reg. 48,727, 48,728 (1988) (calculating the approval phase of the regulatory review period as 2,172 days, in response to a patent term extension request by the manufacturer).

483. *See* 55 Fed. Reg. 39,613 (1990) (codified at 21 C.F.R. § 172.665 (1996)). The original food additive petition had been filed more than four years earlier. *See* 51 Fed. Reg. 687 (1986); *see also* 56 Fed. Reg. 3110 (1991) (calculating the approval phase of the regulatory review period as 1,795 days, in response to a patent term extension request by the manufacturer). Other less significant direct additive approvals include glyceryl tristearate as primarily a formulation aid, 53 Fed. Reg. 21,631 (1988), dimethyl dicarbonate as a yeast inhibitor in wine, 53 Fed. Reg. 41,325 (1988), DL-alanine as a sweetener in pickling mixtures, 56 Fed. Reg. 6968 (1991), cocoa butter substitute, 56 Fed. Reg. 66,969 (1991), certain esters of fatty acids used to dehydrate grapes, 57 Fed. Reg. 12,709 (1992), and curdlan, 61 Fed. Reg. 65,941 (1996); *cf. 1995 Hearings*, *supra* note 1, at 31 (testimony of Linda A. Suydam, Interim Deputy Commissioner for Operations, FDA) (asserting that the FDA approved 42 direct food additives since July 1988, of which at least eight "were of significance").

484. *See 1995 Hearings*, *supra* note 1, at 31 (testimony of Linda A. Suydam, Interim Deputy Commissioner for Operations, FDA) ("[A]bout 75 percent are the indirects."); Hutt, *supra* note 1, at 122 ("It is easy to be misled about the efficiency of FDA regulation of food additives by counting the *Federal Register* food additive notices . . . . More than 80% of these notices relate to obscure indirect food additives that have no possible bearing on the public health."); Rulis & Tarantino, *supra* note 215, at 140.

485. *See* Hutt, *supra* note 1, at 122 (describing the "large number of follow-on amendments" which create "an extraordinary amount of sheer busywork").

486. *See* 59 Fed. Reg. 37,419 (1994) (codified at 21 C.F.R. § 172.841 (1996)).

487. *See* Rulis & Tarantino, *supra* note 215, at 137, 139-41.

488. *Id.* at 140.

489. *Id.* at 148 (Fig. 7).

490. *Id.* at 148 (Fig. 8). Evidently these included both direct and indirect additives.

491. *See* H.R. REP. NO. 436, 104th Cong., 1st Sess. 2 (1995). Earlier oversight hearings had focused on different aspects of the subject. *See, e.g.*, *Oversight of Food Safety, 1983: Hearings Before the Sen. Comm. on Labor and Human Resources*, 98th Cong., 1st Sess. (1983); *Food Additives: Competitive, Regulatory, and Safety Problems: Hearings Before the Sen. Select Comm. on Small Business*, 95th Cong., 1st Sess. (1977).

492. H.R. REP. NO. 436, 104th Cong., 1st Sess. 5-6 (1995) (adding that in no year since 1970 had the average review time for approved direct additives been less than 20 months).

493. *See 1995 Hearings*, *supra* note 1, at 35 (statement of Sanford A. Miller, University of Texas Health Science Center) ("[T]he time required for the Center to reach a conclusion on those petitions for which orders were finally issued had increased from 20 months to 40 months. For pending petitions, the time for consideration increased from about 30 months in 1983 to over 60 months in 1994."); *see also id.* at 42 (statement of Richard L. Hall, Chairman, NAS Food Forum) ("[A]pprovals often are badly delayed even when they simply involve new uses for an already approved additive. When they involve something entirely new the pace becomes glacial.").

494. *See id.* at 10, 14 (statement of Linda A. Suydam, Interim Deputy Commissioner for Operations, FDA). These initiatives are discussed more fully in Part VI.B, *infra*.

495. *See id.* at 25-26 (testimony of Margaret J. Porter, FDA Chief Counsel). After the hearings, FDA officials met with the Subcommittee staff and requested that the statutory deadline be set at 360 days but promised to complete reviews for 90% of all petitions within 180 days. *See* H.R. REP. NO. 436, 104th Cong., 1st Sess. 3 (1995).

496. *See 1995 Hearings, supra* note 1, at 2 (statement of Hon. Christopher Shays, Subcommittee Chairman) (observing that "the statutory deadline has been interpreted out of existence by the FDA"); *id.* at 27 ("What I get a sense of is, from the lack of having a fixed deadline, all other problems follow. And it gives you extraordinary opportunity to do whatever the hell you want."); *see also id.* at 84-85 (expressing surprise at the industry's apparent patience with the Agency and reluctance to seek judicial relief).

497. *See 1995 Hearings, supra* note 1, at 10 (statement of Linda A. Suydam, Interim Deputy Commissioner for Operations, FDA) ("Presently, many petitions, when submitted, have shortcomings in the data needed to support a decision to approve the additive. Similarly, during FDA's review, the data in a petition too often are found to be of poor quality or inadequate."); *id.* at 18 (testimony of Alan M. Rulis, Acting Director of CFSAN's Office of Premarket Review); *id.* at 176 (statement of Michael F. Jacobson, Executive Director, CSPI).

498. *See id.* at 10 (statement of Linda A. Suydam, Interim Deputy Commissioner for Operations, FDA) ("[T]he industry has been reluctant to have the Agency formally deny product petitions. Consistent with industry's preference, FDA's traditional policy for food additives has been to work very closely with each petitioner to develop data . . . instead of simply denying those petitions that lack adequate supporting data."); *id.* at 23 (testimony of Alan M. Rulis, Acting Director of CFSAN's Office of Premarket Review).

499. *See id.* at 84-86 (testimony of Rhona S. Applebaum, Executive Vice President, National Food Processors Association) (explaining that companies have attempted to work within the existing system rather than seek judicial or legislative intervention); *id.* at 106 (testimony of D. Stephen Saunders, Frito-Lay, Inc.).

500. *See id.* at 176-77 (statement of Michael F. Jacobson, Executive Director, CSPI); *see also id.* at 184 ("Perhaps the best way for FDA to get out its message that cooperation with the agency in the pre-filing stage is imperative would be for FDA to implement a policy of quick rejections, without prejudice, of petitions filed with inadequate safety data.").

501. *See Shank: More Emphasis to be Placed on Food Additive Deadlines*, FOOD CHEM. NEWS, Apr. 22, 1996, at 38 ("Because FDA is under the gun to get reviews completed as quickly as possible, the agency will no longer spend time working with petitions to bring them up to par, [according to CFSAN Chief Fred Shank].").

502. *See, e.g., 1995 Hearings, supra* note 1, at 2 (statement of Hon. Christopher Shays, Subcommittee Chairman). Officials from a couple of companies did testify or provide written statements.

503. *See id.* at 70, 86 (statement and testimony of Rhona S. Applebaum, Executive Vice President, National Food Processors Association); *see also Allegations of FDA Abuses of Authority: Hearings Before the Subcomm. on Oversight and Investigations of the House Comm. on Commerce*, 104th Cong., 1st Sess. (1995).

504. *See 1995 Hearings, supra* note 1, at 54, 62 (statement of Stephen A. Ziller, Vice President, Grocery Manufacturers of America) ("This caution is frequently exhibited in requests that reviewers make for more studies and data that have little, if any, relevance to the determination of safety for a food ingredient."); *id.* at 70-71 (statement of Rhona S. Applebaum, Executive Vice President, National Food Processors Association); *id.* at 35 (statement of Sanford A. Miller, University of Texas Health Science Center) (CFSAN "clearly has difficulty in reaching decisions and in particular those decisions that require judgment. It is never possible to have all the data we believe we need to make safety evaluations."); *id.* at 43 (statement of Richard L. Hall, Chairman, NAS Food Forum) ("The most important thing to do is not to make a mistake. It is far safer to delay, usually by asking more questions, than to make a decision."); *id.* at 101 (statement of C. Wayne Callaway, George Washington University Medical Center) ("[T]he current system is too costly, too lengthy, and too much influenced by emotionally-charged issues, promoted by self-appointed 'consumer advocates,' resulting in delays.").

505. *See id.* at 20-21 (testimony of Linda A. Suydam, Interim Deputy Commissioner for Operations, FDA) ("When you have an outlier—for example, if we approve something that we've had in-house for 20 years, then it skews your average. That's why, sometimes, average is not in fact the best."). No effort has been made to update the statistics for petitions which remain pending. In any event, old petitions may remain in pending status long after a company has given up simply because it has not withdrawn the inactive petition. *See id.* at 177 (statement of Michael F. Jacobson, Executive Director, CSPI) (suggesting that the FDA should periodically inquire whether a petition remains active).

506. This survey does not include amendments to tables listing approved flavors and amino acids.

507. If one excludes the 25 supplemental use petitions for acesulfame potassium and aspartame (on the theory that each supplemental use should become progressively easier to review, though possibly offset because of delays triggered by pending objections to earlier approvals), the average review time increases to 39.7 months (n=8).

508. This survey consolidates approvals of petitions for closely related substances which were filed and approved together (even if ultimately reflected in separate regulations), such as the GRAS affirmations of various citrates, enzymes and iron substances. (Note, however, that such consolidated counting actually understates the length of review periods for GRAS affirmation petitions by almost one year when compared to the average if each substance were counted separately.) This survey excludes the few supplemental petitions approved by the FDA to revise an existing GRAS affirmation regulation.

509. *See 1995 Hearings*, *supra* note 1, at 23-24 (testimony of Alan M. Rulis, Acting Director of CFSAN's Office of Premarket Review) (explaining that only 77 of the 295 pending petitions were under active Agency review for more than 180 days). In calculating the approval phase of the regulatory review period for patent extension requests, however, the FDA does not attempt to subtract any time spent waiting for further information from a food additive petitioner. *See, e.g.*, 56 Fed. Reg. 3110 (1991) (gellan gum).

510. *See 1995 Hearings*, *supra* note 1, at 139 (statement of Jerome H. Heckman, on behalf of the Society of the Plastics Industry) ("Typically, a petition will have been pending for at least several months (and in some cases, a year or longer) before a filing notice is published."). The averages reported in the main text reflect the time that elapsed between the dates of publication in the Federal Register of the notice of filing and the final regulation; the sole exception was the GRAS affirmation of high fructose corn syrup where this survey used the much later date of the Agency's notice of proposed rulemaking.

511. *See id.* at 20 (testimony of Linda A. Suydam, Interim Deputy Commissioner for Operations, FDA) ("One thing is that the review time, the trend, has been coming down since 1990. That shows progress."); *id.* at 21 (noting that, since 1988, there has been "a fairly stable number" of approvals and pending petitions, concluding that "[t]he process has not completely shut down"); Rulis & Tarantino, *supra* note 215, at 141, 150 (Fig. 11); *Shank: More Emphasis to be Placed on Food Additive Deadlines*, FOOD CHEM. NEWS, Apr. 22, 1996, at 38 (reporting recent reductions in the backlog and review times for food additive petitions but not GRAS affirmation petitions).

512. *See, e.g.*, SAM PELTZMAN, REGULATION OF PHARMACEUTICAL INNOVATION (1974); GAO, FDA DRUG APPROVAL—A LENGTHY PROCESS THAT DELAYS THE AVAILABILITY OF IMPORTANT NEW DRUGS, No. HRD-80-64 (1980).

513. *See, e.g.*, Robert W. Hahn & John A. Hird, *The Costs and Benefits of Regulation: Review and Synthesis*, 8 YALE J. ON REG. 233, 276-77 (1990); C. Frederick Beckner, III, Note, *The FDA's War on Drugs*, 82 GEO. L.J. 529 (1993). The FDA now contends that it has substantially reduced average review times. *See Agriculture, Rural Development, Food and Drug Administration, and Related Agencies Appropriations for 1997: Hearings Before a Subcomm. of the House Comm. on Appropriations*, 104th Cong., 2d Sess. 328 (1996) (statement of David A. Kessler, Commissioner of Food and Drugs).

514. *See 1995 Hearings*, *supra* note 1, at 9 (statement of Linda A. Suydam, Interim Deputy Commissioner for Operations, FDA) ("Unlike drugs which are ingested for the significant therapeutic benefit they are intended to confer on the patient, food additives are eaten by everyone and, by definition, are not supposed to produce any pharmacological effect. They do not provide direct benefits that justify exposing consumers to risk. This is true even for food additives, such as artificial sweeteners, that may have a beneficial effect on the American diet . . . [because] alternatives [are] available to reduce caloric intake for anyone motivated to do so."); *id.* at 175 (statement of Michael F. Jacobson, Executive Director, CSPI) ("Additives make it possible to market an increased range of processed foods, but it's unusual for additives to provide consumers with measurable health benefits.").

515. *See 1995 Hearings*, *supra* note 1, at 47 (statement of Al S. Clausi, Institute of Food Technologists) ("Food additives are also an important component of food preservation, i.e. in inhibiting microbiological spoilage and reducing the risk of foodborne illness; preventing chemical, physical, and enzymatic deterioration; and in conserving nutritive value."); Rulis, *supra* note 218, at 534 ("Food scientists are aware that some additives enhance the safety of foods . . . [and] make possible the creation of a wider variety of foods, make some foods more palatable, and, in some cases, make it possible to produce foods that may have healthier nutritional profiles (*i.e.*, fewer calories or less fat).").

516. *See* H.R. REP. NO. 436, 104th Cong., 1st Sess. 9 (1995) ("Several companies told the Subcommittee staff in interviews that they had abandoned research into promising food additives because of the delays in the petition review process."); *1995 Hearings*, *supra* note 1, at 2 (statement of Hon. Christopher Shays, Subcommittee Chairman) ("The potential benefits of this technology, both in terms of public health and economic vitality, are too great to permit regulatory

torpor to jeopardize food research and innovation."); *id.* at 35 (statement of Sanford A. Miller, University of Texas Health Science Center) ("The agency's inability to reach decisions on their pending petitions has resulted in nearly a complete stasis in innovation in the food industry."); *id.* at 54 (statement of Stephen A. Ziller, Vice President, Grocery Manufacturers of America) ("The inherent delays resulting from this inability to make final decisions is beginning to turn off major food companies from investing in new additives and technology."); *id.* at 69 (statement of Rhona S. Applebaum, Executive Vice President, National Food Processors Association).

517. *See* Douglas L. Archer & Catherine M. DeRoever, *CFSAN's Program Offices*, 48 FOOD & DRUG L.J. 487, 489 (1993) (describing the new Office of Pre-Market Approval). The FDA also has proposed to coordinate with the USDA any reviews of substances intended for use in meat and poultry products. *See* 60 Fed. Reg. 67,490, 67,492 (1995). In addition, as part of the President's "Reinventing Government" initiative, the FDA published an advance notice of proposed rulemaking for its food additive regulations, though all of the suggested changes represent non-substantive revisions intended to eliminate redundancies or ambiguities in the rules governing specific additives. *See* 61 Fed. Reg. 29,711, 29,712-14 (1996).

518. *See 1995 Hearings*, *supra* note 1, at 10-14 (statement of Linda A. Suydam, Interim Deputy Commissioner for Operations, FDA) (describing initiatives such as performance goals and outreach efforts to better educate petitioners about data requirements, and proposing to reduce environmental assessment requirements for routine petitions); *see also* Rulis, *supra* note 218, at 538-39; *Administrative Reforms Could Significantly Reduce Petition Backlog*, FOOD CHEM. NEWS, Feb. 26, 1996, at 3; *FDA Food Ingredient Review Reform is Ongoing, With More Planned for the Future*, FOOD CHEM. NEWS, Dec. 25, 1995, at 33; FDA Staff Manual Guide, *Policies, Authority, and Procedures for Food and Color Additive Petitions and GRAS Affirmation Petitions* (Apr. 1993). Many of these guidelines are available through CFSAN's home page, http://vm.cfsan.fda.gov/~dms/opa-toc.html.

519. *See 1995 Hearings*, *supra* note 1, at 78 (statement of Robert C. Gelardi, Executive Vice President, Calorie Control Council).

520. *See* Rulis & Tarantino, *supra* note 215, at 141 (conceding that most "improvements in the efficiency of the process will take place at the margin, that is, improvements by factors of 10% to 20%"); *OPA Contract Looks at Petition Review While Headway Seen on Backlog*, FOOD CHEM. NEWS, Oct. 28, 1996, at 17 (reporting that the inventory of active petitions had been reduced from 295 in June 1995 to 240); *see also 1995 Hearings*, *supra* note 1, at 10-14 (statement of Linda A. Suydam, Interim Deputy Commissioner for Operations, FDA) (cautioning that "the zeal to speed up the process not be allowed to override the credibility and integrity of that process"); Hutt, *supra* note 1, at 128 (doubting that the FDA will "reform itself from within, and restore the efficiency and effective regulatory approach taken in the early 1960s").

521. *See 1995 Hearings*, *supra* note 1, at 72 (statement of Rhona S. Applebaum, Executive Vice President, National Food Processors Association) ("We have no reason to expect that new resolve by FDA to mend its ways, in response to current public concerns about its performance, will be sustained over the long term that is necessary for achievement of real action."); *id.* at 49 (testimony of Sanford A. Miller, University of Texas Health Science Center) ("I don't believe they are going to meet even their performance standards."); *see also id.* at 2 (statement of Hon. Christopher Shays, Subcommittee Chairman) (noting that, in the week preceding the hearings, the FDA finally acted on several GRAS affirmation petitions that had been pending since 1972).

522. For petitions classified in Tiers I and II, the goal "is to issue an Agency response—that the submission is adequate, or provide a complete description of why it is not adequate—within" 90 and 180 days respectively. *See 1995 Hearings*, *supra* note 1, at 13 (statement of Linda A. Suydam, Interim Deputy Commissioner for Operations, FDA). Moreover, for most Tier III petitions, the announced goal is to provide such an *initial* response within 360 days, *id.*, double the maximum statutory time frame for *final* action. *See id.* at 25-27 (statement of Hon. Christopher Shays, Subcommittee Chairman); *see also Protecting the U.S. Consumer from Food Borne Illnesses: Hearings Before the Subcomm. on Human Resources and Intergovernmental Relations of the House Comm. on Government Reform and Oversight*, 104th Cong., 2d Sess. (1996) (testimony of Michael Friedman, Deputy Commissioner for Operations, FDA) (announcing hopes to complete reviews on 50% of new direct food additive petitions within 12 months during the first year after the existing backlog is cleared).

523. *See* S. 1477, 104th Cong., 2d Sess. § 103 (1996) (calling for a reduction in backlogs within two years and requiring the publication of annual reports of progress in satisfying the existing statutory deadlines).

524. *See* H.R. REP. NO. 436, 104th Cong., 1st Sess. 14 (1995) (additional views of Hon. David M. McIntosh and Hon. Mark E. Souder) (concluding that the "inertia" within the FDA "cannot be eliminated without a significant enforcement hammer," and suggesting that the Agency be given a short period of time after a more realistic review period to either approve the additive or deny the petition if it "can demonstrate that an additive has not been found to be safe"); S. 1477,

104th Cong., 2d Sess. § 404 (743(c)) (1996) (providing that an additive already approved in the European Union or the United Kingdom would be deemed approved at the petitioner's request if the FDA fails to act on a petition within the statutory timeframe); *1995 Hearings*, *supra* note 1, at 71, 83 (statement of Rhona S. Applebaum, Executive Vice President, National Food Processors Association) ("[W]ithout amendments to the Act that establish an effective forcing mechanism, there can be no real prospect for substantial improvement in the food additive approval process."); *id.* at 87 (statement of Stephen A. Ziller, Vice President, Grocery Manufacturers of America).

525. *See, e.g.*, H.R. 2245, 83d Cong., 1st Sess. § 6 (407(d)) (1953).

526. *See, e.g.*, Nutrition Labeling and Education Act of 1990, Pub. L. No. 101-535, §§ 2(b), 3(b), 104 Stat. 2356, 2360; Safe Medical Devices Act of 1990, Pub. L. No. 101-629, § 3(c)(2), 104 Stat. 4511; Hazardous and Solid Waste Amendments of 1984, Pub. L. No. 98-616, § 201, 98 Stat. 3226 (codified at 42 U.S.C. § 6924(c) (1994)); *see also* M. Elizabeth Magill, *Congressional Control Over Agency Rulemaking: The Nutrition Labeling and Education Act's Hammer Provisions*, 50 FOOD & DRUG L.J. 149 (1995).

527. *See 1995 Hearings*, *supra* note 1, at 177 (statement of Michael F. Jacobson, Executive Director, CSPI) ("[I]ndustry should realize that a rigid time limit for the review process could well mean that the FDA would simply reject a petition that currently would be put in abeyance pending further research and analysis."); Hutt, *supra* note 1, at 128 ("[I]t is all too easy for FDA simply to issue continual denials . . . on the ground that further testing is needed."); *see also* 43 Fed. Reg. 27,507, 27,509 (1978) (ACUS recommendation against the imposition of strict deadlines); Alden F. Abbott, *The Case Against Federal Statutory and Judicial Deadlines: A Cost-Benefit Appraisal*, 39 ADMIN. L. REV. 171 (1987).

528. *See, e.g.*, Weinberger v. Bentex Pharmaceuticals, Inc., 412 U.S. 645, 654 (1973) ("Threshold questions within the peculiar expertise of an administrative agency are appropriately routed to the agency, while the court stays its hand."); Biotics Research Corp. v. Heckler, 710 F.2d 1375, 1376 (9th Cir. 1983). Thus, unsuccessful applicants rarely prevail on judicial review and, therefore, frequently do not even bother appealing from an unfavorable Agency decision. *See* HUTT & MERRILL, *supra* note 170, at 533-34 (canvassing case law involving FDA denials of applications for new drug approval).

529. *See* H.R. REP. NO. 436, 104th Cong., 1st Sess. 8 (1995) ("The leveling of FDA resources for foods in recent years is in sharp contrast with the increased responsibilities CFSAN has assumed due to new legislation . . . ."); *1995 Hearings*, *supra* note 1, at 35-36 (statement of Sanford A. Miller, University of Texas Health Science Center) (noting that CFSAN is "under funded and overly-committed" but that "it is highly improbable" that it could get the 200-300 extra reviewers it needs for food additives); *id.* at 54 (statement of Stephen A. Ziller, Vice President, Grocery Manufacturers of America); *cf.* *id.* at 53 (Reduced resources are "more of a symptom and not a root cause" of the breakdown in the food additive approval process. "The fundamental causes are lack of a clear mission, a steady decline in priority over the years, and the increasing lack of incentive and ability of the agency to make a final positive decision on a petition against the statutory criteria.").

530. *See* 60 Fed. Reg. 36,582 (1995); *see also* Jerome H. Heckman, *Closing in on Zero*, 45 FOOD DRUG COSM. L.J. 599 (1990) (discussing long-running industry efforts at trying to convince the FDA to adopt a threshold of regulation policy); Alan M. Rulis et al., *FDA's Priority-Based Assessment of Food Additives*, 4 REG. TOXICOL. & PHARMACOL. 37 (1984).

531. *See* Rulis & Tarantino, *supra* note 215, at 141 (noting that this "could free up a considerable amount of person power for work on petitions of greater consequence to the food supply and public health protection"); *1995 Hearings*, *supra* note 1, at 64 (statement of Stephen A. Ziller, Vice President, Grocery Manufacturers of America) ("Under the proposed process for indirects, a notification would be submitted to FDA . . . and take effect in ninety days and use of the substance therefore allowed, unless FDA concluded that there existed substantial evidence to show" migration or lack of safety).

532. *See* 21 C.F.R. § 170.39 (1996). The threshold is set at a concentration of 0.5 ppb or, in the case of an approved direct food additive being used in a food-contact material, at 1% of the ADI. *Id.* § 170.39(a)(2). The substance may not be exempted (much less approved) if it has been shown to induce cancer. *Id.* § 170.39(a)(1). The 0.5 ppb threshold attempts to ensure an upper-bound lifetime risk of cancer of less than one-in-one million in the event that a substance later proves to be carcinogenic. *See* 60 Fed. Reg. at 36,583. The Agency rejected a suggestion that it extend the policy to substances added directly to foods at low levels. *Id.* at 36,585.

533. *See* 60 Fed. Reg. at 36,589-60 (observing that "such reviews can usually be completed within 3 to 4 months," but fearing that a formal deadline would restrict the Agency's flexibility in allocating resources among competing priorities); *cf.* S. 1477, 104th Cong., 2d Sess. § 802(a) (1996) (proposing to force the FDA to act on premarket notifications for indirect additives within 90 days); S. REP. NO. 284, 104th Cong., 2d Sess. 62 (1996) ("This simple procedure will allow the FDA to quickly dispose of its existing inventory" of indirect food additive petitions.); *Kessler Objects to Hammer Provisions, Shorter Review Times at Senate Hearing*, FOOD CHEM. NEWS, Feb. 26, 1996, at 25.

534. *See 1995 Hearings*, *supra* note 1, at 133-41 (statement of Jerome H. Heckman, on behalf of the Society of the Plastics Industry) (explaining that exemption petitions under the threshold of regulation policy already have become backlogged at about six months, and proposing a substantially less formal procedure for reviewing indirect food additives); Hutt, *supra* note 1, at 122 (supporting the threshold of regulation concept but criticizing the replacement of food additive petitions with exemption petitions).

535. *See* 60 Fed. Reg. at 36,586-87, 36,589 (rejecting suggestions that companies be permitted to make their own judgment that a substance is exempt under the threshold of regulation policy, though noting that companies remain free to decide that a substance is not a "food additive" to begin with because it is not likely to migrate). Once the FDA issues a letter granting an exemption, any company wishing to utilize the substance under the same conditions of use may rely on the exemption. *See id.* at 36,587, 36,591-92.

536. *See* Dietary Supplement Health and Education Act of 1994, Pub. L. No. 103-417, § 8, 108 Stat. 4331 (codified at 21 U.S.C. § 350b(a)(2) (1994)); *supra* note 6.

537. *See* S. REP. NO. 513, 101st Cong., 2d Sess. 15 (1990) ("Over 95% of the devices marketed since the passage of the [1976] Amendments have been found 'substantially equivalent' to a predicate device."); GAO, MEDICAL DEVICES: FDA REVIEW TIME, No. PEMD-96-2 (1995); Robert B. Leflar, *Public Accountability and Medical Device Regulation*, 2 HARV. J.L. & TECH. 1 (1989) (arguing that Section 510(k) has been used inappropriately to circumvent full approval requirements); Lawrence S. Makow, Note, *Medical Device Review at the Food and Drug Administration: Lessons from Magnetic Resonance Spectroscopy and Biliary Lithotripsy*, 46 STAN. L. REV. 709 (1994). To address growing backlogs, the Agency recently exempted numerous classes of low-risk devices from the notification requirement. *See* 59 Fed. Reg. 63,005 (1994).

538. *See 1995 Hearings*, *supra* note 1, at 79 (statement of Robert C. Gelardi, Executive Vice President, Calorie Control Council); *cf. id.* at 13 (statement of Linda A. Suydam, Interim Deputy Commissioner for Operations, FDA) (suggesting that most such petitions would fall within Tier I, for which the performance goal time frames are just 90 days for an initial response); 48 Fed. Reg. 48,457, 48,458 (1983) (explaining that GRAS self-determination would be possible for an additional use of a substance affirmed as GRAS but not for one approved as a food additive).

539. *See* H.R. REP. NO. 436, 104th Cong., 1st Sess. 8 (1995) (noting that the FDA "utiliz[es] a 'first in, first out' review system which does not devote the greatest resources to the applications with the greatest resource requirements"); *1995 Hearings*, *supra* note 1, at 12, 19 (statement and testimony of Linda A. Suydam, Interim Deputy Commissioner for Operations, FDA) ("We need to get rid of the backlog so that we can start fresh in this program.").

540. *See supra* notes 310-13 and accompanying text.

541. *See* GAO, NEW FOOD TECHNOLOGIES, *supra* note 9, at 63-64 (noting that the Edwards Committee "concluded that FDA must recognize that approving useful and safe new products can contribute as much to public health as preventing the marketing of harmful or ineffective products," adding that some "have proposed that FDA establish a fast track for processing petitions for food additives that provide some positive public health benefit"); *The Need for FDA Reform: Hearing Before the Subcomm. on Health and Environment of the House Comm. on Commerce*, 104th Cong., 2d Sess. 100 (1996) (statement of Michael W. Pariza, Director of the Food Research Inst.); *1995 Hearings*, *supra* note 1, at 104-05 (testimony of Michael H. Davidson, Medical Director, Chicago Center for Clinical Research) (describing potential benefits of fat substitutes, and recommending that "at least priority be given to those food additives that do have health benefits, that they receive expedited approvals, or reviews").

542. *See* 21 C.F.R. pt. 314(h) (1996) (establishing expedited approval procedures for new drugs indicated for the treatment of serious or life-threatening illnesses); HUTT & MERRILL, *supra* note 170, at 529-31 (describing previous system for prioritizing new drug reviews according to therapeutic potential).

543. *See 1995 Hearings*, *supra* note 1, at 13 (statement of Linda A. Suydam, Interim Deputy Commissioner for Operations, FDA).

544. *See* GAO, NEW FOOD TECHNOLOGIES, *supra* note 9, at 89-95.

545. *See* Prescription Drug User Fee Act of 1992, Pub. L. No. 102-571, tit. I, 106 Stat. 4491 (codified at 21 U.S.C. § 379h (1994)); Bruce N. Kuhlik, *Industry Funding of Improvements in the FDA's New Drug Approval Process: The Prescription Drug User Fee Act of 1992*, 47 FOOD & DRUG L.J. 483 (1992).

546. *See 1956 Hearings*, *supra* note 19, at 141 (HEW memorandum) ("We cannot absorb this important new function without serious neglect of other essential responsibilities. And the cost of obtaining governmental review of scientific data to assure safety of a new chemical is a legitimate charge to the cost of doing business."). Industry representatives expressed

strong opposition to the request for such authority. *See, e.g., id.* at 95 (statement of Glenn G. Paxton, appearing as counsel for various food industry associations).

547. *See* Pub. L. No. 83-518, § 3 (408(o)), 68 Stat. 517 (codified at 21 U.S.C. § 346a(o) (1994), as repealed and replaced by the Food Quality Protection Act of 1996, Pub. L. No. 104-170, § 405 (408(m)), 110 Stat. 1529).

548. *See, e.g.*, H.R. 4014, 85th Cong., 1st Sess. § 6 (1957); *see also* 104 CONG. REC. 17,424 (1958) (statement of Hon. Leonor K. Sullivan) (calling for adequate appropriations so that the FDA could execute its significant new responsibilities in reviewing food additives). An early draft of Congressman Dingell's recent bill, H.R. 5952, 102d Cong., 2d Sess. (1992), had included provisions applicable to food additive but not GRAS affirmation petitions, establishing an interim annual user fee of $75,000. (Although a one time filing fee might make sense, an annual fee imposed after approval would unfairly tax the petitioner, and a fee imposed only during the pendency of the FDA's review might create a perverse incentive to delay approval.)

549. *See* National Cable Television Ass'n v. United States, 415 U.S. 336, 340-341 (1974); *see also* Skinner v. Mid-America Pipeline Co., 490 U.S. 212, 223 (1989); Clayton P. Gillette & Thomas D. Hopkins, *Federal User Fees: A Legal and Economic Analysis*, 67 B.U. L. REV. 795, 826-45 (1987).

550. *See supra* notes 231-35 and accompanying text.

551. *See 1995 Hearings*, *supra* note 1, at 29 (testimony of Linda A. Suydam, Interim Deputy Commissioner for Operations, FDA) ("[A] user fee program is difficult in the food additive area because a manufacturer is not given a product license as one is in the drug and devices area."); *id.* at 170 (testimony of Stuart M. Pape, on behalf of the National Soft Drink Association); *cf. id.* at 141 (statement of Jerome H. Heckman, on behalf of the Society of the Plastics Industry) (noting that "modest filing fees could be charged for [proposed indirect food additive premarket] notifications since they would be basically proprietary"); *id.* at 169. In fact, based on conversations held after the conclusion of the hearings, it appears that the FDA "may propose user fees to fund pre-filing consultation activities with sponsors." H.R. REP. NO. 436, 104th Cong., 1st Sess. 3 (1995).

552. *See 1995 Hearings*, *supra* note 1, at 186 (statement of Keith C. Triebwasser, Procter & Gamble) ("Patents alone do not provide this security, since patents are difficult to obtain in the food industry and difficult to enforce. Margins in the food industry are too low to support protracted patent battles."); Hutt, *supra* note 1, at 126 ("Without a statutory period of market exclusivity, American industry cannot be expected to invest in new food additives that cannot be patented, even if the regulatory process itself is reformed.").

553. *See* Elizabeth C. Price, *Teaching the Elephant to Dance: Privatizing the FDA Review Process*, 51 FOOD & DRUG L.J. 651 (1996); Charles J. Walsh & Alissa Pyrich, *Rationalizing the Regulation of Prescription Drugs and Medical Devices: Perspectives on Private Certification and Tort Reform*, 48 RUTGERS L. REV. 883, 987-1016 (1996). *See generally* Ronald A. Cass, *Privatization: Politics, Law, and Theory*, 71 MARQ. L. REV. 449 (1988); Harold J. Krent, *Fragmenting the Unitary Executive: Congressional Delegations of Administrative Authority Outside the Federal Government*, 85 NW. U. L. REV. 62 (1990); Douglas C. Michael, *Federal Agency Use of Audited Self-Regulation as a Regulatory Technique*, 47 ADMIN. L. REV. 171 (1995).

554. *See supra* notes 128-33 and accompanying text.

555. *See 1995 Hearings*, *supra* note 1, at 12 (statement of Linda A. Suydam, Interim Deputy Commissioner for Operations, FDA). The FDA also has initiated a limited pilot program allowing third-party reviews of premarket notifications for certain medical devices. *See* 61 Fed. Reg. 14,789 (1996). The EPA makes use of extramural reviews for pesticide data submissions. *See* 7 U.S.C. § 136w(d) (1994); 40 C.F.R. § 155.27 (1996).

556. *See, e.g.*, *1995 Hearings*, *supra* note 1, at 116-17, 171 (statement and testimony of Kenneth D. Fisher, Former Director of LSRO, FASEB); *id.* at 44-45 (statement of Richard L. Hall, Chairman, NAS Food Forum); *id.* at 54-55, 62-67 (statement of Stephen A. Ziller, Vice President, Grocery Manufacturers of America); *see also id.* at 36 (statement of Sanford A. Miller, University of Texas Health Science Center) (explaining that extramural reviews could provide a method of leveraging the Agency's limited resources, but emphasizing that the FDA cannot abdicate its regulatory duties and must, therefore, closely supervise external reviews); Stuart M. Pape, *Food Industry Initiatives to Improve the FDA's Food Ingredient Review Processes*, 51 FOOD & DRUG L.J. 413, 417-20 (1996).

557. *See* 5 U.S.C. app. 2 (1994); 21 C.F.R. pt. 14 (1996); Food Chem. News v. Young, 709 F. Supp. 5, 6-9 (D.D.C. 1989) (holding that a FASEB expert panel under contract to prepare a food safety report for the FDA was subject to the provisions of the Federal Advisory Committee Act, including requirements for balanced membership and open meetings), *rev'd*, 900 F.2d 328 (D.C. Cir.), *cert. denied*, 498 U.S. 846 (1990); *see also* Animal Legal Defense Fund, Inc. v. Shalala,

1997 U.S. App. LEXIS 353 (D.C. Cir. Jan. 10, 1997) (holding that FACA applied to NAS guidance concerning the care of laboratory animals); Washington Legal Found. v. United States Sentencing Comm'n, 17 F.3d 1446 (D.C. Cir. 1994); Steven P. Croley, *Practical Guidance on the Applicability of the Federal Advisory Committee Act*, 10 ADMIN. L.J. 111 (1996).

558. *See 1995 Hearings*, *supra* note 1, at 84 (statement of Stephen A. Ziller, Vice President, Grocery Manufacturers of America) ("[T]he check can surely go through FDA's hands, provided a service charge is not excised during the process.").

559. *See* H.R. REP. NO. 436, 104th Cong., 1st Sess. 10, 12 (1995) (recommending this approach); H.R. 3200, 104th Cong., 2d Sess. § 105(c)(3) (1996); *1995 Hearings*, *supra* note 1, at 36 (statement of Sanford A. Miller, University of Texas Health Science Center) ("If for example FDA does not issue a regulation or a report defending an opposing view within the prescribed time, then an assumption of approval is made."); *id.* at 63 (statement of Stephen A. Ziller, Vice President, Grocery Manufacturers of America) ("The presumption of approvability arising from a favorable report of the independent review organization would be rebuttable by FDA only if it concluded that there existed substantial evidence to demonstrate that the additive had not been shown to be safe."); Hutt, *supra* note 1, at 128 ("FDA would not be permitted, in its review of that recommendation, to veto marketing of the product on the ground that it still needs further testing.").

560. *See* Degnan, *supra* note 98, at 580-82.

> The GRAS concept provides the agency with a mechanism for concentrating its resources in these [novel food] areas—and for shifting some of its traditional food additive type functions away from substances which do not raise safety issues that only the agency is qualified to address. As a result, the general pace of decisionmaking could quicken because the scientific and technical staffs available for the review of safety issues would be subject to less diversions and able to concentrate on matters of high priority.

Id. at 582; *see also 1995 Hearings*, *supra* note 1, at 170 (testimony of Kenneth D. Fisher, Former Director of LSRO, FASEB) (observing that the FDA "has made the GRAS affirmation process analogous to the food additive petition process," and applauding the Agency's recent suggestion "to separate these and make the GRAS affirmation process perhaps what it was originally meant to be: a way to separate food additives and GRAS substances").

561. *See supra* notes 128-33 and accompanying text.

562. *See 1995 Hearings*, *supra* note 1, at 80 (statement of Robert C. Gelardi, Executive Vice President, Calorie Control Council).

563. *See 62 Fed. Reg. 18, 938, 18,941 (1997)* ("This streamlining would allow FDA to redirect its resources to questions about GRAS status that are a priority with respect to public health protection . . . [and] to its statutorily mandated task of reviewing food and color additive petitions.").

564. *See supra* Part II.B.2.

565. *Cf.* Heckman, *supra* note 60, at 49 ("A food packaging manufacturer often files a food additive petition because he would rather be safe than sorry. But by the time he emerges from the petition ordeal, he will certainly be sorry and may not be one whit more safe.").

566. *See* 21 C.F.R. § 180.1(c)(3) (1996) ("[I]f the Commissioner concludes that the studies are not being pursued promptly and diligently or if interim results indicate a reasonable likelihood that a health hazard exists, an order will promptly be published in the FEDERAL REGISTER revoking the interim food additive regulation effective on publication.").

567. *See* Degnan, *supra* note 98, at 567 ("Because FEMA's GRAS determinations are independent, they do not bind the FDA. It is standard practice, however, for food processors to rely upon FEMA's GRAS determinations. The FDA has deferred to FEMA's practice and has only rarely taken issue with a FEMA determination.").

568. *See id.* ("While FEMA's far-reaching GRAS review might seem a challenge to the FDA's authority and to the principle of premarket approval, the group's scientific and professional approach to making thorough GRAS determinations actually has provided important assistance to the FDA in its efforts to implement the [Food Additives Amendment] efficiently.").

569. *Cf.* Lars Noah & Barbara A. Noah, *Liberating Commercial Speech: Product Labeling Controls and the First Amendment*, 47 FLA. L. REV. 63, 72 & 107-11 (1995) (discussing the FDA's guidelines for industry sponsorship of continuing medical education programs).

570. *See 1995 Hearings*, *supra* note 1, at 89 (testimony of Stephen A. Ziller, Vice President, Grocery Manufacturers of America) ("I think the people who don't want additives, virtually of any type, any way, will see this as moving decisions away from a group that they think they have greater political power over."); *id.* at 177-79, 184-85 (statement of Michael F. Jacobson, Executive Director, CSPI) (doubting that third party reviews would reduce delays substantially, fearing "conflicts of interest among reviewers and forum shopping by additive manufacturers," and concluding that "safety evaluations should be made by FDA officials, who are publicly accountable, not by outsiders").

571. *See id.* at 88 (statement of Hon. Edolphus Towns).

572. *See id.* at 124 (statement of Stuart M. Pape, on behalf of the National Soft Drink Association) ("Contrary to some suggestions, this is not a radical reversal of the burden [of] proving that the additive is safe . . . [but the] FDA should not be able to frustrate the purpose of independent review and prevent the approval of the additive merely by identifying some question or issue that is unresolved."); *id.* at 168 ("The proposal we made would require FDA to have substantial evidence, not to demonstrate that the additive is unsafe, but simply substantial evidence to demonstrate that safety hasn't been shown.").

573. Lars Noah, *Sham Petitioning as a Threat to the Integrity of the Regulatory Process*, 74 N.C. L. REV. 1 (1995).

574. *Id.* at 3.

575. *See* 21 C.F.R. § 171.1(h) (1996). Certain confidential information and protected trade secrets are exempt. *See, e.g.*, *id.* §§ 171.1(h)(1)(iii) (exempting from public disclosure identifying information in adverse reaction reports and consumer complaints), 171.1(h)(2) (exempting from public disclosure manufacturing methods, sales data and quantitative formulas).

576. *See supra* notes 207-13 and accompanying text.

577. 52 Fed. Reg. 17,475 (1987); *see also* 51 Fed. Reg. 34,503 (1986) (notice of filing of a food additive petition for alitame, another sweetener that the FDA continues to review ten years later).

578. *See Formal Comment Period on Food Additive Petitions Requested*, FOOD CHEM. NEWS, July 6, 1992, at 36-37 (suggesting that the tardy submission by the Center for Science in the Public Interest of old data about sucralose, data which purportedly was received from an anonymous source, may have reflected bad faith intervention by a company seeking to retain its competitive advantage in the market for non-nutritive sweeteners). *But see 1995 Hearings*, *supra* note 1, at 181 (statement of Michael F. Jacobson, Executive Director of CSPI) (responding that CSPI "has not been used by anti-competitive forces to delay decisions on pending petitions").

579. *See* H.R. REP. NO. 436, 104th Cong., 1st Sess. 5 (1995); *see also* Ron Wasik, *A Sweet New Alternative*, FOOD IN CANADA, June 1991, at 27 (describing review of the sucralose petition in Canada).

580. *See FDA Delay in Sucralose Approval Gets "Golden Grinch" Award from Sen. Mathews*, FOOD CHEM. NEWS, Aug. 29, 1994, at 46 (quoting Sen. Harlan Mathews as complaining that "'any third party could indefinitely delay approval of [a food] additive simply by repeatedly submitting their interpretation of data'"); *see also 1995 Hearings*, *supra* note 1, at 78 (statement of Robert C. Gelardi, Executive Vice President, Calorie Control Council) (noting that "the careful timing of their submissions can hold up a review numerous times just short of approval"); *id.* at 90-91 (describing anonymous submissions as a method of delaying FDA approval of a food additive petition for competitive reasons); *House Patent Extension Hearing*, *supra* note 438, at 186, 204, 383 (statement of Edwin L. Artzt, Chairman and CEO of the Procter & Gamble Co.) (suggesting that Unilever, a competitor developing an additive like olestra, "funded a group of scientists who wrote to the FDA, urging caution and more testing" on Procter & Gamble's pending petition).

581. *See* Letter from George H. Pauli, Ph.D., CFSAN's Office of Premarket Approval, to Sandra Schlicker, Ph.D., Director of the NAS's Food Forum, Sept. 27, 1996, at 7 (copy on file with the author) ("All outstanding issues still have not been resolved, and it is misleading to attribute to comments a delay in reaching a decision based on the original data. Comments that have little merit will not cause lengthy delays.").

582. *See* H.R. REP. NO. 436, 104th Cong., 1st Sess. 9 (1995); *see also id.* at 12-13 ("Manipulation of the food additive review process for anti-competitive purposes is inconsistent with the purposes of pre-market review.").

583. *See* Cutler v. Hayes, 818 F.2d 879, 896-97 (D.C. Cir. 1987) ("[E]xcessive delay saps the public confidence in an agency's ability to discharge its responsibilities and creates uncertainty for the parties, who must incorporate the potential effect of possible agency decisionmaking into future plans." (internal quotation marks omitted)); Noah, *supra* note 573, at 58 ("[T]he largely unrestricted opportunity to participate brings with it the possibility for strategic manipulation of the regulatory process in pursuit of anticompetitive ends.").

584. *See In re* International Chemical Workers Union, 958 F.2d 1144 (D.C. Cir. 1992) (issuing a writ of mandamus after a six year delay by OSHA); Public Citizen Health Research Group v. Commissioner, 740 F.2d 21, 32 (D.C. Cir. 1984) ("[C]ourts are certainly not without power to address the interests of a regulatory beneficiary . . . when unwarranted agency delay prejudices those interests."); Nader v. FCC, 520 F.2d 182, 206 (D.C. Cir. 1975) ("There comes a point when relegating issues to proceedings that go on without conclusion in any kind of reasonable time frame is tantamount to refusing to address the issues at all—and the result is a denial of justice.").

585. Abbott Laboratories v. Harris, 481 F. Supp. 74, 76 (N.D. Ill. 1979) ("It is undisputed that the administrative process has gone on for six years without an order from which plaintiff could seek judicial review.").

586. Southeastern Minerals, Inc. v. Califano, Civ. No. 77-51-THOM (M.D. Ga. Jan. 31, 1978). Counsel for the government in that case admitted that the FDA's delay in responding to the petition was "outrageous" and "unjustified;" the Agency "wisely decided not to appeal from that portion of the district court's judgment." Southeastern Minerals, Inc. v. Harris, 622 F.2d 758, 768 (5th Cir. 1980). The court of appeals in that case noted that the "FDA's disregard for the statutory and regulatory requirement that the agency act on a pending petition within a maximum of 180 days is equally regrettable and inexcusable." *Id.* at 767; *see also In re* Center for Auto Safety, 793 F.2d 1346, 1353-54 & n.55 (D.C. Cir. 1986).

587. *See* 21 U.S.C. § 348(c)(2) (1994); 21 C.F.R. § 171.100 (1996).

588. Sierra Club v. Costle, 657 F.2d 298, 397 (D.C. Cir. 1981) ("Most likely the drafters [of the Clean Air Act Amendments] envisioned promulgation of a rule soon after the close of the public comment period, and did not envision a months-long hiatus where continued outside communications with the agency would continue unabated.").

> [Interested parties] cannot force an agency to delay rulemaking simply because some new rebuttal evidence may be forthcoming; this is particularly so when the statute mandates speedy promulgation of the rule. Were it otherwise, participants could delay promulgation indefinitely since new information continually comes to light on the subject of many proposed rules.

Id. at 399-400; *see also* Community Nutrition Inst. v. Block, 749 F.2d 50, 58 (D.C. Cir. 1984) ("Rulemaking proceedings would never end if an agency's response to comments must always be made the subject of additional comments.").

589. 60 Fed. Reg. 57,586, 57,587 (1995).

590. *See* 21 C.F.R. § 330.10(a)(6) (1996); 45 Fed. Reg. 31,422, 31,424 (1980) ("[T]he agency's decision in a tentative final monograph will be based solely on the administrative record developed through the 90-day comment and 30-day rebuttal comment period."). The FDA requires that petitions for reconsideration be filed within 30 days of a decision, 21 C.F.R. § 10.33(b), "in order to make certain that such matters are settled promptly. Although filing such petitions would not operate to delay any administrative action, the uncertainty that would be generated by permitting such petitions at any point in time would undermine effective implementation of the act." 40 Fed. Reg. 40,682, 40,687 (1975).

591. *See* Cutler v. Kennedy, 475 F. Supp. 838, 854 (D.D.C. 1979) (deciding that the FDA's regulation of OTC drugs, by "formally authoriz[ing] the continued marketing of Category III drug products in the absence of an administrative determination that those products are" GRAS/GRAE, "flies in the face of statutory scheme"). Indeed, the FDA considers a food additive petition automatically withdrawn if the petitioner fails to submit, in response to a timely request from the Agency, a sample before the 180-day deadline. 21 C.F.R. § 171.1(j) (1996).

592. *See, e.g.*, 57 Fed. Reg. 11,325 (1992). GRAS affirmation petitions allow 60 days for comment, 21 C.F.R § 170.35-(c)(3) (1996), and this is also the amount of time provided in the FDA's general procedures for rulemaking. *Id.* § 10.40(b)(2); *see also* 55 Fed. Reg. 49,576 (1990) (petition to prohibit BHA).

593. *See* 60 Fed. Reg. 57,586, 57,587 (1995) ("Any data, information, or comments received after that [deadline] will be filed in an administrative file and will be evaluated along with any objections to the final decision" on the olestra petition.); *1995 Hearings*, *supra* note 1, at 79 (statement of Robert C. Gelardi, Executive Vice President, Calorie Control Council) (recommending the adoption of this procedure); *see also* H.R. REP. NO. 436, 104th Cong., 1st Sess. 13 (1995) (recommending that the FDA refuse to consider any information from anonymous sources). One industry representative suggested that the FD&C Act be amended to shift food additive approvals from formal to informal rulemaking procedures, thereby hoping to speed reviews by reducing the pressure to anticipate objections and requests for an administrative hearing. *See FDA Blueprint for Additive Petition Reform Goes to HHS*, FOOD CHEM. NEWS, Oct. 30, 1995, at 37, 40.

Although it is not clear that officials would be any less worried about the prospect of judicial review, late-filed objections would then become a petition for reconsideration or to amend the final rule.

594. *See* 45 Fed. Reg. 31,422, 31,424 (1980) ("New data and information may be submitted after the 90-day comment period but will not be included as part of the administrative record for consideration by the agency until after the administrative record is reopened following publication of a [TFM] . . . ."); *see also* Noah, *supra* note 573, at 72 ("[L]egislators and regulators must ensure that opportunities for intervention are circumscribed so that incumbent firms cannot inappropriately inhibit competition.").

595. *See* 21 C.F.R. § 330.10(a)(7)(v) (1996) (unless "good cause has been shown that warrants earlier consideration"); 45 Fed. Reg. at 31,424 (the FDA "will not include such [late-filed] data in its consideration of the content of a final monograph."); *see also* Noah, *supra* note 573, at 67 ("For example, intervention might be permitted only at a particular stage in the proceedings and in such a way as not to delay agency action.").

596. *See* 21 C.F.R. § 171.130(b) (1996) ("Any such petition shall include an assertion of facts, supported by data, showing that new information exists with respect to the food additive or that new uses have been developed or old uses abandoned, that new data are available as to toxicity of the chemical, or that experience with the existing regulation or exemption may justify its amendment or repeal.").

597. Existing certification requirements suffer from certain limitations, however, especially a lack of effective monitoring and enforcement by the responsible agencies. *See* Noah, *supra* note 573, at 53-58. "Although agencies might do well to demand closer adherence to the rules of professional responsibility or impose certification requirements akin to Rule 11, ultimately more stringent restrictions on participation may be necessary to combat abuse of the regulatory process." *Id.* at 58.

598. 21 C.F.R. § 10.30(b) (1996). A food additive petition must be signed by the petitioner or by its attorney or agent, *id.* § 171.1(e), and it "shall not omit without explanation any reports of investigations that would bias an evaluation of the safety of the food additive." *Id.* § 171.1(c)(E); *see also 1995 Hearings*, *supra* note 1, at 78 (statement of Robert C. Gelardi, Executive Vice President, Calorie Control Council) (complaining that "nonpetitioner submissions are accorded a full review without hard data, or peer review, and when indeed they often are no more than opinion").

599. *See supra* Part II.B. Although the FDA has published "positive" GRAS lists, these do not exhaust the range of possible GRAS substances. *See* 21 C.F.R. §§ 170.30(d), 182.1 (1996). The only substances for which GRAS status could never be asserted include those subject to a food additive regulation or an outright prohibition. *See id.* §§ 170.38, 182.1(d), 189.1. Absence from one of these "negative" lists would not, however, automatically authorize the use of a substance unless it also satisfies the general criteria for GRAS status.

600. *See generally* ROGER D. MIDDLEKAUFF & PHILIPPE SHUBIK eds., INTERNATIONAL FOOD REGULATION HANDBOOK 329-479 (1989) (summarizing regulatory approaches to food and food additives in Belgium, France, Denmark, Israel, Egypt, Thailand, and Australia).

601. *See, e.g.*, 60 Fed. Reg. 53,078, 53,080 (1995) (describing the FDA's participation in international activities related to the establishment of food standards); 60 Fed. Reg. 11,260-87 (1995) (announcing international guidelines for the testing of human pharmaceuticals); Joseph G. Contrera, Comment, *The Food and Drug Administration and the International Conference on Harmonization: How Harmonious will International Pharmaceutical Regulations Become?*, 8 ADMIN. L.J. 927 (1995).

602. *See Interim Patent Extension Hearing*, *supra* note 438, at 16 (testimony of Bruce A. Lehman, Commissioner of Patents and Trademarks) ("[W]e are fairly advanced in the biotechnology, biochemical area and . . . normally we are the first country to have these regulatory review problems."). *But cf.* Burros, *supra* note 434, at C1 (reporting that olestra has been under review for a number of years in Britain and Canada).

603. *See 1995 Hearings*, *supra* note 1, at 162, 166 (testimony of Donald Farley, President, Food Science Group, Pfizer, Inc.) ("[S]ome companies are conducting research offshore simply for that purpose; they obtain faster approvals in foreign countries, who have a professional regulatory authority who review detailed safety petitions.").

604. In contrast, comparative data exist for drug approval times. *See, e.g.*, Rosemarie Kanusky, Comment, *Pharmaceutical Harmonization: Standardizing Regulations Among the United States, the European Economic Community, and Japan*, 16 HOUS. J. INT'L L. 665, 686 (1994).

605. R.S.C., ch. F-27 (1985) (Can.).

606. *See* D.G. Chapman, *Current Topics in Canadian Food Regulatory Affairs*, 30 FOOD DRUG COSM. L.J. 654, 655-56 (1975); A.B. Morrison, *The Canadian Approach to Food and Drug Regulations*, 30 FOOD DRUG COSM. L.J. 632 (1975); Ron O. Read, *Food Safety and Regulations—A Canadian Perspective*, 36 FOOD DRUG COSM. L.J. 120 (1981).

607. R.S.C. ch. F-27, §§ 4(a), 30(1)(b)(iv).

608. C.R.C. ch. 870, § B.01.001 (1996).

609. *See id.*; *see also* Read, *supra* note 606, at 125 ("The major reason for some of the exemptions such as flavors and packaging materials at the time of drafting the food additive regulations was based on the premise that there was only a remote possibility of hazard to health because of the small amount added or migrating into foods."). Instead, the HPB issues regulations prohibiting these substances when necessary. *See* Chapman, *supra* note 606, at 655 ("We have found this practice [of "negative" listing] to be a good alternative to the [FDA] policy of attempting to list all permitted flavoring materials and components of packaging materials.").

610. *See 1995 Hearings*, *supra* note 1, at 168 (statement of Jerome H. Heckman, on behalf of the Society of the Plastics Industry) ("[T]hey use a system in Canada that is more like pre-market notification . . . . There are three people that work on indirect additive no objection letter requests, and last year they processed 900 of them. They don't have any backlog to speak of."); Read, *supra* note 606, at 125 ("[W]hile there is no legal requirement to do so, most manufacturers who supply packaging materials to the food industry make submissions to the [HPB] on a continuing basis, requesting the Branch's opinion on the acceptability of their various products.").

611. C.R.C. ch. 870, § B.01.001 (1996).

612. *See* Blake, Cassels & Graydon, *Developments in Canadian Law Relating to Food, Drugs, Devices, and Cosmetics as of December 1992*, 49 FOOD & DRUG L.J. 323, 342 (1994); Katharine E. Gourlie, *NAFTA Countries: Convergence and Fracture*, 51 FOOD & DRUG L.J. 423, 429-31 (1996) (adding that special labeling would not routinely be required); *see also* HPB, *Guidelines for the Safety Assessment of Novel Foods* (1994).

613. C.R.C. ch. 870, § B.16.100 (1995). The regulations include fifteen separate tables listing various classes of approved food additives, along with any restrictions on use. For a summary of recent revisions to these regulations, see the "Food Additive Update" section of the annual *Encyclopedia of Food Ingredients* published in the April issue of FOOD IN CANADA, *available in* LEXIS, News Library, FDCAN File.

614. C.R.C. ch. 870, § B.16.002(d) & (e) (1996).

615. *See id.* § B.16.003.

616. *See id.* § B.16.002; Chapman, *supra* note 606, at 655-56.

617. *See* Erik Millstone, *Food Additive Regulation in the UK*, 10 FOOD POL'Y 237, 244-45, 252 (1985). *See generally* David Jukes, *Regulation and Enforcement of Food Safety in the UK*, 18 FOOD POL'Y 131 (1993).

618. Food Safety Act, 1990, ch. 16, §§ 7(1), 16(1)(a). For a list of food additive regulations issued under the authority of this statute and its predecessors, see 18 HALSBURY'S STATUTES 502-06 (4th ed. 1991).

619. *See* Millstone, *supra* note 617, at 239, 245 (explaining that, as of 1985, 314 additives in 23 different classes were listed (accounting for less than 10% of all additives in use) and that other classes were subject only to limited negative lists).

620. *See* Sweeteners in Food Regulations, S.I. 1995, No. 3123; Colours in Food Regulations, S.I. 1995, No. 3124; Miscellaneous Food Additives Regulations, S.I. 1995, No. 3187; *United Kingdom Removes Numerous Outdated Food Composition Regulations*, FOOD & DRINK WKLY., Jan. 15, 1996, *available in* Westlaw, Foodrd File ("Fourteen food additive regulations, dating to 1967, have been revoked and replaced by three sets of regulations that introduce new European Union requirements for colors, sweeteners and other additives.").

621. *See* John Abraham & Erik Millstone, *Food Additive Controls: Some International Comparisons*, 14 FOOD POL'Y 43, 47 (1989) ("This means that [the additive] must perform a function which is not yet performed by any additive already permitted, or else perform it more effectively or more safely."); *see also id.* at 49 ("It has been a long-standing policy of successive FR German governments not to permit any new additives, or any new uses for those additives which are already permitted, unless there are particularly strong grounds for doing so.").

622. *See id.* at 46-47; Millstone, *supra* note 617, at 245-46. As of 1985, it was estimated that "it takes from three to 10 years to complete the tests and gain a regulatory decision." Millstone, *supra* note 617, at 252. (The estimate in the U.S. at that time was 5-7 years for direct additives. *See* 49 Fed. Reg. 50,856, 50,859 (1984).)

623. *See* CHARLES LISTER, REGULATION OF FOOD PRODUCTS BY THE EUROPEAN COMMUNITY (1992).

624. *See* EEC Treaty arts. 30 & 36.

625. *See, e.g.*, Case 178/84, Commission v. Germany, [1987] E.C.R. 1227, [1988] 1 C.M.L.R. 780; Case 304/84, Ministère Public v. Muller & Kampfmeyer-France Sàrl, [1986] E.C.R. 1511, [1987] 2 C.M.L.R. 469; Case 247/84 State v. Motte, [1985] E.C.R. 3887, [1987] 1 C.M.L.R. 663; Case 174/82, Officier van Justite v. Sandoz B.V., [1983] E.C.R. 2445, [1984] 3 C.M.L.R. 43; *see also* Communication on the Free Movement of Foodstuffs Within the Community, 1989 O.J. (C271) 13, at ¶ 38 (interpreting "reasonable time" as 90 days).

626. *See* Council Directive 89/107, 1989 O.J. (L40) 27, art. 1(2), *amended by* 94/34, 1994 O.J. (L237) 1.

627. *See id.* art. 1(3). "Processing aid" is defined as a substance used during treatment or processing "which may result in the unintentional but technically unavoidable presence of residues of the substance or its derivatives in the final product, provided that these residues do not present any health risk and do not have any technological effect on the finished product." *Id.* n.1.

628. *See* Common Position 25/95, 1995 O.J. (C320) 1, arts. 3(4) & 5 (proposing to subject certain novel foods and food ingredients to a premarket notification rather than premarket approval process).

629. Council Directive 89/107, 1989 O.J. (L40) 27, annex II(1).

630. *Id.* annex II(2) ("[I]n other words it is necessary to establish the case for what is commonly referred to as 'need.'"). The directive sets forth four purposes—preservation of nutritional quality; provision of a constituent for a special dietary need; enhancement of "keeping quality or stability" or organoleptic properties; and assistance in manufacture, processing, preparation, treatment, packing, transport or storage—but emphasizes that utility for one or more of these broad purposes would not demonstrate "need" unless the purpose(s) cannot be achieved by other practicable means. *See id.*

631. *Id.* annex II(3) (adding that "[t]he evaluation should also take into account, for example, any cumulative, synergistic or potentiating effect of its use and the phenomenon of human intolerance to substances foreign to the body"). Approval of a food additive must take into account, among other things, "any acceptable daily intake, or equivalent assessment, established for the food additive and the probable daily intake of it from all sources." *Id.* annex II(6)(c); *see also* EC Commission, *Presentation of an Application for Assessment of a Food Additive Prior to its Authorization* (1989) (specifying the safety data and other information required in a dossier).

632. Council Directive 89/107, 1989 O.J. (L40) 27, art. 2(1). Such substances also must abide by any applicable limitations on use. *Id.* art. 3(2). Subject to certain conditions, individual member states may provisionally authorize the use of an unlisted additive for no more than two years. *See id.* art 5.

633. *See* Council Directive 2645/62, 1962 O.J. (L279) 1.

634. *See* Council Directive 64/54, 1964 O.J. (12) 161; Council Directive 70/357, 1970 O.J. (L157) 31; Council Directive 74/329, 1974 O.J. (L189) 1.

635. *See* Council Directive 94/36, 1994 O.J. (L237) 13; Council Directive 94/35, 1994 O.J. (L237) 3; *see also* Council Directive 95/31, 1995 O.J. (L178) 1 (establishing purity criteria for colors and sweeteners).

636. *See* Council Directive 95/2, 1995 O.J. (L61) 1.

637. *See supra* note 620.

638. *See* Charles Lister, *Discord and Change: An Assessment of the European Community's Food Packaging Laws*, 48 FOOD & DRUG L.J. 589 (1993); Jean-Philippe Montfort, *"The Article 30 Solution": An Alternative to Market Food-Contact Materials in the European Union*, 51 FOOD & DRUG L.J. 161 (1996).

639. *See* Council Directive 88/388, 1988 O.J. (L184) 61 (framework directive concerning the approximation of flavoring laws); *see also* Mitzi Elkes, *Europe 1992: Its Impact on Nontariff Trade Barriers and Trade Relations with the United States*, 44 FOOD DRUG COSM. L.J. 563, 581-82 (1989).

640. *See* Common Position, 25/95, 1995 O.J. (C320) 1, arts. 1 & 2. (GMOs were defined in Council Directive 90/220, 1990 O.J. (L117) 15 (concerning deliberate environmental releases).) Because the Council plans to issue regulations rather than a directive, member states will not first have to modified their domestic laws.

641. *See* Common Position, 25/95, 1995 O.J. (C320) 1, arts. 3(1)-(2), 4, 6, 7 & 13. The EU's Scientific Committee for Food (SCF) would play an advisory role. *Id.* art. 11.

642. *See id.* art. 8. The labeling issue has created significant controversy and delayed work toward adoption of a directive on the subject. *See Council to Agree Novel Foods Conciliation*, REUTER E.C. REP., July 11, 1996, *available in* LEXIS, Intlaw Library, ECNews File.

643. *See* Peter B. Edelman, *Japanese Product Standards as Non-tariff Trade Barriers: When Regulatory Policy Becomes a Trade Issue*, 24 STAN. J. INT'L L. 389, 392-94 (1988); Frank K. Upham, *The Legal Framework of Japan's Declining Industries Policy: The Problem of Transparency in Administrative Processes*, 27 HARV. INT'L L.J. 425 (1986); Ken Duck, Comment, *Now That the Fog Has Lifted: The Impact of Japan's Administrative Procedures Law on the Regulation of Industry and Market Governance*, 19 FORDHAM INT'L L.J. 1686 (1996); *see also* David Cohen & Karen Martin, *Western Ideology, Japanese Product Safety Regulation and International Trade*, 19 U.B.C. L. REV. 315, 348-49 (1985) (mentioning positive list and approval process for food additives).

644. *See Highlights of U.S. Trade Barrier Report*, JAPAN WKLY. MONITOR, Apr. 8, 1996, *available in* LEXIS, News Library, Iacwld File; Hiroshi Nakamae, *USTR Report Targets Japan as Closed Market*, NIKKEI WKLY., Apr. 4, 1994, *available in* LEXIS, Busfin Library, Nikkei File; *see also Commission Statement on EU-Japan Ministerial Meeting*, REUTER E.C. REP., Apr. 29, 1996, *available in* LEXIS, Eurcom Library, Reuec File (noting that "a dialogue on food additive regulation will soon begin"); *Japan Joins West in Food-Safety Research*, NIKKEI WKLY., Mar. 11, 1996, *available in* LEXIS, Busfin Library, Nikkei File.

645. *See* MINISTRY OF HEALTH AND WELFARE, JAPANESE STANDARDS FOR FOOD ADDITIVES (6th ed. (English) 1994), *reviewed in* JAPAN CHEM. WEEK, May 19, 1994, at 8.

646. *See Japan: Koseisho to Relax Standards for Nine Food Additives*, REUTER TEXTLINE, Oct. 3, 1992, *available in* LEXIS, World Library, Txtlne File (adding that the approvals for over 200 of these compounds include restrictions on use); *see also* MICHAEL ASH & IRENE ASH, HANDBOOK OF FOOD ADDITIVES 999-1017 (1995).

647. *See Consumer Groups Target Food Additives*, NIKKEI WKLY., Sept. 18, 1995, *available in* LEXIS, Busfin Library, Nikkei File ("Japan's Food Sanitation Law was revised last May for the first time in 23 years. The amendments added Japan's first controls on natural food additives . . . [and the] Ministry released a list of 466 natural additives that will be approved under the new law.").

648. *See* Ministry of Health & Welfare, *Draft Guidelines for Designation of Food Additives and for Revision of Standards for the Use of Food Additives* (1995); *Japan: Draft on Food Additive Deregulation Prepared*, REUTER TEXTLINE, July 17, 1995, *available in* LEXIS, World Library, Txtlne File (reporting that the draft "calls for a sweeping revision of the 1965 report with respect to the range of toxicity tests required for safety evaluations and the need for guidelines showing the standard test methods and is aimed at greater speed and transparency in the procedures to designate food additives").

649. *See Japan's Bioindustry—Genetic Recombination Starting to Bear Fruit*, JAPAN CHEM. WEEK, Nov. 17, 1994, at 7; *Great Expectation for Foodstuffs*, JAPAN CHEM. WEEK, Nov. 18, 1993, at 4.

650. Ministry of Health & Welfare, *Guidelines for Safety Assessments of Foods and Food Additives Produced by Recombinant DNA Techniques* (1992).

651. *See Japan: Group Confirms Safety of rDNA Chymosin*, REUTER TEXTLINE, June 27, 1994, *available in* LEXIS, World Library, Txtlne File; *Japan Trials of Recombinant Chymosin to Begin*, REUTER TEXTLINE, Jan. 18, 1994, *available in* LEXIS, World Library, Txtlne File.

652. *See supra* note 401.

APPENDIX B

Case Studies of the Implementation of the Direct Food and Color Additives Amendments to the Federal Food, Drug, and Cosmetic Act of 1938[a]

TECHNOLOGICAL AND SOCIAL FACTORS THAT HAVE AFFECTED INTRODUCTION OF NEW DIRECT FOOD INGREDIENTS AND PROCESSES

Introduction

The companion paper by Lars Noah (1997) provides a well-documented history of the development and application of the legal and regulatory background of the present processes for the review and approval of new direct food ingredients and technologies into the marketplace.

The case histories that follow are intended to illustrate how that legal and regulatory structure has operated in actual practice over the past four decades. The purpose of these case studies is *not* to point out error or assess blame. Instead, the value that can be extracted from these histories is to learn what specific features of process and procedure have been effective in protecting public health while permitting innovation, and why they have been effective. We wish also to learn which features have not been effective, and why. Efforts to improve the overall structure will be more effective when it is possible to draw carefully and dispassionately from experience.

The cases summarized did not evolve in an atmosphere defined solely by statutory and regulatory boundaries. Rather, they have been heavily, and sometimes decisively, influenced by changes in available technology and in society in general. This brief introduction cannot examine these influences in detail. Simply listing them with minimal comment, however, begins to suggest the impact they have had on attitudes and lifestyles, and most importantly, on the approval processes that are the subject of this exercise.

Developments in Analytical Chemistry

Since 1958, one of the most significant developments in technology has been the dramatic increase, approximately six orders of magnitude, in the sensitivity of instrumental methods of chemical analysis. Discrimination and speed have increased almost as much, with a consequent, and comparable, reduction in cost per analysis. As a consequence, there is now far more information on the enormous complexity and variability of the trace constituents in the food supply (IFBC, 1990; NAS, 1996). The great majority of these constituents occur naturally. A small minority, but still very many, are present as a result of human activity. Analytical

[a] Prepared by Food Forum members and consultants, John Kirschman, Ph.D., Kirschman Associates, C.K. Gund, Ph.D., and Clyde Takeguchi, Ph.D., Phoenix Regulatory Associates, Ltd.

methodology is now at the point where it is almost possible, with sufficient effort, to find traces of almost anything, in virtually everything. This awareness has complicated enormously the task of devising appropriately protective specifications for food-grade ingredients. Particularly for pesticide residues, it has also undermined the simplistic black-or-white, permit-or-prohibit, zero-tolerance assumptions on which the Delaney clause was based.

Developments in Toxicology

In the past four decades the cost in constant dollars and complexity of toxicological tests, particularly the two-year chronic (carcinogenicity) bioassay, have increased several fold. A fundamental tenet of toxicology is dose/response—the higher the dose, the more frequent and severe will be the adverse effects. Humans are almost always exposed to comparatively very low doses—doses at which the chance of finding adverse effects in a reasonable number of animals would be negligible. In order to be likely to detect adverse effects, particularly carcinogenicity, dose levels have increased, often to the "maximum tolerated dose" (MTD). This greater assurance of finding adverse effects is purchased at the cost of possible, and sometimes demonstrated, lack of relevance to humans at the low doses humans normally ingest.

Since 1958, the number of animals per test level has more than doubled and the number of tissues and organs typically examined has increased from 10 to 50. In addition to traditional endpoints such as carcinogenicity, neurological, behavioral, and immune-system effects are now being studied. However, the debate about how to measure, analogize, or transfer results in test animals to humans continues.

In 1973, a quick, inexpensive screening test was developed by Ames and co-workers (Ames, 1973) with the aim of predicting carcinogenicity of a broad range of substances. This test measures the mutagenic potential of substances using, as the test organism, a genetically modified bacterial strain, *Salmonella typhimurium*. Mutagenesis is the ability of chemicals to cause changes in DNA, RNA, and other cellular macromolecules. This hoped for relationship between mutagenicity and carcinogenicity that underlies the Ames test was questioned when substances with no known carcinogenicity tested positively. Mutagenic potential, however, remains a serious concern even though, as yet, no heritable human disease has been traced to a chemical mutagen. The Ames test, and the later genetic toxicology tests it stimulated, have become a useful way of distinguishing those ("genetic") carcinogens that act through attack on DNA and RNA from "epigenetic" carcinogens acting by more indirect mechanisms.

Obviously, these changes have vastly increased the volume and complexity of data that must be collected, recorded, analyzed, and evaluated as part of the approval process.

The Emerging Understanding of Mechanisms

Lagging greatly behind the advances in analytical chemistry, and the increasing power of toxicological testing, has been the development and acceptance of the sciences that are coming to be increasing useful in the design of, and the interpretation of, the results of analytical and toxicological testing. Among these interpretive sciences are:

- Comparative Metabolism—studying the similarity or differences between test animal and human metabolism of a substance;
- Structure /Activity Relationships (SAR)—the study of the effect of the chemical structure of a substance on its biological activity;

- Physiologically-Based Pharmacokinetics (PBPK)—detailed study of the rates, volumes, and capacities of a test animal's metabolic pathways at varying doses; and
- Molecular Biology—the internal biochemistry of the individual cell, with particular focus on the role of the nucleic acids in determining cellular response.

These interpretive sciences have begun to contribute heavily to understanding the gross results of toxicological studies. They help to separate adverse effects relevant to humans from those that are not relevant, and genuine effects from spurious ones. The above sciences greatly improve the estimation of actual human health risks. Unfortunately, they involve a broad range of cutting-edge science not available in-house to any single organization—governmental, industrial, or academic. All organizations, therefore, require extensive outside expertise in order to be effective.

Only in the past 10 to 15 years has it been widely accepted that cancer is a genetic disease, that is, due to changes in the genetic makeup of cells. These changes are usually triggered and heavily influenced by environmental and lifestyle factors. This is a key portion of our current understanding, far broader and more specific than in 1958, of the extent to which diets and lifestyles affect the risk of chronic diseases, including cancer, coronary heart disease, and stroke. This improved understanding of cancer is a direct outcome of molecular biology, in particular.

Sound toxicology has always held that no single test or criterion can be decisive. All of the data must always be examined. These newer interpretive sciences, however, have resulted in a gradual, but major diminution in the role of the once controlling chronic study, and an insistence on additional supporting and interpretive data before applying the results of such studies.

Changes in Risk and Safety Assessment

The more obvious safety decisions on direct food ingredients (substances intentionally added) and constituents (substances naturally or unavoidably present) have been made simply and easily. Some substances are so clearly toxic that regulations specifically exclude them (dulcin, CFR Sec. 189.145). Others are so obviously safe because of lack of toxicity (sugar or salt) or because of trivial exposure (hydrogen cyanide, cucurbiticin E, and other natural toxicants), that regulations do not specifically deal with them and they are treated under the general provisions of the FD&C Act. In such cases, a formal process of risk assessment is neither needed or used. It is the large group of "in between" substances, too useful and not toxic enough to prohibit, too risky to leave totally uncontrolled, that require some level of risk assessment, and that may also require risk management. This can range from good manufacturing practices (GMPs) or labeling to tightly restricted uses.

Until 30 years ago the only internationally recognized method of establishing a safe level of exposure (consumption) of a substance was to take the highest dose that produced no observed adverse effects in animals (the NOEL), and divide it by a suitable safety factory, often 100, to obtain the acceptable daily intake (ADI) which humans might safely consume. For most toxic endpoints, such as neurotoxicity or non-carcinogenic organ damage, this approach continues to be used and well serves human health. FDA commonly uses the concept, although seldom employs it explicitly, preferring instead to rely on "the weight of all of the evidence."

In the last few decades, however, and particularly for substances that show carcinogenic effects in test animals, that approach has been replaced by "quantitative risk assessment" (QRA). Although it can be mathematically complex, QRA usually involves a series of conservative "default" assumptions. These default assumptions are made where the needed biological data simply do not yet exist. They typically deal with:

• The estimated incidence of adverse effects that would be found at the levels to which humans are exposed, usually several orders of magnitude below the lowest animal dose (extrapolation);

• The assumption that humans will react like the most sensitive test animal (analogy);

• The maximum possible level of lifetime human exposure, because actual human exposures are often not well known.

All of these assumptions are fraught with uncertainty.

• Depending on the particular assumptions used, extrapolation may grossly under- or overstate human risk. The default assumption is therefore conservative to avoid understatement.

• Because of metabolic differences, the test animal may be a poor model for human risk, and better understanding of mechanisms (see previous discussion) is intended to minimize this problem. However, QRA can seldom factor in human differences in susceptibility, except in the same way that the safety factor is used in the ADI.

• Exposure estimates range from the mean or 95th percentile, when available, to the maximum possible, or something in between. They, too, tend to be conservative.

This process leads to what might reasonably be called a "probable upper bound" of risk which is usually expressed as a lifetime risk of one-in-a-million or some other large number. Unfortunately, it is often carelessly and misleadingly called "the risk." QRA has some clear merit, particularly when default assumptions can be replaced by biological data. It also appears to deal more comfortably with those undesirable trace constituents chemical analysis indicates are present. But it also has the deceptive appeal of a "hard number" that often conceals the softness of the underlying data.

We are never exposed simply to one chemical substance, natural or synthetic. We are constantly exposed to a shifting pool of complex mixtures of substances, most of which we encounter at very low levels. How to assess the safety of mixtures has become a matter of increasing interest, because testing them all, in every conceivable proportion, is obviously impossible. In addition, there is pressure from various interest groups to reduce the use of animals in toxicology testing.

Substances that are metabolized by different routes are very likely not to be additive, in either load or risk. Where, because of exposure or toxicity, a formal risk assessment is appropriate, each substance should be evaluated independently, not lumped together. Absent special reason for concern, very low level exposures can be safely ignored.

Substances that act by the same routes may constitute additive risks. However, if the level of exposure is many orders of magnitude below the levels at which effects have been observed in test animals or humans, the significance of possible synergistic effects is still likely to be negligible. This is not true as exposure to a component of a mixture approaches the ADI, or some other appropriately conservative interpretation of the available biological data. A useful discussion of this complex problem is found in 1997 report of the Presidential Commission on Risk Assessment and Risk Management.

Changes in Agriculture

In 1958, classical genetics had already demonstrated its power with hybrid corn, and the "green revolution" was about to begin. But the family farm, which produced enough food to feed 27 people, was already disappearing. Today, each farmer produces food to feed 128 people at home and abroad. Thus, farming techniques have changed dramatically.

Agricultural technology seemed always to favor larger operations with the resources to make use of new technologies including irrigation control, herbicides, pesticides, plant and animal hormones, and low-dose antibiotics. This trend added to the perceived distance, geographic, economic, and technologic; which separated consumers from the source of their food, and with this increasing distance inevitably came increasing uncertainty and discomfort.

Environmental Concerns

Rachael Carson's *Silent Spring* was published in 1962. Prescient in some respects, erroneous in others, its poetry and power mainstreamed the environmental movement, and promoted an often healthy, but poorly informed, skepticism of new technologies. Current awareness of the potential environmental consequences of industrial and governmental activities was largely lacking in 1958. Environmental impact assessments are a permanent feature of new ingredient and technology development.

Consumer Activity

Consumers as individuals and as organizations have contributed significantly to raising and debating public health and economic issues. Consumer pressure and publications were prominent in the passage of the 1906 and 1938 Food and Drug Acts and in activity leading to the Food Additives Amendment of 1958. Since then, they have been frequent, often vocal, but unevenly effective contributors to food safety issues. Part of this uneven effectiveness may be due to thinly spread resources and limited access to the expertise necessary for dealing with large volumes of data and complex issues. In addition, it may also be due to their continuing concern with social and economic issues, as well as the science. Social and economic issues, however important, lie outside the regulatory authority of FDA. Their perceived urgency may lead to an artificial and unproductive prolongation of the safety discussion as the only forum in which a new technology can be discussed and opposed or delayed.

Changes in Food Marketing and Consumption Trends

Consumer purchasing trends, visible in the marketplace, do not necessarily reflect the agendas of consumer organizations, and these purchasing trends often are contradictory. Forty-three percent of food dollars are now spent on meals eaten away from home and this trend continues. The percent of foods subjected to prior processing before reaching their point-of-sale continues to increase. Since 1958 there has been a generally, although unevenly, increasing number of new food products introduced each year. Most new food products fail, but there are some monumental successes. New food processes have been introduced that include extrusion cooking, pulsed light, aseptic packaging, membrane filtration, and supercritical carbon dioxide extraction. Food costs by families and individuals as a percent of disposable income have continued to decrease, and now stand at 11.2 percent. Nutrition has become a far more prominent and widespread concern, with a consequent interest in lower fat, lower calorie, reduced salt, and higher fiber foods and the "food pyramid," even in elementary schools. And, somewhat contradictorily but simultaneously, "minimally processed," "organic," and "natural" foods, often at substantially increased prices, have moved from niches into supermarkets.

These developments in the U.S. food supply have depended on new or modified ingredients and processes. For example, lower calorie and lower fat foods require new processes, such as microparticulated protein (Simpless™), non-metabolizable fat replacements (Olestra), and non-

or low-calorie sweeteners (saccharin, Nutrasweet™, Acesulfame K, etc.). Thus the list of substances and processes seeking market entry grows steadily.

Congress has enacted laws to increase information and economic protection for consumers, including Fair Packaging and Labeling Act (FPLA) and the Nutrition Labeling and Education Act (NLEA).

The Impact on FDA

In summary, all of the following factors have added enormously to FDA's task load since 1958:

- the knowledge of the presence of trace constituents and contaminants in food;
- more sensitive, more complex toxicological testing, involving much more data and the need for far more interpretive expertise;
- the understanding of the means, the biological mechanisms, by which substances exert their toxic effects;
- the growing need for a broad range of external expertise;
- the need of assessing the environmental impact of every major action;
- the increasing globalization, diversity, and complexity of the food supply;
- increasing dependence on new ingredients and processes; and
- FPLA, NLEA, and the higher level of consumer interest in nutrition, in "healthy lifestyles," and in influencing regulatory decisions.

By contrast, in recent years, the resources of the FDA have remained almost level in constant dollars. The overwhelming competing pressures on the federal budget strongly suggest that the future will be no brighter.

FDA has responded to these pressures with a number of changes in the premarket evaluation of food additives, including the Prioritizing the Assessment of Food Additives (PAFA), the concept of the "threshold of regulation," "levels of concern" in the Redbook, "fast-track" approvals for straightforward and well-supported petitions, and other measures discussed in this symposium. All of these measures are aimed at prioritizing tasks and sensible use of limited resources. That directly complements the purpose of this symposium.

Provisions That Continue to Work Well after Six Decades

Surprisingly, in the midst of all these changes, two provisions of the FD&C Act have continued to serve the public health well. The "does not ordinarily render it [the food] injurious to health" standard applies to foods themselves. If that standard were significantly more strict, there would be little left to eat, for nearly all foods contain natural toxicants capable of causing harm under improper circumstances and with relatively narrow margins of safety (NAS, 1996, 1973; IFBC, 1990; Hall, 1977). The standards, "may render it injurious," in the statute, and "reasonable certainty of no harm," from the legislative history of the 1958 Food Additives Amendment, are more stringent standards that are appropriate for those changes that are intentional and which are therefore under human choice and control.

Conclusion

The thoughtful reader of the case studies that follow will note the pervasive impact of these technological, social, and economic factors, not only on the cases themselves, but on the lessons that can be extracted from them.

CYCLAMATE

Overview

In 1969, the FDA banned cyclamate from use in food after studies suggested that it might be an animal carcinogen. The reintroduction of this food additive petition, by Abbott Laboratories, Inc. in 1973, placed FDA under tremendous scrutiny by all interested parties. The agency had to consider whether to reverse its previous decision while assuring the public that the statutory safety standard would be met.

Cyclamate's previous regulatory history led to heightened sensitivities for both the agency and the petitioner resulting in the FDA Commissioner's direct involvement from the time of initial submission. Over 300 published and unpublished studies were submitted. Some studies were poorly designed but reported adverse effects, such as carcinogenic bladder tumors, testicular atrophy, and cardiotoxicity which caused major concerns to the regulatory scientific reviewers. When scientists from various disciplines review complex issues, there are often disagreements about final interpretations and when placed under tight review time frames, most regulatory scientists will exercise the worst-case scenario. There were several rounds of scientific review and debate about incomplete data and interpretation of data. Some issues were resolved while others remained as major scientific safety concerns. Lack of communication between the agency and the petitioner led to distrust between them.

Another major point of departure from a typical review was the Commissioner's public announcements through talk papers at every decision point and the placement of the entire food additive petition minus trade secrets at the public docket for review. The agency moved very quickly in reviewing the enormous data package and found many deficiencies which led to a rejection letter within the first year. When the Commissioner found the petition inadequate a second time, he assured the public that FDA would not act alone in its scientific review but would ask an outside expert panel to review and provide recommendations. The National Cancer Institute (NCI), a sister agency, served as the expert panel. NCI played a major role in the government's decision to ban cyclamate in 1969. The introduction of the NCI's Temporary Committee's review delayed the final decision for nearly three years.

Another departure from a typical review was the manner in which the final decision was reached. Although the FDA reviewing scientists concluded that the NCI's Temporary Committee had resolved the carcinogenic question and the FDA's management recommended limited approval, the Commissioner, after personally analyzing NCI's Temporary Committee report, concluded that cyclamate could not be approved for use in food.

With the formal denial, Abbott requested a formal evidentiary hearing. This administrative procedure took another four years with vast resources utilized by both the agency and the petitioner. Although the Commissioner's final denial came as no surprise to some observers, there were many from the scientific community that felt a total miscarriage of regulatory decision-making had taken place.

Chronology

1961 FDA advise Abbott laboratories that sodium cyclamate was GRAS as a food substance.

1969 An independent laboratory conducting a two-year feeding study in rats, using the 10:1 ratio of cyclamate:saccharin, reported the presence of bladder tumors. NCI concurred with the finding of carcinogenic bladder tumors and cyclamate was removed from general purpose use in food. There was no evidence that cyclamate caused cancer in humans.

1973 On November 13, Abbott submitted a petition to gain approval for cyclamates as a new food additive. The petition provided all relevant data for cyclamate and the cyclamate/saccharin mixture for the twenty years that it had been used in the United States, plus new unpublished data on cyclamate and cyclohexylamine (CHA).

1973 On December 21, FDA sent Abbott a letter of filing.

1974 FDA toxicology review stated that no conclusions based on the reference articles submitted could be drawn, but concluded that cyclamate must be considered a weak carcinogen. The agency concluded that the mutagenicity data were sufficient.

1974 On September 5, FDA sent a letter to Abbott asking that the petition be withdrawn without prejudice for a future filing. The letter included a discussion of the inadequacies of the toxicology data and the various problems found in the chemistry review.

1974 On September 10, Abbott met with the FDA Commissioner and the agency's staff. The petitioner took exception to the request for additional studies.

1974 On November 1, Abbott responding to the rejection letter, submitted additional data. They disagreed with nearly every issue raised by the agency and noted that 22 long-term studies in rats, mice, and hamsters had been negative for carcinogenic potential for cyclamate and CHA, while bladder tumors were observed in only two rat studies, neither of which had been designed to test for carcinogenic potential of cyclamate. These two studies were further complicated by the presence of bladder calculi and parasites and Abbott declared "the suggestion of carcinogenicity of cyclamate has no scientific validity." Abbott found no significant testicular changes based on two other studies in which researchers fed CHA to rats over 24 months and mice over 80 weeks and concluded that testicular changes probably emanated secondary to dietary inanition.

1974 On November 13, FDA held a public meeting. Abbott provided scientific expert opinions on the inappropriate interpretation by the FDA of the submitted studies and indicated that data were available to demonstrate that cyclamate does not cause teratogenic effects in mice, rats, and rabbits.

1975 In March, FDA rescinded the request to withdraw the petition based on the evaluation of data submitted by Abbott on November 1, 1974, and the transcripts of the November 13, 1974 public meeting.

1975 On March 14, FDA requested that NCI convene a blue ribbon panel of oncologists to decide the carcinogenic issue.

1975 On November 17, Abbott submitted more data and concluded the following: NOEL of CHA in the diet was 5,000 ppm; testicular changes in rats treated for long duration (18–28 months) with large doses of cyclamate (3–5%) probably resulted as a secondary response to nutritional imbalances; no testicular changes had been seen in monkeys treated with 500 mg/kg/day cyclamate for 5 or 7.5 years; no testicular effects observed in rats fed 10% cyclamate for 12 months; and the data indicated that an ADI for cyclamate of 3 g could be established.

1976 On March 8, the NCI Committee concluded that the evidence did not establish the carcinogenicity of cyclamate or CHA in experimental animals. No conclusion could be made on potential carcinogenicity in humans due to the short post-exposure observation time and the insensitivity of epidemiological studies to detect relatively small changes in cancer incidence and other factors.

1976 FDA final toxicology memorandum offered several additional conclusions as follows: (1) the NCI Committee appeared to have resolved the carcinogenesis issue; (2) the ADI could range from about 200–300 mg/day for the average 60 kg adult, but should be proportionally less for children; (3) with this ADI, general use of cyclamate could not be approved; (4) the tablet and drop form for home use should be the item of choice for the individual who needed artificial sweeteners; (5) specific label instruction would be helpful because the ADI could be exceeded by some individuals; and (6) use in soft drinks should be prohibited because excessive use by the young would soon exceed the ADI.

1976 The agency informally recommended limited use of cyclamate for consideration by the Commissioner.

1976 On May 11, because of concerns raised by the NCI Committee, the FDA denied the Abbott petition and requested withdrawal without prejudice to a future filing.

1976 In a June 16 letter, Abbott decided not to withdraw the petition and stated that the Chairman of the NCI Committee believed that the conclusions in the agency's letter were not consistent with the NCI report. The petitioner offered to submit additional data and to conduct an experiment to demonstrate that the proper NOEL of CHA would be 5,000 ppm rather than 2,000 ppm. This compromise was offered if the Commissioner modified his position and allowed cyclamate to return to the marketplace.

1976 On October 4, FDA announced the formal denial of the petition to re-market the artificial sweetener.

1976 On November 3, Abbott requested a formal evidentiary hearing.

1977 The formal hearing with oral testimony and cross-examination took place.

1978 On August 4, the administrative law judge concluded that cyclamate has not been shown to be safe, to not cause cancer in humans or animals, and to not be a mutagen. In addition, if the carcinogenicity and mutagenicity questions are resolved, the record would not support a finding that the ADI is 5 mg/kg/day or less and does not establish probable consumption patterns of cyclamate to the extent necessary to establish safe conditions of use.

1979 On June 29, the FDA published a Notice of Interlocutory Decision that reopened the proceeding to develop the record more fully for the identified areas of concern.

1979 At an October 22 hearing, testimony concerning statistical and biological significance was presented by both the FDA and Abbott.

1980 On February 4, the administrative law judge concluded that the evidence suggests that cyclamate may be a carcinogen, but that the record falls short of establishing that cyclamate is a carcinogen. However, Abbott has failed to establish that cyclamate is not a carcinogen.

1980 On September 16, the FDA published the Commissioner's Final Decision denying the food additive petition for cyclamate.

Comments

During these above seven years, many congressional and consumer inquiries were received—some mandating that FDA place cyclamate back in the marketplace and some adamant that this non-nutritive sweetener was unsafe and lauding the agency for its sound decision-making in banning it. All letters were answered, thereby depleting resources that could have been used to review scientific documents and develop appropriate regulatory policy for this matter.

Although this case study ends with the Commissioner's decision to uphold the denial of cyclamate for use in food, the process is still ongoing. Another petition for cyclamate's use is pending before FDA. In addition, other major government regulatory bodies (European Union, Canada, Australia) have reassessed the regulatory status of cyclamate and allowed it back into the marketplace, with some countries acting within a few years after the initial U.S. ban.

Lessons Learned

1. Communication has to be mutual between the petitioner and agency.
2. When a chemical's history results in notoriety, the agency can decide on new procedures to manage the approval process.
3. Petitioners and the FDA both need to follow the rules.
4. Petioners need to understand the basic petition requirements before submitting a formal petition.
5. When homework on scientific issues presented in the petition is not adequate, the petitioner is the loser.
6. A petitioner of a controversial substance needs to recognize the in-depth scrutiny and resolve issues satisfactorily at the first encounter.
7. Incomplete submissions lead to extensive questions and resource utilization by the agency and ultimately the petitioner.
8. Identical data can be interpreted differently by competent scientists leading to lost time, resources, and difficult decision-making, because the regulatory process typically feels compelled to support the most conservative interpretation and outcome.
9. Scientific positions change as new information become available (e.g., the percent cyclamate converted to cyclohexylamine) illustrating that communicating findings and documenting with data facilitates resolution.
10. In-house conflicts on scientific issues result in lost time.
11. Careful selection of outside expert panels and educating their members on the regulatory safety evaluation process is mandatory for assuring relevant and sound recommendations.
12. Rushing the process does not necessarily result in a sound decision.
13. Decisions involving a controversial subject will always require an unusually long time for closure.
14. The Commissioner is the senior manager and final decision maker of FDA and he/she should carefully consider the final recommendations of the agency's scientists together with those from outside experts and other regulatory bodies when making a controversial decision.

IRRADIATED POULTRY

Overview

Work on the use of radiation to reduce or eliminate microbiological and insect contamination of food, inhibit sprouting, and for other purposes, began shortly after World War II. This was the first new food preservation technique to be developed since the invention of canning by Appert early in the 19th century. It was therefore, the first major food process to be tested for safety by the modern methods of analytical chemistry, microbiology, and toxicology. It also resulted, for the first time, in foods which could not be tested by conventional toxicological methods because test animals cannot be fed enough of the test food to provide conventional margins of safety. Attempts to do so cause nutritional and toxicological problems in the test animal unrelated to the irradiation.

Much of the early testing of irradiated foods, done in the 1950s and 1960s, did not fully recognize these problems, was poorly designed, and gave uninterpretable results that can be attributed to the irradiation conditions, palatability of the irradiated food, and the effect of feeding animals a diet that was nutritionally compromised. Thus, there was little useful background for successful rulemaking on which later petitions could draw.

The rulemaking process for the irradiated poultry regulation is unique because it involves two petitions, one from a contract radiation company, Radiation Technology, Inc. (RTI), and the second, from USDA's Food Safety and Inspection Service. RTI submitted safety studies generated in foreign countries by other sponsors that were originally submitted as data for the safety of food irradiation in those countries. FDA requested additional studies on the effect of irradiation on *C. botulinum* and competitive vegetative bacteria. In addition, FDA had specific questions about some of the safety studies submitted by RTI. However, RTI could not respond adequately to specific questions about the studies because it was not the designer or sponsor of the some of the studies.

Because food additive regulations are generic, the agency utilized information submitted by the petitioner as well as other information in its files. The USDA petition referenced the availability of safety studies in FDA's files and emphasized its knowledge of poultry processing, packaging, labeling, transporting, and quality control.

Chronology

1978 RTI submitted petition describing a process to irradiate chilled poultry at a dose range of 3–7 kGy.

1978 FDA stated need for data on rates of growth of *C. botulinum* in poultry at good refrigeration and higher temperatures.

1979 FDA established the Bureau of Foods Irradiated Foods Committee (BFIFC) to focus on how the safety of irradiated foods can be scientifically evaluated, applying scientific principles and rationale. Thus, much of the insight needed to draw the conclusions FDA eventually reached had not been developed when the petition was submitted.

1979 The FDA review of toxicology data resulted in a request for additional data from the animal feeding studies by the Central Institute for Food and Nutrition Research, TNO Laboratories, The Netherlands, and Bio Research Laboratories.

1981 Joint FAO/IAEA/WHO Expert Committee on the Wholesomeness of Irradiated Food (JECIF) concluded that the irradiation of any food commodity up to the overall average dose of 10 kGy presents no toxicological hazard.

1981 BFIFC recommended that (1) food irradiated at doses below 1 kGy (100 krad) was wholesome and safe, (2) food (e.g., dried spices) that comprise only a small fraction of the diet and irradiated at doses up to 50 kGy (5 Mrad) is safe, and (3) food irradiated at doses exceeding 1 kGy be subject to toxicological testing consisting of a battery of four short-term mutagenicity tests and two 90-day feeding studies.

1983 RTI changed maximum permitted dose to 3 kGy based on a report that demonstrated that *C. botulinum* type E does not pose a problem for poultry irradiated at a maximum dose of 3 kGy and under adverse conditions.

1986 FDA reviewed and evaluated the individual data on irradiated chicken studies in rats and dogs and found the studies acceptable and suitable for safety evaluation.

1986 FDA issued omnibus regulation permitting the use of irradiation to inhibit growth and maturation of fresh foods, to disinfest food of arthropod pests, and to sterilize dried vegetable substances.

1986 USDA submitted petition proposing to use a dose range of 150–300 krad (1.5–3 kGy) to reduce food-borne pathogens such as *Salmonella*, *Campylobacter*, and *Yersinia*.

1987 Resolution on Bio Research data in RTI petition occurred after sponsor of research admitted an error in the incidence of hepatomas that occurred in transposing data to a table.

1987 FDA filed the USDA and RTI petition. FDA entered into a notice and comment rulemaking based on a reevaluation by internal committees that dealt with resolving issues on safety, labeling, processing, and the environment. This reevaluation also included issues regulated by the Nuclear Regulatory Commission, the Department of Transportation, and the Occupational Safety and Health Administration. These issues needed to be resolved before a regulation on irradiated poultry could be approved.

1988 Based on a review of the USDA microbiology data, FDA recommended against vacuum and modified atmosphere packaging for irradiated poultry products.

1990 FDA issued a final rule to provide for the safe use of sources of ionizing radiation for the control of food-borne pathogens in poultry at doses not to exceed 3 kGy with the limitation that any packaging used shall not exclude oxygen.

1992 USDA proposed to amend the poultry products inspection regulations to permit the use of ionizing radiation sources to treat (1) fresh or frozen, uncooked whole poultry carcasses or parts known as "ready to cook poultry," which includes such poultry products as fresh or frozen, uncooked ground, hand-boned, and skinless poultry, and (2) mechanically separated poultry product. Additionally, the proposed rule included regulations regarding packaging, labeling, application for inspection, and a quality control system.

1992 The final USDA rule issued. Currently, there are seven facilities with partial quality control procedures for irradiating poultry that have been approved by USDA.

Comments

Time from original submission of the RTI petition until FDA's filing letter took over 100 months (over 8 years). Time from submission until publication of the final rule took over 140 months (over 11 years). During that time, there were six (6) chemistry memoranda, 16 toxicology memoranda, eight (8) microbiology memoranda, four (4) environmental staff memoranda, and one (1) memorandum from nutrition. It was difficult to analyze the amount of time FDA took to review the petition compared to the time that the petitioner needed to provide additional data and information. FDA provided partial responses to the petitioner on a timely basis after receipt of the technical review and the petitioner's response varied from immediate reaction to a response dependent on the time necessary to obtain the required information.

The USDA petition took less than a month from submission to the filing letter but more than the 15 days specified by regulation. Time from submission until publication of the final rule in the *Federal Register* took over 43 months (3.5 years).

Consumers, interest in irradiation increased after the 1981 publication of FDA's advanced notice of proposed rulemaking for irradiated foods. Initially consumers were concerned about induced radioactivity in foods treated with radiation, the production of toxic products, destruction of essential nutrients, microbiological efficacy, worker safety, and labeling. FDA has responded to all issues of concern to consumers but their questions, especially on the safety, labeling, and environmental effects of irradiated foods continue to be issues of concern. Of particular concern to food manufacturers are the consumer groups, such as Food and Water, Inc., that are threatening "economic blackmail" to prevent use of food irradiation.

Lessons Learned

1. A petition needs to address all safety issues. For the irradiation petition, FDA required additional studies or collection of data to address an outstanding issue on microbial safety. Data on the effect of irradiation on competition between *C. botulinum* and other spoilage organisms were not submitted to FDA until late in the process.
2. FDA does not limit its review to the information submitted by the petitioner but includes all data in its files relevant to the petition.
3. Novel ingredients and processes that involve large amounts of data and that excite substantial and vocal public interest are nearly certain to require long periods for approval, although care in preparation and well organized outside expertise, can improve the process.
4. Poor and poorly presented data result in: (1) failure, or, at best, (2) wasted effort, (3) long delays, and (4) adversely affected public acceptance.
5. Irradiated foods are examples of "food additives" (by statutory definition only) that cannot be tested or evaluated by the traditional methods of toxicology. Among several other reasons, it is not possible to run high-dose feeding studies that provide the large safety factors used in traditional safety evaluation.
6. A new test design should be subject to careful peer review and independent validation before it is used, directly or indirectly, for any regulatory purpose. Petitioners intending to use a new test design must realize that the FDA will not apply lower standards to toxicology and safety evaluation of food ingredients and technologies than would be applied to medical devices, drugs, analytical methods or any new scientific discovery. Indeed, the standards applied to food ingredient testing will necessarily be more stringent that those used for other purposes.
7. In proper circumstances (e.g., absence, after extensive testing of any adverse effect; known, easy, safe, metabolism; or apparently large safety margins), experienced professional judgment can bridge data gaps on a specific subject, or even can rise above the poor quality of some data.

OLESTRA

Overview

On January 30, 1996, the FDA approved Procter & Gamble's (P&G's) food additive petition for the use of its non-caloric fat replacer olestra in certain snack foods. Olestra is the first food additive approved as a macroingredient and the final regulation describes vitamin fortification, special labeling, and the submission of postmarketing surveillance reports. P&G spent more than \$200 million in the 25 years that elapsed between their initial contact with FDA in 1971 and final approval.

Chronology

1971 First meeting with FDA and P&G. Patent granted to P&G on sucrose polyester (SPE), the class of non-digestible fats which includes olestra, as fat replacers.
1975 Procter & Gamble (P&G) files Investigative New Drug Exemption on SPEs.
1979 P&G meets with FDA because of the unclear regulatory status of SPEs.
1982 P&G meets with FDA to review the SPE testing program.
1984 FDA recognizes that SPE, as a food macroingredient, introduces a new dimension for low-calorie ingredients.
1986 P&G meets with FDA to present all safety data and discuss products to be covered in a Food Additive Petition.
1987 Food Additive Petition submitted—covers olestra in conventional oil blends to prepare savory snacks and for food service and home use in shortening and oils.
1988 FDA defines additional absorption and toxicology data.
1990 P&G narrows the petition to savory snacks. FDA defines nutrition testing needed to facilitate the review.
1993 Last data requested by FDA submitted.
1995 Substantial majority of the FDA's Food Advisory Committee found that olestra meets the FDA safety standard of "reasonable certainty of no harm."
1996 FDA approval.

Lessons Learned

1. Fully, effective two-way communication between the agency and petitioner is essential. Part of the reason that olestra took so long was that often effective two-way communication was not taking place. When it did, progress toward a decision was made.

2. The FDA involved substantial expertise from outside of FDA and ultimately outside government. This perspective was essential in ultimately bringing issues to resolution so a decision could be made.

3. There is a correct way to use an outside expert committee. The FDA Foods Advisory Committee meeting on olestra created an administrative record which FDA found constructive as evidenced by the preamble to the regulation published in the *Federal Register*.

4. Any complex, novel case, involving large amounts of data and substantial public interest, will almost certainly present some unresolved, and perhaps unresolvable, issues. These will be used by interested parties for their own ends.

5. Unanticipated scientific questions and issues usually arise during a research program on new food additives, before or after market introduction, requiring close and frequent interaction between the petitioner and FDA as well as with outside experts, and later, with the public at large.

6. The use of senior decision teams and outside experts by the FDA helped in addressing issues of in-house scientific disagreement.

7. Novel ingredients and processes that involve large amounts of data and that excite substantial and vocal public interest are nearly certain to require long periods for approval, although care in preparation and well organized outside expertise, can improve the process.

8. P&G's original submission was not as well organized as it could have been, resulting in delays in understanding what conclusions could be drawn from the original package.

9. FDA can develop processes for decision making on tough issues, but this requires clear priority and effective leadership. Unfortunately, often the pressure of inadequate resources and multiple, conflicting priorities prevent this from getting done in a timely manner.

FD&C RED NO. 2 (AMARANTH)

Overview

Amaranth is red monoazo dye that serves as a red color in many food systems. Its high water solubility and tinctorial power, and its "true red" hue make it a very useful color for which there is no adequate substitute.

Chronology

1907 Red No. 2 was on the original list of seven food colors approved for use in the United States by the USDA.

1908 Red No. 2 became part of the USDA voluntary certification program for synthetic color additives.

1938 Red No. 2 became part of the FD&C Act mandatory certification for food, drug, and cosmetic colors.

1960 Having been on the original list of seven food colors permitted by the USDA (1907), it remained on the provisional list, based on toxicological studies before and after adoption of the 1960 Color Additive Amendments.

1964 The FAO/WHO Joint Committee on Food Additives (JEFCA) evaluated amaranth (Red No. 2) and assigned it an ADI of 0–1.5 mg/kg/day.

1970 Amaranth was reported to be embryotoxic, gonadotoxic, and carcinogenic in rats by Russian scientists.

1971 FDA requested teratology and reproduction studies on all FD&C and D&C colors. FDA Commissioner promised to perform new chronic studies on FD&C Red No. 2 and requested no new studies from industry.

1971 Health Research Group petitioned FDA to ban Red No. 2.

1972 While control data in numerous other laboratories showed greater variations and higher control incidences of early resorptions, the FDA took the position that Red No. 2 caused an adverse effect by increasing early resorptions. This effect was not seen in either the industry-supported teratology or the three-generation reproduction studies.

1972 National Academy of Sciences (NAS) originally declined to hold a special review but then convened a committee to review the available toxicity data on Red No. 2. The committee recommended no restrictions but asked for more studies.

1972 Despite the fact that FDA's scientists considered the Russian 1970 study to be questionable on a number of accounts, the FDA undertook a new chronic feeding study as an extension of a three-generation reproduction study.

1972 JEFCA reevaluated amaranth and assigned it a temporary ADI of 0–0.75 mg/kg/day.

1973 Teratology studies were repeated at Industrial Biotest, FDA, and NCTR. Metabolic studies were subsequently performed by General Foods Corporation.

1974 All three of the above collaborative studies showed no difference in the incidence of early resorptions between treated and control rats. By the time these studies were completed, more teratology testing had been done in FDA's laboratories and their control data was similar with those of other laboratories.

1974 Comparative absorption, metabolism, and distribution (AMD) studies between Red No. 2 given via drinking water, diet, or gavage provided dose-response data which demonstrated that blood levels of amaranth and its metabolites were significantly higher in animals fed the high dose of color in the negative three-generation reproduction study than would result from the gavage doses at which increased early resorptions were reported in FDA's original teratology study.

1975 An FDA internal report found the 1972 *in utero* chronic study to have flaws, including a few lost and misdosed animals. These flaws could have been prevented by observance of good laboratory practices (GLPs). The GLP regulations, however, did not then exist. The FDA believed the study was still useable, and supported the safety of Red No. 2. A working group of scientists from FDA, NCI, and the agency's Toxicology Advisory Committee was doubtful, and the FDA Commissioner decided otherwise.

1976 Termination of the provisional listing of this color was opposed by industry but upheld by the court, because no scientific investigations to support safety were underway. The administrative law judge denied industry's petition for permanent listing of the color.

1980 The FDA Commissioner issued a final denial of the petition for permanent listing of the color.

1984 JEFCA reevaluated amaranth and assigned it a permanent ADI of 0–0.5 mg/kg/day.

Comment

It was never documented by the Russian scientists that amaranth was actually tested in 1970. In fact, Dr. V. Wodicka (then Director, Bureau of Foods, FDA) reported, following a visit to Russia, the substance actually tested was a red textile dye rather than amaranth. Although the possible carcinogenicity of FD&C Red No. 2 was the central issue, the presence in the color of carcinogenic impurities fueled concern over trace contaminants. This resulted in the banning of Ext. D&C Yellow No. 1, and D&C Nos. 10, 11, 12, and 13, and ultimately, to the evolution of FDA's constituents policy.

Federal Register notices on Red No. 2 repeatedly mention the frequency and intensity of consumer interest expressed over the safety of the substance. However, 47 countries, including Canada and the European Union, have approved amaranth (FD&C Red No. 2) for use in food.

Lessons Learned

1. Scientific issues, placing a food ingredient's safety into question, can arise anytime from anywhere around the world. Even the poorest and non-confirmed hypothesis or "scientific" sightings can lead to loss of an additive if the concerned industry has not maintained a close and continuing program for assurance of safety.

2. Inadequate experience with a test procedure and the concomitant database from untreated control animals is costly in time and dollars to both regulators and industry.

3. Comparative AMD studies can be extremely helpful in resolving discrepancies between different toxicity test results.

4. There is a wrong way to use an outside expert committee. That is to wait for a crisis to become acute, appoint a "balanced" committee, many of whom are unfamiliar with the problem; many of whom do not know, or even trust, each other, and require them to reach a consensus in an impossibly short time.

5. Regulatory actions made administratively, that are contrary to FDA's internal scientific staff as well as a worldwide scientific consensus based on substantial data, will place the United States out of step internationally and raise questions about FDA's scientific credibility. This has greater implications today under GATT than it did heretofore.

6. If it is to exercise independent judgment on the results, a regulatory agency probably should not run its own tests.

7. The events surrounding FD&C Red No. 2 reveal a good example of a risk management/risk communications failure. As a result, the public lost faith in all colors and became increasingly suspicious of food additives. Had FD&C Red No. 2 been properly managed, the listing of other provisionally listed colors likely would have occurred in a much more rational manner.

FD&C RED NO. 3 (ERYTHROSINE)

Overview

Erythrosine (2,4,5,7-tetraiodofluorescine) is a synthetic xanthene color additive used primarily to color confectionery products, cherries, and canned fruits and vegetables. Each molecule of erythrosine contains four covalently bound iodine atoms.

Chronology

1907 Red No. 3 was first listed for foods in the United States.

1960 The Color Additives Amendment to FD&C Act required premarket approval for color additives.

1962 FD&C Red No. 3 was permanently listed by FDA for use in food and ingested drugs, provisionally listed for all other uses. Red No. 3 lake was provisionally listed for all uses.

1977 FDA required new lifetime toxicity/carcinogenicity studies of Red No. 3 and other FD&C colors as a condition of maintaining provisionally listed uses.

1981 Results from Red No. 3 rat studies indicated thyroid toxicity at highest feeding levels, and tumors at the highest level (4.0%, 2464 mg/kg/day) in male rats. No effects were seen in mice.

1982 to 1987
A series of studies showed that Red No. 3 inhibits conversion of T4 to T3 *in vitro* and *in vivo* in rats resulting in increased TSH-mediated stimulation of the thyroid leading to thyroid follicular cell hyperplasia and tumors. Clear thresholds for the effect were far above the estimated human exposure to Red No. 3. Clinical studies failed to show any effects of large doses of Red No. 3 on the human thyroid.

1985 Color Additives Scientific Review Panel (organized by NCTR) reviewed data on Red No. 3 and related colors and failed to provide a clear conclusion on risks associated with color additives, including Red No. 3.

1986 Lin and Brusick, in a critical review, found Red No. 3 not genotoxic.

1987 FD&C Red No. 3 Peer Review Panel did not come to any conclusion concerning the exact mechanism Red No. 3 induced thyroid tumors in rats. However, they believed it operated through a secondary mechanism of carcinogenesis.

1988 EPA published a report which concluded that the mechanism for thyroid tumors is a threshold mechanism for which clear no-effect levels can be established.

1990 FDA sided with the uncertainties expressed in 1985 by the (NCTR) Color Additives Scientific Review Panel and the 1987 Peer Review Panel rather than with the 1988 EPA report, or with JECFA's action. It did not conclude that genotoxicity was excluded. FDA denied the petition and terminated provisional listings for Red No. 3 dye and lake, and stated its intent to propose termination of permanent listing of dye for use in food and ingested drugs. Although FDA viewed Red No. 3 cancer risks as small, about 1 in

100,000 over a 70-year lifetime, the agency terminated the provisional listing due to the Delaney clause.

1990 JECFA established an ADI of 0–0.1 mg/kg/day which is high enough to account for existing uses of Red No. 3 in food.

1990 Multigeneration reproduction study in rats showed no significant effects, including no thyroid pathology.

1993 FDA-sponsored teratology study showed no effects of Red No. 3 in rats.

1994 Publication of clastogenicity study showed no effect of Red No. 3.

1997 Red No. 3 dye remains permanently listed. FDA has not published a proposal to de-list the dye, nor has the agency responded to requests, made in 1990, for a color additive advisory committee to review the de-listed uses.

Comments

During the two decades from 1960 to approximately 1980, FDA was reluctant to follow any course with respect to the interpretation of carcinogenicity data other than that dictated by a conservative reading of the Delaney clause. Such a course was repeatedly urged by consumer organizations and their representatives, in comments on various substances that were before the agency for decision, among them, a number of food colors.

In the 1980s, the agency attempted to introduce some flexibility by the development and use of the "constituents policy" and the *de minimis* concept. The application of *de minimis* was litigated in a suit involving not FD & C colors, but D & C Red No. 19 and Orange No. 17. These had been determined to be carcinogenic but the agency had concluded that under the circumstances of use, the risk was negligible (*de minimis*) (*Public Citizen v. Young*, 831 F.2d 1108 [D.C. Cir. 1987]. In its decision, the court decided that the "plain language" of the Delaney clause should apply. The court made clear that its decision applied only to the clause in the Color Additives Amendment, not the Food Additives Amendment, where, although the wording was closely similar, "the context is clearly different." Since then, the FDA dropped any explicit use of *de minimis* but has continued to develop and apply its "constituents policy" to direct and indirect food additives. This policy has been sustained in court (*Scott v. FDA*, 728 F.2nd 322, 325 [6th Cir. 1984]).

Not until the late 1980s and the 1990s had the interpretive sciences (see introductory paper to the case studies) developed enough to give strong support to indirect mechanisms of carcinogenesis (secondary mechanisms) for which thresholds have been demonstrated. The use of secondary mechanisms as a basis for holding that an animal carcinogenicity test does not show that a substance "induces cancer" within the meaning of the Delaney clause has not yet been tested in court.

Lessons Learned

1. Determining a chemical's genotoxic potential is well established as an important step towards characterizing its carcinogencity potential.

2. Mechanisms of action can be very important for evaluation of a chemical's potential risk for man.

3. In the two decades following passage of the 1958 Food Additive Amendments to the FD&C, the FDA, urged on by many consumer groups, chose, with few exceptions, to apply a conservative and literal reading of the Delaney clause to data showing carcinogenic effects in animals.

4. In the 1980s and 1990s the agency increasingly sought some flexibility to avoid the "zero tolerance" approach to the clause. A court decision denied it the use of the *de minimis* concept under the Color Additives Amendment. The FDA has continued to employ the *de minimis* principle, although not explicitly, in the formulation and use of its "constituents policy."

5. Although the agency has not explicitly adopted the secondary mechanisms approach to the interpretation of animal data on carcinogenic effects, when the data are solid and persuasive, it seems willing to rely on that concept as a basis for not taking action. That concept has not yet been tested in court.

TCE AND DCM

Overview

Trichloroethylene (TCE) and Dichloromethane (DCM; methylene chloride) are two of the most widely used chlorinated solvents. While these chemicals were used as degreasers in paints, and in other industrial products, they served important roles in the food industry, as well. One role was in the decaffeination of coffee.

Chronology

Trichloroethylene (TCE)

1975 NCI announced in a Memorandum of Alert that TCE caused liver tumors in mice but not in rats. However, this announcement disregarded many unusual circumstances surrounding the study in mice, including the fact that 17 other chemicals, many known potent carcinogens among them, were under test in the same room. The National Coffee Association (NCA) immediately began discussions with FDA and NCI and started a search for alternate decaffeination processes.

1975 Although no compound-related effects were found in the rat study, NCI immediately began to retest TCE chronically in four different strains of the rat. One strain showed a slight elevation in kidney tumors; the other three strains were negative.

1976 to 1997
While TCE has long since been dropped from use by the food industry, its importance to other industries brought continued research on its safety.

1997 The results of 35 chronic studies supported by in-depth biochemical and PBPK evaluations have led to the following findings (Bogen, 1997):

a. TCE causes greater liver damage when administered by oil gavage than via drinking water.

b. Increased tumor incidence is unlikely to occur in the absence of chronic cytotoxicity.

c. Liver toxicity in mice correlates with the total amount of TCE metabolized. This indicates that major forms of TCE-induced chronic cytotoxicity are almost certainly caused by TCE metabolism or metabolites rather than by TCE itself.

d. Elevated SGPT levels in mice were observed at daily doses of 1,600–3,200 mg/kg body weight, but not at 200–800 mg/kg body weight. The authors consider this evidence of a threshold for induction of liver cytotoxicity.

e. The occurrence of TCE-induced rat kidney tumors is unlikely in the absence of chronic kidney damage.

1975 to 1997

TCE continues to be listed by FDA for use as a solvent in food processing, including coffee decaffeination.

Dichloromethane (DCM, Methylene chloride)

1975 Although FDA did not move to de-list the food uses of TCE, the affected industries felt that with the cloud over the substance, they needed alternatives. An intensive search began for a technically adequate and commercially feasible alternative decaffeination solvent. While DCM had not undergone long-term carcinogenicity testing comparable to the NCI bioassay, there were chronic feeding studies on coffee products decaffeinated with DCM, showing no adverse effects. Also, SAR analysis suggested that DCM did not form an epoxide intermediate similar to TCE, which was suspected to mediate TCE-induced cancer effects. Based on this evidence, coffee manufacturers that had been using TCE switched to using DCM, and the NCA immediately began discussions with NCI and FDA expressing its commitment to supporting the very best research program possible for evaluating the safety of DCM for use as a decaffeination solvent.

1976 NCA began a research and testing program on DCM. In the course of that effort and related activities by individual firms, General Foods spent $300,000 for metabolism studies for use in PBPK evaluation and for designing chronic drinking water studies in rats and mice.

1978 NTP's chronic gavage studies on DCM in rats began at Gulf South Laboratories.

1979 Through the Interagency Regulatory Liaison Group, FDA scientists agreed to use the MTD approach to dose selection despite their expressed reservations over its use for testing this substance. NCA began its chronic rat and mouse drinking water studies on DCM at Hazleton Laboratories.

1980 The NCA unprecedented "dancing mice," not DCM or dose-related. This phenomenon required urgent assembly of a wide variety of specialists. This observation was attributed to the single housing of the B6C3F1 mice, never before seen at NCI, NTP, or animal suppliers, where mice are group housed.

1982 NCA studies on DCM reported no adverse effects.

1984 The Nutrition Foundation sponsored a Food Solvents Workshop. Dr. Robert Squire, formerly head of the NCI Bioassay Program, stated: "NCA's testing program for DCM is an example of how a material should be tested. In 8 years at NCI, this is the first chemical tested by industry we discussed with industry representatives."

1984 Chronic studies under contract from NTP on DCM, 1,1,1-trichloroethane, and methyl chloroform, were so seriously flawed that the toxicology unit of Gulf South Laboratories was shut down.

1986 Test results showed orally administered DCM not to be carcinogenic at high, but less than MTD doses, in either rats or mice.

1986 The NTP reported finding elevated liver and lung tumors in mice, but not rats, exposed to DCM in inhalation at the MTD.

1996 Research continues. Twenty years of intense and costly research, including the first use of PBPK modeling of a food-use chemical has shown the species specificity for liver and lung tumors in the mouse to be a direct consequence of the high activity and specific localization of a glutathione S-transferase theta enzyme in the mice. In the absence of such high or localized enzyme activity in other species, the metabolites of the glutathione S-transferase pathway are too unstable to interact with DNA. Thus, DNA interactions were not detectable in short-term mammalian mutagenicity assays in rats *in-vivo* or in hamster and human hepatocytes exposed to toxic dose levels of DCM *in-vitro*.

Circumstances have not been identified under which the effects seen in mice could occur in other species, including humans.

1975 to 1997

DCM continues to be listed by FDA as a solvent for certain uses in food processing, including coffee decaffeination (CFR 173.255, 172.560, and 73.1)

Comments

The finding of tumors in the NCI inhalation studies, while not directly relevant to oral consumption, continued to cast a cloud over TCE and was responsible for much of the later research to remove this compound. While industries often work cooperatively on research to solve common problems, they typically are highly competitive in marketing. (See Lesson Learned No. 3.)

In the late 1970s and early 1980s, FDA based its decision to continue the listings of TCE and DCM on the *de minimis* principle. The court rejected this principle, but only for food colors, in the case of *Public Citizen v. Young*, 831 F.2nd 1108 [D.C. Cir. 1987]. On the basis of that decision however, and the results of the NCI inhalation studies on DCM, FDA terminated cosmetic uses of DCM, but stated that it would take some time to assess the impact of that decision on the food uses, for which listing continues (FR 54, 124, 27328 ff.).

Lessons Learned

1. Pace-setting chronic toxicology is extremely expensive, twice that for following standard protocols. But it can lead to some success for the test material itself and help advance the science generally. Nevertheless, few industrial research funds are allocated purely for the purpose of advancing the sciences.

2. Once a report of carcinogenic effect is attributed to a food-related chemical, the only economically reasonable thing an industry can justify doing is to stop using the material, unless defense of the material is the last resort for remaining in business. Having a safety cloud over one's product brands, over a 5 to 10-year span required to scientifically resolve a safety issue, is very costly.

3. In the case of both TCE and DCM, the industries reacted far more precipitously than did FDA, partly out of justified fear of customer and consumer reaction, and partly, by finding a better alternative first, to acquire a competitive advantage. This contributed heavily to the rush to move from TCE to DCM, and from DCM to other solvents.

4. The then existing policies and practices of the NTP bioassay program, and the resulting political and public relations climate, made it extremely difficult to obtain support for the practice of good in-depth science even after professional consensus (e.g., The report of the Task Force of Past Presidents of the SOT, 1982). Fortunately, support was ultimately found.

5. Once FDA makes the decision to approve a substance, it feels that it has acquired some "ownership" that makes it difficult and embarrassing to change its mind. It understandably does not like to find that later data have cast doubt on an earlier approval. This tends to make FDA extremely cautious about new approvals, particularly if they involve highly novel substances or technologies. Conversely, it also, as in this case, can make the agency reluctant to be pushed into a premature decision to restrict or ban the substance.

d-LIMONENE

Overview

d-Limonene is a monoterpene hydrocarbon found in more than 30 species of fruits and vegetables, especially in citrus oils, and particularly in oil of orange. In addition to its natural occurrence, d-limonene is widely used as a flavor additive in foods and beverages including a variety of juices and non-alcoholic beverages, baked goods, gelatins, puddings, and chewing gums. Daily U.S. consumption is estimated to be approximately 0.27 mg/kg, but depending on citrus juice consumption, exposure can be as high as 1.2 mg/kg/day for young children. In addition to exposure to d-limonene in foods, this monoterpene is also widely used as a fragrance in perfumes and a variety of household products and as an industrial solvent and degreaser. Recently, its use as a cancer chemopreventive and chemotherapeutic agent has been reported.

Chronology

1960 FDA recognized d-limonene to be GRAS as a synthetic flavoring substance.

1965 FEMA expert panel determined d-limonene to be GRAS.

1976 FEMA expert panel reviewed all available data on d-limonene and affirmed the previous GRAS status.

1987 Published data demonstrated that d-limonene caused a male rat specific nephrotoxicity mediated by the accumulation of α2u-globulin.

1989 Researchers found that renal toxicity seen with d-limonene treatment was caused by the binding of d-limonene epoxide metabolite to α2u-globulin. This prevented its degradation and caused it to accumulate in renal phagolysosomes only in male rats.

1990 NTP reported evidence of carcinogenic activity of d-limonene in male F344 rats, as indicated by increased incidence of renal tubular cell adenomas and adenocarcinomas. No evidence of carcinogenic activity in female F344 rats or in male or female B6C3F1 mice. There was no evidence of mutagenic activity of d-limonene.

1990 d-limonene given GRAS status by the expert panel of FEMA. They reviewed the data and were convinced that the evidence supported a unique response in the male rat that was not predictive of a similar risk for humans.

1991 EPA Risk Assessment Forum published criteria document for chemicals that caused male rat specific renal tubular tumors. EPA concluded that data would not be used if male rat tumors arose from process involving α2u-globulin. d-limonene was one of the standards from which these criteria were developed.

1992 International Agency for Research on Cancer (IARC) reviewed data on d-limonene and classified it as a Group 3 carcinogen (not classifiable as to its carcinogenicity in humans).

1993 JECFA reviewed d-limonene and decided that it did not represent any hazard to human health. A "not specified" ADI was published by this group.

Lessons Learned

1. There are chemicals that may be found to be carcinogenic in laboratory animals but for which the response is not relevant for humans. In the case of d-limonene, this qualitative difference is based solely on the presence of a unique protein, α2u-globulin. As such, the human risk assessment should be based on this qualitative difference, and no quantitative risk analysis can or should be developed.

2. The mechanism developed to explain the carcinogenic activity of d-limonene has been substantiated across a broad class of compounds, and these data support further the unique male rat specific response associated with the presence of α2u-globulin. However, a significant research effort was invested to deduce the biochemical and cellular changes that linked the acute nephropathy to renal cancer and which established the lack of human relevance of these events. The level of detailed mechanistic information provided for d-limonene is likely to be the standard by which other efforts to deviate from default assumptions for human risk assessment will be judged. In this manner, it will likely take many years to convince regulatory bodies of a unique mechanism of action. Regulatory agencies were generally patient and restrained during the development of the essential data for d-limonene, and such judgment is needed in all cases.

3. The major vehicle for human exposure to d-limonene is natural fruits. Further, the consumption of natural fruits that are high in d-limonene is associated with reduced rates of human cancer. Clearly, this knowledge had considerable impact on the patience and restrained action of the regulatory agencies.

BENZYL ACETATE

Overview

Benzyl acetate is used primarily as a component of perfumes for soaps and as a flavoring ingredient. As a flavoring ingredient, it is found in a variety of baked goods, soft and hard candy, various beverages, frozen dairy, and chewing gum products. Benzyl acetate is also a naturally occurring component of traditional foods, such as tomatoes, apples, mushrooms, and strawberries. The Consumption Ratio (CR), which compares the average intake of added flavoring materials to the quantities consumed as components of traditional foods, indicates that benzyl acetate is consumed about as much as a flavor ingredient as it is as a constituent of traditional foods. Its reported consumption volume of 22,500 kg in 1970 drew the interest of the NTP in testing and evaluating the toxicity of benzyl acetate.

Chronology

1964 FDA approved benzyl acetate as a flavoring ingredient in foods.

1965 FEMA expert panel judged benzyl acetate to be GRAS.

1980 FEMA expert panel evaluated the available data and affirmed the previous GRAS status.

Pre-1986 NTP conducted toxicity and carcinogenicity investigations of benzyl acetate (>99% pure). Positive trends for several types of neoplasms, none of which were statistically significant or dose-related, were noted. These positive trends included acinar-cell adenomas of the exocrine pancreas in F344/N male rats; neoplasms of the preputial gland; hepatocellular adenomas in mice of each sex; and squamous cell papillomas or carcinomas of the forestomach in male mice. No evidence of carcinogenicity was found for female F344/N rats.

1982 Reviewers of benzyl acetate NTP draft technical report were in agreement with the studies' conclusions, with only minor modifications. One reviewer believed that the known metabolites of benzyl acetate were non-mutagenic and likely not carcinogenic.

1983 Draft NTP technical report again reviewed with increased concern for the quantitative and qualitative limitations of the study. The use of corn oil was a

	confounding variable that left the causation of pancreatic acinar-cell adenomas in male F344/N rats unclear. Additionally, the non-random mortality of female mice due to intercurrent disease was excessive, prohibiting a proper analysis of the association between incidence of liver adenomas and benzyl acetate. Thirdly, the incidence of liver adenomas in the vehicle control group was unusually low, and the incidence of liver adenomas in the benzyl acetate group was comparable with those found in historical corn oil gavage control groups.
1984	Metabolism studies show ring-labeled ^{14}C-benzyl acetate to be rapidly excreted in adult male F344 rats and B6C3F$_1$ mice, with no detectable tissue retention, or diminution of clearance, even at high doses in two-year NTP studies. NTP short-term genotoxicity studies found no statistically significant mutagenic activity in test objects exposed to benzyl acetate. The audit confirmed the forestomach as a target organ for carcinogenicity in the mouse.
Pre-1993	NTP further studied benzyl acetate using the dosed feed route. No evidence of carcinogenic activity was shown in either male or female F344/N rats, or in male or female B6C3F$_1$ mice at highest doses given (600 mg/kg/day). NTP suspected rats may have tolerated higher doses.

Comments

Peer Review Panel objections to NTP's 2-year study protocol of benzyl acetate have emphasized two major study concerns: (1) that B6C3F$_1$ mice are a poor model for human carcinogenicity, and (2) corn oil gavage may be a significant confounding factor in the study of carcinogenicity. The high tumor incidence observed in rodent controls of NTP carcinogenicity studies raised concern within the scientific community, and led to independent investigations. A study considering the use of historical control data in the evaluation of tumor incidences for carcinogenicity studies observed liver nodules, adenomas, or carcinomas in 31 percent of untreated control male B6C3F$_1$ mice. Further studies have noted that hepatocellular hyperplasia may occur secondary to necrosis or a degenerative process in the liver, and that high incidence of hepatocellular neoplasms in control male B6C3F$_1$ mice should elicit some concern. Inflammation, necrosis/ulceration, and hyperplasia of the forestomach squamous mucosa have been observed in many long-term studies utilizing corn oil gavage, making it difficult to interpret potential carcinogenic responses.

Other concerns for the NTP benzyl acetate study have been raised. After careful review of the NTP draft report on its bioassay of benzyl acetate, the FEMA and Fragrance Manufacturers Association (FMA) expert panels noted several troubling issues. A high degree of infection noted in mice of both sexes; poor handling of the untreated control groups; a lack of significant tumor incidence between the benzyl acetate treated groups and historical controls; and poor statistical analysis led the FEMA and FMA expert panels to disagree with the NTP finding of carcinogenicity. It was attention to points raised by independent review committees and investigations that led the NTP expert panel to push for a second 2-year NTP benzyl acetate study using a microencapsulation feed protocol.

Lessons Learned

1. Failure to address the limitations of standard protocols, even if they are widely utilized, limits the significance of such studies, and can create undue public concern. NTP's continued use of corn oil gavage and B6C3F$_1$ mice in its two-year rodent studies, without proper regard for

their potential as confounding factors, raises concerns about study results and the clarity of interpretation. Such factors, without appropriate evaluation, can impugn the safety of a substance that presents no significant hazard whatever under its conditions of use.

2. The NTP MTD/1/2 MTD bioassay was never originally intended to be any more than a screen for serious toxicity, and was not intended for, nor should it serve as, an appropriate source of data for risk analysis.

3. Poor data from a defective study are a waste of time and resources.

4. The expert review committee members should not only be experts in carcinogenesis, but must also be able to properly interpret information for safety assessments. This point is well illustrated by the case history of benzyl acetate. Prior concerns for NTP's testing protocols provided the foundation for issues raised during the Peer Review Panel's critique of the NTP 1986 publication, and the subsequent retesting of benzyl acetate by NTP. The results from this 1993 publication proved to be consistent with the scientific literature as a whole, supporting the 1964 FDA and the FEMA GRAS approvals of benzyl acetate as a synthetic flavor ingredient.

5. The FEMA expert panel's 37 years of activity demonstrate how to properly use independent expert opinion. The depth of experience provided by panel members in the most relevant fields, the appropriate balance of system and flexibility in procedures, and total independence in reaching conclusions permits quick decisions on simple, negligible-risk matters.

6. The FDA wisely exercised restraint in not responding precipitously to the defective first study by NTP.

ISO-AMYL ACETATE

Overview

Iso-amyl acetate occurs in nature and has been reported in cider, rum, and malt whiskey. The Consumption Ratio (CR), which compares the average intake of added flavoring materials to the quantities consumed as components of traditional foods, indicates that *iso*-amyl acetate is consumed about equally from both the two categories. Studies show that *iso*-amyl acetate is rapidly absorbed and metabolized.

Chronology

1965 FEMA expert panel determined *iso*-amyl acetate to be GRAS.

1975 FEMA expert panel affirmed the previous GRAS status for *iso*-amyl acetate.

1994 FEMA expert panel reaffirmed *iso*-amyl acetate as GRAS based upon its facile hydrolysis and oxidative detoxification of its alcohol and acetic acid, its very low level of flavor use, the safety factor calculated from results of subchronic studies for *iso*-amyl alcohol and *iso*-amyl *iso*-valerate, and its very low acute oral toxicity.

1997 Midwest Research Institute conducted an *in vitro* study using whole rat blood and showed that the half-life of *iso*-amyl acetate is very short *in vivo*; 4 minutes in blood and 2 minutes in plasma.

Comments

Iso-amyl acetate has not been the subject of a significant amount of scientific research or toxicological testing. It was therefore necessary to draw upon experienced professional judgment in determining the potential risk *iso*-amyl acetate poses to the population. In conducting a safety assessment, the FEMA expert panel deemed *iso*-amyl acetate GRAS based upon studies addressing structurally similar compounds, its low level of flavor use, and its rapid metabolism and excretion.

Lessons Learned

1. The case of *iso*-amyl acetate illustrates how important it is to have a contextual understanding of related scientific literature in conducting an assessment of the safety-in-use of a substance as a flavor ingredient.

2. The FEMA expert panel's 37 years of activity demonstrate how to properly use independent expert opinion. The depth of experience provided by Panel members in the most relevant fields, the appropriate balance of system and flexibility in procedures, and total independence in reaching conclusions permits quick decisions on simple, negligible-risk matters. More complex problems may require many months of scrutiny, and can be appropriately addressed by the expert panel because of its depth of experience and flexibility. There can be little doubt that this is a cost-effective, timely method of providing highly expert decisions on safety-in-use.

FURFURAL

Overview

Virtually ubiquitous in nature, furfural is a naturally occurring component of many fruits and vegetables. The CR, which compares the average intake of added flavoring materials to the quantities consumed as unavoidable components of traditional foods, indicates that furfural is almost entirely found in traditional foods. In addition, the formation of furfural during the thermal decomposition of carbohydrates, makes it a component of many processed food, products such as baked goods, meat products, and alcoholic and non-alcoholic beverages. NTP included furfural in its testing program based upon its widespread natural occurrence in food and historical data indicating exposure to high concentrations may be hepatoxic.

Chronology

1960	FEMA expert panel judged furfural to be GRAS.
1975	FEMA expert panel affirmed the previous GRAS status of furfural for use as a flavor ingredient.
Pre-1990	NTP conducted toxicity and carcinogenicity investigations of furfural (>99% pure). There was evidence of carcinogenic activity for male F344/N rats based upon the occurrence of uncommon cholangiocarcinomas and bile duct dysplasia. Additionally, there appeared some evidence of carcinogenic activity in male and female B6C3F$_1$ mice based on increased incidences of heptocellular adenomas. No evidence of carcinogenicity was identified in female F344/N rats at the highest dose level.
1989	Reviewers of furfural NTP draft technical report found general agreement on the findings of the study with respect to male rats, and male and female mice.
1993	JECFA determined furfural was not an appropriate flavor addition, and could not be allocated an ADI. The NTP studies, taken with the perceived "relatively high"

concentrations of furfural found in some foods, caused JECFA to "consider the direct addition of furfural as a flavor to be inappropriate."

1995 The International Agency for Research on Cancer (IARC) concluded that there was inadequate evidence in humans and limited evidence in animals for the carcinogenicity of furfural. IARC found furfural to be a component of 150 foods, including a wide range of fruits and vegetables.

1996 FEMA expert panel conducted a comprehensive review of the scientific literature and determined that furfural be reaffirmed as GRAS based upon its rapid absorption and metabolism in *in vivo* systems, its ubiquity in nature, a lack of evidence indicating any risk to human health under conditions of use as a flavor ingredient, and a lack of evidence implicating furfural as a carcinogen. Its only significant finding for carcinogenicity was two-year NTP bioassays, showing increased incidence of hepatocellular adenomas and carcinomas in the high-dose group of male mice. Review of these findings determined that the observed carcinogenicity was secondary to pronounced hepatotoxicity.

Comments

Despite the pervasive presence of furfural at low concentrations in the native food supply, concerns have been raised about its toxicological characteristics, particularly with respect to carcinogenicity. Low molecular weight aldehydes like furfural may undergo oxidation or condensation reactions associated with the aldehyde function either in digestive fluids prior to absorption, or in body fluids prior to entering the cell. Reactivity of these aldehyde groups has been demonstrated to produce toxic effects including the induction of tumors when administered under non-physiological conditions at high dose levels.

Lessons Learned

1. The testing and review history of furfural is a strong example of how results from chronic, high-dose testing can be given inappropriate weight. The 1990 NTP study publication on furfural noted some evidence of carcinogenic activity, which proved to be a strong factor in JECFA's failure to allocate furfural an ADI. In contrast, IARC and FEMA conducted critical reviews of the literature, concluding furfural to be of no carcinogenic risk to humans. The FEMA expert panel's GRAS conclusion, and subsequent affirmation and reaffirmation were based upon a contextual understanding of the wide range of studies conducted with furfural. Institutions that conduct primary research with regulatory implications must hold themselves to a high protocol standard, just as regulatory agencies that utilize these studies must be able to place referred studies into context with the questions of human risk. Therefore, regulatory bodies must critically evaluate the relevance of high-dose chronic studies to the safety evaluation of substances ubiquitous in the food supply at far lower levels of exposure.

2. The FEMA expert panel's 37 years of activity demonstrate how to properly use independent expert opinion. The depth of experience provided by panel members in the most relevant fields, the appropriate balance of system and flexibility in procedures, and total independence in reaching conclusions permits quick decisions on simple, negligible-risk matters. More complex problems, such as those posed by furfural, require many months of scrutiny, and can be appropriately addressed by the expert panel because of its depth of experience and flexibility. There can be little doubt that this is a cost-effective, timely method of providing highly expert decisions on safety-in-use.

PULSED LIGHT

Overview

FDA was first contacted about the possible use of pulsed light as a surface antimicrobial treatment for food in the spring of 1993. PurePulse (then Foodco Corp) had developed a technology that used short, high-intensity, broad spectral bandwidth pulses from specialized flashlamps to destroy a variety of microorganisms (bacteria, yeast, molds, etc.) commonly found on the surfaces of food. Although the flashlamp technology had been used in other applications, it had not previously been used for food treatment. The company sought FDA guidance on the regulatory steps that would be necessary before the novel technology could be commercialized.

Since the law categorizes sources of radiation used to treat food as a "food additive" unless they are GRAS, submission of a food additive petition, and its subsequent approval by FDA, were necessary. Because a source of radiation is not actually added to food, nor does it come in contact with food, a petition for pulsed light would need to contain different information than a petition for a more typical food additive (direct or indirect). FDA worked with the petitioner to identify the type and amount of data and supporting information that would be submitted.

Because of the potential public health impact of the technology, FDA further committed to an up-front "review" of sections of the petition, while still in draft, by the Consumer Safety Officer responsible for coordinating the technical review of the petition. Sections of the petition that provided the basis for critical quantitative arguments received detailed review, as did the environmental assessment.

Chronology

1994 In March, pulsed light petition filed by PurePulse.
1994 In May, FDA review of the photochemical data and extensive quantitative arguments completed.
1994 FDA initial scientific review of the petition completed in August.
1995 In January, FDA questions in the area of microbiology, specifically, the area of competitive microbial populations, sent to petitioner.
1995 In March, petitioner sent FDA information needed to fill in the gaps in the petition.
1995 FDA completed review of March information in June.
1995 In June, *Federal Register* document that would grant approval was drafted and received scientific clearance as well as clearance by OPA management.
1996 Higher level clearance of *Federal Register* document, including review and clearance by the Office of General Counsel, complete in May.
1996 In August, final rule published.

Lessons Learned

1. Early consultation and communication between FDA and the petitioner is necessary on a novel food technology.
2. FDA and the petitioner worked to reach a mutual understanding of the types and amount of data and information that would be needed to establish safety. The goal was to ensure a "good" petition.
3. FDA committed priority resources to a "good" petition that had potential for positive public heath impact: an investment of agency resources in a limited review of draft petition materials, and a focused "team approach" in review once the complete petition was filed.

4. Constraints included many urgent competing demands not within the agency's control. These involved serious outbreaks of foodborne illness that required immediate response from the agency and constituted a serious drain on personnel resources needed to complete review of the petition. In addition, many urgent competing demands on FDA and other agency staff and officials, including General Counsel, resulted from increased congressional interest in the food additive premarket approval program and in other premarket approval programs throughout the agency.

CHYMOSIN

Overview

In 1988 and 1989, petitions were filed independently by three separate companies seeking FDA's affirmation of the GRAS status for chymosin, the active enzyme component of rennet, used in cheese production. Because these chymosin preparations were produced through modern biotechnological means, all three petitioners awaited final FDA affirmation before marketing their products because of the potential for consumer rejection in the marketplace. FDA affirmation of GRAS status was critical for public acceptance of these newly developed food ingredients.

The information provided herein is based on the record and on personal communications with FDA personnel who were involved in the review of the petition filed by Pfizer Inc., which was submitted in 1988 and affirmed in 1990 (a total of 25 months). The two other companies filed their GRAS petitions in May 1989 and October 1989, and were affirmed in 33 and 43 months, respectively.

Chronology

1987 Pfizer had informal consultations with FDA to identify and elaborate issues of concern. FDA realized that although biotechnology presented new questions related to safety, those questions could be answered with the available scientific procedures, including those provided by biotechnological procedures. The inherent safety of the final chymosin product was confirmed from feeding studies in rats and dogs, and from a genotoxicity test battery.

1988 Pfizer submitted both a Food Additive Petition (FAP) and GRAS affirmation petition for chymosin. The FDA wanted to affirm the GRAS status of chymosin because a) traditional rennet was already GRAS affirmed, and b) it desired a review process open to public scrutiny during the petition review process. Pfizer submitted an FAP to ensure that the FDA would abide by the 180-day statutory deadline for FAP approval.

1989 FDA scientific review completed within 15 months of filing (circa July 1989).

1990 FDA affirmed chymosin as GRAS, 25 months after submission of the petition.

Comment

Although the scientific aspects of the review had been comprehensively elaborated, some effort was needed to establish a record that supported *general recognition* and to educate FDA management regarding the biotechnological aspects of the petition. It is important to keep in mind that the FDA had to answer policy questions subsequent to the scientific review period, yet most policy questions were dealt with rather expediently (i.e., within a few months) because the scientific review conducted was definitive and conclusive to affirm GRAS status.

Lessons Learned

1. Good data and joint agency/petitioner planning permit reasonably prompt and effective decisions, especially on noncontroversial topics. Before the petition was submitted, the FDA met with the petitioner on an informal basis to identify issues and to develop a framework to answer questions to determine the safety of the product.

APPENDIX C

Enhancing the Regulatory Approval Process for Food Ingredient Technologies
A Workshop

Sponsored by the Food Forum
Food and Nutrition Board
Institute of Medicine
May 6–7, 1997

WORKSHOP AGENDA

Tuesday, May 6, 1997 — National Academy of Sciences Auditorium

I. WELCOME AND INTRODUCTION TO THE TOPIC

8:15 am — Welcome and Introduction
Sandra A. Schlicker, Director, Food Forum
Michael W. Pariza, Chair, Workshop

II. LEGAL BACKGROUND
Moderator: *Richard A. Merrill*

8:45 am — Purpose of Session
Richard A. Merrill

Perspectives and Issues Raised in the Legal Background Document
Lars Noah, University of Florida

Reactor Panel
Government—*Catherine Copp*
Industry—*Steve McNamara*
Consumer—*Marsha Cohen*

10:40 am — Break

11:00 am — Audience Discussion with Presenter and Reactor Panel

12:00 noon — Lunch

III. INTERPRETATION OF THE SCIENCE AND THE APPROVAL PROCESS
Moderator: *Jerry Hjelle*

1:00 pm — Purpose of Session
Jerry Hjelle

Document	Perspectives and Issues Raised in Technical and Commercial Practices
	John Kirschman, Kirschman Associates
	C.K. Gund and Clyde Takeguchi, Phoenix Regulatory Associates, Ltd.
	Reactor Panel
	Government—*Alan M. Rulis*
	Industry—*Stephen Ziller*
	Consumer—*Michael Jacobson*
2:55 pm	Break
3:15 pm	Audience Discussion with Presenters and Reactor Panel
5:00 pm	Summary of Sessions II and III *Michael W. Pariza*
5:15 pm	Adjourn

Wednesday, May 7, 1997 — National Academy of Sciences Auditorium

8:30 noon	Opening Remarks *Michael W. Pariza,* Chair, Workshop

IV. OPPORTUNITIES FOR CHANGE
Moderator: *Robert Drotman*

8:35 am	Purpose of Session *Robert Drotman*
	FDA Considerations *Fred R. Shank*
	Industry Considerations *Fred Degnan*
	Legislative Considerations *Congressman Scott Klug*
	Consumer Considerations *Edward Groth*
	Audience Discussion

V. CONCLUSION

12:00 noon	"Where Do We Go from Here?" *Eileen Madden*
12:20 pm	Closing Remarks *Michael W. Pariza*

APPENDIX D

Enhancing the Regulatory Approval Process for Food Ingredient Technologies

May 6–7, 1997

Participants List

Cathy Badami
Government Relations Manager
Council for Responsible Nutrition
Washington, DC

Catherine J. Bailey
Science Policy Analyst
FDA/CFSAN
Washington, DC

Sarah Barnett
Vice President Public Affairs
Sugar Association
Washington, DC

R. Daniel Benz
Review Toxicologist
USFDA/CFSAN
Washington, DC

Sanford Bigelow
Director
Medical Nutritionals Regulatory Affairs
Ross Products Division
Columbus, OH

Herbert Blumenthal
Consultant
12545 Two Farm Drive
Silver Spring, MD

Margaret Bogle
Coordinator Delta NIRI
USDA/ARS—National Program Staff
Beltsville, MD

Camille Brewer
Nutritionist
Food and Drug Administration
Washington, DC

Nancy M. Childs
Saint Joseph's University
Philadelphia, PA

David B. Clissold
Associate
Hyman, Phelps and McNamara, P.C.
Washington, DC

Catherine Copp
Associate Chief Counsel for Foods
Food and Drug Administration
Rockville, MD

Nancy Crane
Nutritionist
FDA/CFSAN
Washington, DC

Eunice Cuirle
Manager, Regulatory Affairs
FMC Corporation
Philadelphia, PA

Frances Davidson
USAID
Washington, DC

Fred H. Degnan
Lawyer
King & Spalding
Washington, DC

Anne Depman
Science Policy Analyst
FDA/CFSAN
Washington, DC

Adrienne Dern
Reporter
Food Chemical News
Washington, DC

Lynn Dickey
Branch Chief
FSIS/USDA
Fort Washington, MD

Charlene Dieter
Nutritionist
WIC Program
Springfield, VA

Sean Donohue
Labor and Human Resources Committee
Washington, DC

Patricia A. Dozier
Public Health Nutritionist
DC Government
Washington, DC

Robert Drotman
Vice President
Food Safety
Frito-Lay
Plano, TX

Robert Earl
Director of Public Health
International Food Information Council
Washington, DC

James T. Elfotrum
Manager, Regulatory Affairs
Rhone-Poulenc Inc.
Cranbury, NJ

Kathryn A. Finerty
Corporate Counsel
Universal Foods Corporation
Milwaukee, WI

Kenneth D. Fisher
Executive Director
Commission on Dietary Supplement Labels
Washington, DC

Carol Fletcher
Nutritionist
USDA/FSIS
Washington, DC

Frank Flora
Food Scientist
USDA/CSREES
Washington, DC

Victor Frattali
Deputy Director for Programs
FDA/CFSAN
Washington, DC

Mary Beth Fritz
Manager Regulatory Assurance
Pepsi Cola Company
Valhalla, NY

Mary Virginia Garza
Ellicott City, MD

Walter H. Glinsmann
Consultant
Glinsmann, Inc.
Washington, DC

John W. Gordon
Science Policy Analyst
Food and Drug Administration
Office of Policy Planning and Strategic Initiatives
Washington, DC

Rodney J.H. Gray
Manager, Regulatory Affairs
Hercules Incorporated
Wilmington, DE

Carolyn K. Gund
Phoenix Regulatory Associates, Ltd.
Sterling, VA

Mercy Hammond
Dietitian
Mitchellville, MD

Barbara Harland
Professor, Department of Nutrition Science
Howard University
Washington, DC

John Hathcock
Director
Nutritional & Regulatory Science
Council for Responsible Nutrition
Washington, DC

James T. Heimbach
TAS, Inc.
Washington, DC

Jerry Hjelle
Vice President, Nutrition and Consumer Products
MONSANTO Company
Deerfield, IL

Margaret Hoke
Nutritionist
USDA/ARS/NDL
Riverdale, MD

William J. Hudnall
Assistant Deputy Administrator-OPPI
USDA/FSIS/OPPDE
Washington, DC

Jayne Hurley
Senior Nutritionist
Center for Science in the Public Interest
Washington, DC

Michael F. Jacobson
Executive Director
Center for Science in the Public Interest
Washington, DC

Sally Jones
Food Technologist
USDA/FSIS
Washington, DC

Timothy Kanaley
Program Coordinator
International Food Information Council
Washington, DC

Mark A. Kantor
Associate Professor
University of Maryland
College Park, MD

Lisa Kelly
Associate
N. Chapman Associates
Washington, DC

John C. Kirschman
Consultant
Kirschman Associates
Emmaus, PA

The Hon. Scott Klug
U.S. Congress
Washington, DC

Ian Knight
President
Knight International
Tappahannock, VA

Daniel A. Kracov
Partner
Patton Boggs, L.L.P.
Washington, DC

Naomi Kulakow
Coordinator, Food Labeling Education
Food and Drug Administration
Washington, DC

Evelyn Lashley
Dietitian
U.S. Department of Agriculture
Beltsville, MD

Helen Lee
Toxicologist
Food and Drug Administration
Washington, DC

Anne Lindsay
Director, Field and External Affairs Division
Environmental Protection Agency
Washington, DC

Ronald J. Lorentzen
Strategic Manager for Risk
Assessment/Communication
Food and Drug Administration
Washington, DC

William B. Luth
Director, Corporate Quality
Universal Foods Corporation
Milwaukee, WI

R. Jane Mandell
Nutrition Program Coordinator
U.S. Department of Agriculture
Alexandria, VA

Anita Manka
Food Technologist
U.S. Department of Agriculture
Washington, DC

Kendra Martello
Legal Assistant
Morgan, Lewis and Bockius
Washington, DC

Stephen H. McNamara
Partner
Hyman, Phelps, McNamara
Washington, DC

Lyn O'Brien Nabors
Executive Vice President
Calorie Control Council
Atlanta, GA

Juan Navia
Principal Scientist
McNeil Specialty Products
Athens, GA

Rosetta Newsome
Senior Food Scientist
Institute of Food Technologists
Chicago, IL

Lars Noah
University of Florida College of Law
Gainesville, FL

Owen Olesen
Director of Quality
Red Star BioProducts
Milwaukee, WI

Regina A. Payne
Child Adult Care Food Program
Coordinator
United Planning Organization
Washington, DC

Robert C. Post
Deputy Director
Food Safety and Inspection Service
Washington, DC

Sharan A. Prasad
Dietitian
Vivra Renal Care
Washington, DC

Daniel J. Raiten
Senior Staff Scientist
Life Sciences Research Office/FASEB
Bethesda, MD

Jim G. Rasekh
Food Technologist
Food Safety and Inspection Service
Washington, DC

Joe M. Regenstein
Legislative Science Fellow
United States Senate
Washington, DC

Alison Reich
Regulatory Project Manager
TAS, Inc.
Washington, DC

Richard R. Reo
Associate Director, Regulatory Affairs
McNeil Specialty Products
New Brunswick, NJ

Lourdes Sandoval
Dietitian
Gambro Health Care Service
Washington, DC

Bob Scheuplein
Consultant
Winberg Consultant Group
Washington, DC

David Schnakenberg
10108 Tamarack Drive
Vienna, VA

Marilyn D. Schorin
Group Manager, Nutrition and Science
Pepsi Cola Company
Valhalla, NY

Prabhdip Sekhon
Nutritionist
PSI Services Inc.
Washington, DC

Carol Shivezy-Knight
Vice President
Knight International
Tappahannock, VA

Thomas J. Sobotka
Research Neurotoxicology
Food and Drug Administration
Laurel, MD

Dan. Steffen
Manager Scientific Relations
Kraft Foods
Tarrytown, NY

Mary K. Stone
Clinical Dietitian
Springfield Hospital Center
Sykesville, MD

Junko Alice Tamaki
Nutritionist
Agricultural Research Service
Beltsville, MD

Susan Thompson
Chemist
Food and Drug Administration
Washington, DC

Toni M. Thrush
Clinical Dietitian
Springfield Hospital Center
Ellicott City, MD

Dorothy W. Tousignant
Food and Drug Administration
Washington, DC

Liz Turner
Executive Director
Sustain
Washington, DC

Richetta Webb
Public Health Nutritionist
Department of Health
Washington, DC

Ronald Weiss
Research Program Manager
Food Research Institute
Madison, WI

Patricia N. White.
Nutritionist
U.S. Department of Administration
Cheverly, MD

Mary Woo
Potomac, MD

John T. Woodard
Food and Drug Regulatory Specialist
Dow Corning Corporation
Midland, MI

Elizabeth A. Yetley
Director, Office of Special Nutritionals
Food and Drug Administration
Washington, DC

Irene E. Yuhaniak
Nutritionist
Agricultural Research Service
Riverdale, MD

Acronyms

ADI	Acceptable daily intake
AMD	Absorption, metabolism, and distribution
BFIFC	Bureau of Foods Irradiated Foods Committee
CFSAN	Center for Food Safety and Applied Nutrition
CHA	Cyclohexylamine
CR	Consumption ratio
D&C Act	Drug and Cosmetic Act
DCM	Dichloromethane
DNA	Deoxyribonucleic acid
EPA	Environmental Protection Agency
FAO	Food and Agriculture Organization (of the United Nations)
FD&C Act	Food, Drug, and Cosmetic Act
FEMA	Flavor and Extract Manufacturer's Association
FMA	Fragrance Manufacturers Association
FPLA	Fair Packaging and Labeling Act
FR	Federal Register
GATT	General Agreement on Tariffs and Trade
GLP	Good laboratory practices
GMP	Good manufacturing practices
GRAS	Generally recognized as safe

IAEA	International Atomic Energy Agency
FAO	Food and Agriculture Organization
IARC	International Agency for Research on Cancer
JECIF	Joint Expert Committee on the Wholesomeness of Irradiated Food
JEFCA	Joint Committee on Food Additives
MTD	Maximum tolerated dose
NAS	National Academy of Sciences
NCA	National Coffee Association
NCI	National Cancer Institute
NCTR	National Center for Toxicological Research
NLEA	Nutrition Labeling and Education Act
NOEL	No observed effects level
NTP	National Toxicology Program
P&G	Procter & Gamble
PAFA	Prioritizing the assessment of food additives
PBPK	Physiologically-based pharmacokinetics
QRA	Quantitative risk assessment
RNA	Ribonucleic acid
RTI	Radiation Technology, Inc.
SAR	Structure/activity relationships
SGPT	S glutathione protein transferase
SOT	Society of Toxicology
SPE	Sucrose polyester
TCE	Trichloroethylene
TSH	Thyroid stimulating hormone
USDA	United States Department of Agriculture
WHO	World Health Organization